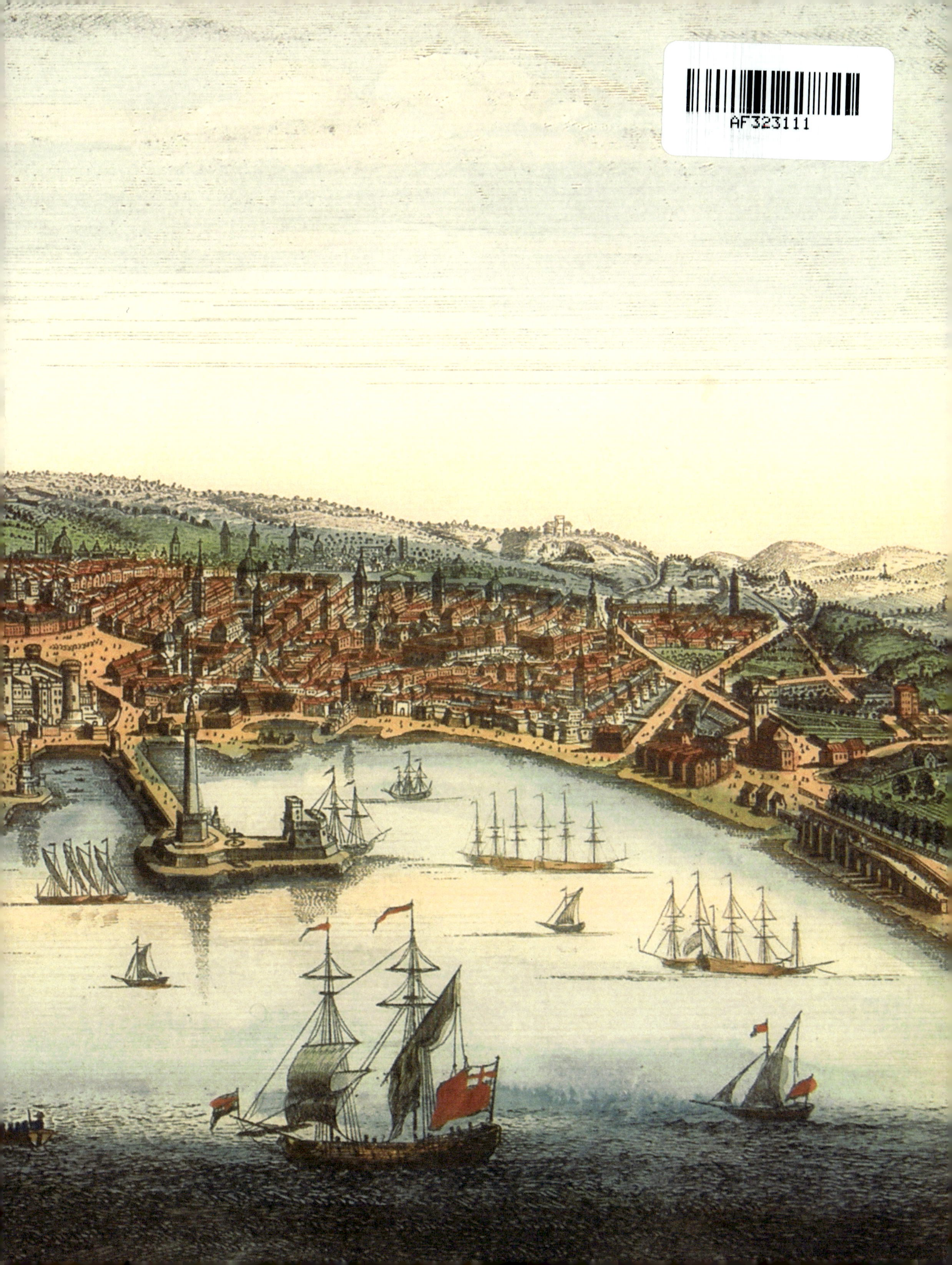

# THE ENCHANTRESS

*Emma, Lady Hamilton*

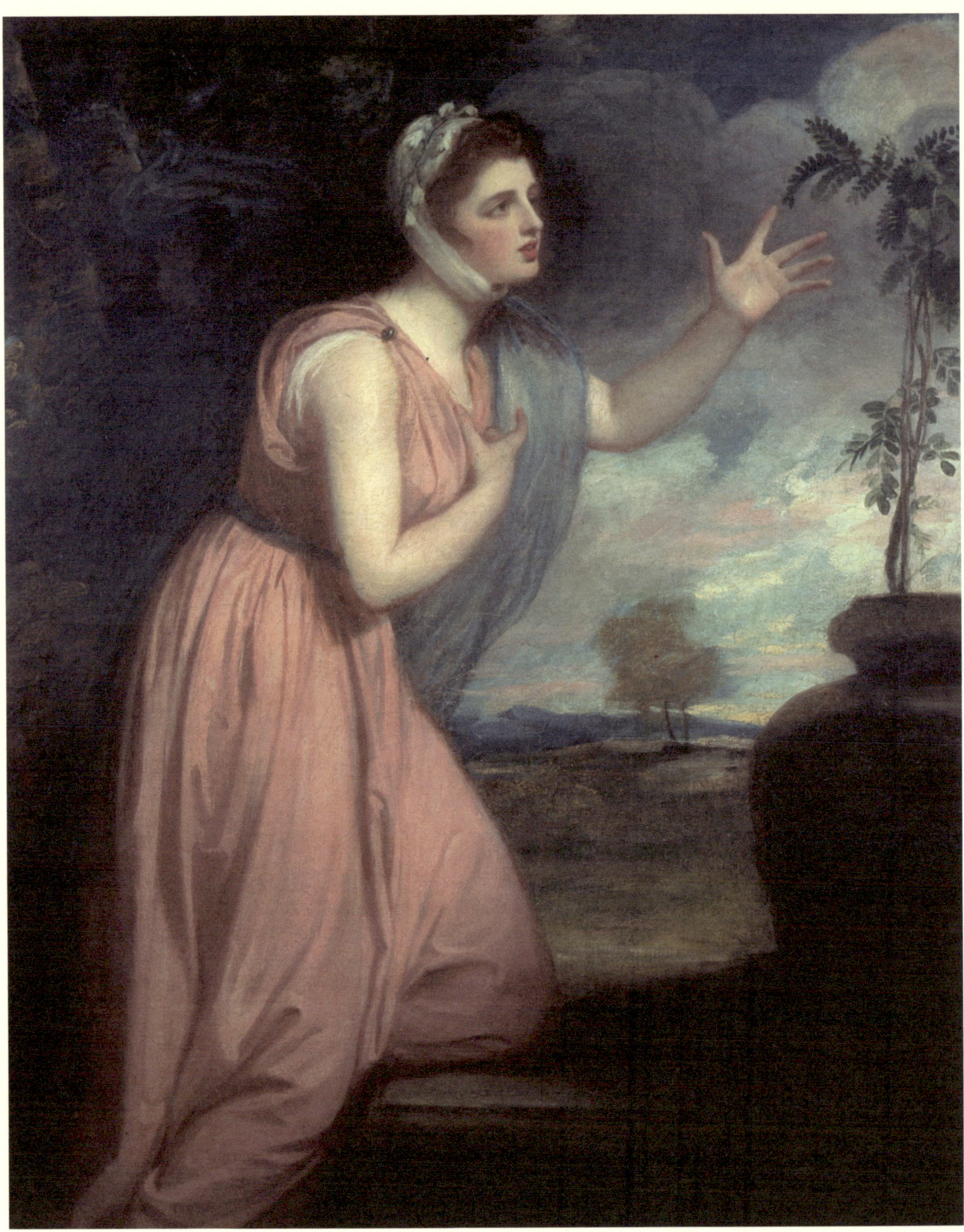

# THE ENCHANTRESS

## *Emma, Lady Hamilton*

### THE JEAN KISLAK COLLECTION

*Edited by*

Arthur Dunkelman

*With essays by*

MARTYN DOWNER · FLORA FRASER

ALEX KIDSON · MICHAEL NASH

KATE WILLIAMS

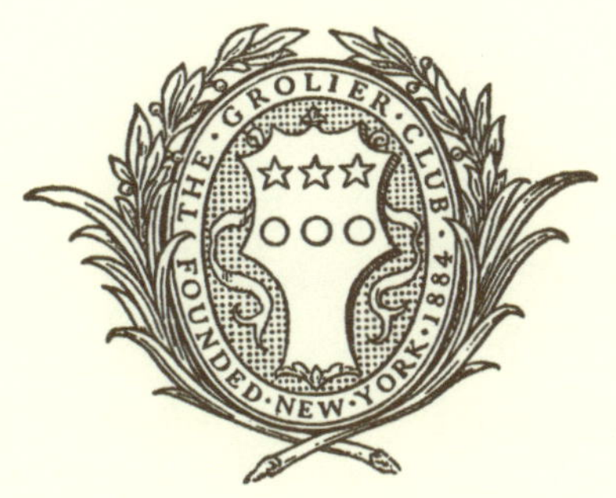

NEW YORK

THE GROLIER CLUB

MM · XI

ISBN 978–1–60583–034–6

FRONTISPIECE:

PORTRAIT OF EMMA HART AS *Sensibility*

(see page 27)

# CONTENTS



## *Catalogue*

## *Introduction & Acknowledgments*

THE REAL EMMA is elusive—to be found somewhere between the layers of romantic myth and spiteful biography that are her legacy.

The details of her early life are obscure. Rather than fact we have suggestion, gossip, and innuendo. Modern biographers—including two who generously have contributed to this volume—have described the details of her life, but no one has fully captured her magic.

She was a creative spirit, an artist of self-invention, endlessly fascinating to men and totally engaged with life. She rose from humble origins to become the wife of the British envoy to the Kingdom of Naples and the mistress of England's greatest naval hero.

Emma had many detractors and there is no doubt that she was flawed—she was a woman larger than life, whose extravagance combined with her generosity contributed to her undoing.

Jean Kislak's collection is remarkable and intimate, yet one-sided. The collection includes many romantic and dramatic letters to Emma from Nelson, but none of hers to him. They made a pact to destroy their letters in order to preserve their privacy and her dignity. With military discipline, Nelson scrupulously destroyed all the letters he received. She could not abide by their compact and saved all. Purloined and published during her lifetime, they caused a sensation and established the immortality of their love.

Men were infatuated and inspired by Emma the enchantress. Yet she was not simply one of the great beauties of her age. She was bright, a hard worker, and a quick study. Although it is doubtful she received any schooling as a child, once given an opportunity learning came quickly. She applied herself and was fluent in both French and Italian and able to read and perform the complex musical scores of Hayden.

One of the great beauties of her time, she sat for many important artists, including George Romney, who painted her image more than fifty times.

She was a fashion diva who set trends throughout Europe and quite possibly can be credited with introducing the Regency or Empire style, based on her study and adaptation of the classical dress that she saw on the Greek and Roman pottery in Sir William Hamilton's collection of vases.

She was a performance artist of *tableaux vivants* who could render a series of dramatic poses that held audiences in her thrall for hours. As a dancer she pioneered a coquettish "shawl dance" that took London by storm and was copied throughout Europe.

She was a behind-the-scenes political operative who used her contacts and influence in service to her country and to the benefit of her friends. She charmed the great and the near great, among them travellers, artists, princes, and kings.

After the death of Sir William Hamilton and Nelson, Emma wrote pitiful pleas to the government for recognition for her services and financial compensation—all went without official reply.

Nearly two hundred years after her death, Emma continues to fascinate. I have spent the past several months sleuthing the archives, reading many books, and yet she remains a mystery.

The challenge in creating *The Enchantress: Emma, Lady Hamilton* was to establish the context of events and personalities within which she lived, loved, and lost all. Like the many art works inspired by Emma, this exhibit could not possibly reveal the full depth of this remarkable woman. But it presents, I hope, a closer look at the many aspects of her talent, character, and historic impact.

◀═══▶

IT REQUIRES many talented individuals to create an exhibition, beginning always with an idea and the material. For *The Enchantress*, we thank Jean Kislak for both. Her two-decade pursuit of all things Emma has resulted in the nearly two hundred items that comprise this unique collection.

It has been an adventure and a great deal of fun to explore Emma's life and legacy with Jean, whose passion, patience, and persistence are ably abetted by the discerning eye of a connoisseur. Along the way we have had many wonderful opportunities to learn about Emma, Lady Hamilton, and her time.

We have been assisted in this venture by our essayists, Flora Fraser, Martyn Downer, Alex Kidson, and Kate Williams. Special thanks are due Michael Nash of The 1805 Club who recounted the creation of the monument to Emma, Lady Hamilton, in Calais and who volunteered his comprehensive knowledge of the Royal Navy during the Georgian period, and to Rear Admiral Joseph Callo for reading the proofs. We also want to thank Michael T. Ryan, Carton Rogers, Daniel Traister, and Andrea Gottschalk of the University of Pennsylvania Libraries, for their early research and exhibition of this collection.

We have benefited greatly from the generosity of donors who offered photographs and artifacts for the exhibit: Jackie Danicki, Lawrence Rutherford, Gunnar Bengtsson, and Iain Macfarlaine.

Our admiration and respect go to Mark Argetsinger, our nonpareil designer, whose patience would earn praise from Job. Thanks to our editor, Phyllis Shapiro, who smoothed many rough patches in the text, and to our assistant, Stephanie Chace.

To the staff of the Grolier Club, especially Director Eric Holzenberg, Maev Brennan, and Exhibitions Coördinator Megan Smith, our gratitude for keeping us on track and on schedule; to Publications Committee Chair George Ong, for his careful review of the catalogue, and the member-volunteers of the Exhibitions Committee, for their skill and care installing the exhibition.

And, finally, we want to thank Jean's husband, Jay Kislak, for his support and encouragement of our creative explorations.

Any errors or omissions in this catalogue are mine and have been committed despite the efforts of advisers.

—ARTHUR DUNKELMAN

## *Emma, Lady Hamilton*

BY MARTYN DOWNER

EMMA HAMILTON came into my life through my chance discovery—whilst working for Sotheby's—of a cache of letters and artefacts once belonging to her lover, Britain's greatest naval hero Admiral Lord Nelson. The circumstances of discovery were dramatic enough but they failed to match the impact of first reading her words in letters left untouched for almost two centuries. Principally addressed to Nelson's former agent Alexander Davison in the days following the admiral's death at Trafalgar, the letters were charged with a high-intensity almost hysterical sentiment which nevertheless failed to disguise a highly intelligent, cultivated mind. At the time of writing, Emma was the focal point not only for the outpouring of national grief at Nelson's untimely death but for the storm of controversy which surrounded his scandalous private life. Even as Nelson's body was interred at St. Paul's Cathedral amid the pomp of a State funeral, all minds, even among the most noble in the land, were turned towards Merton in Surrey where Emma, excluded from the ceremony, lay prostrate with grief. They did so with a mixture of sympathy, prurience, and undoubted anxiety. That Emma occupied their thoughts on such a day was the culmination of an extraordinary public career made more astonishing by the squalid nature of its beginning.

Emma Hamilton began life on 26 April 1765 as Amy Lyon. Far from the glittering ballrooms or sun-soaked palazzos of her later celebrity, her infant eyes saw only the smoke-stained bare walls of a low hovel in Ness, a small coal-mining village near Liverpool. She had no memory of her blacksmith father, Henry Lyon, as he died soon after her birth, compelling Emma's mother Mary to return with her baby to her own people, the Kidds, in Hawarden outside Chester. There, amid grinding rural poverty, Mary Lyon slowly forged a close understanding with her child, giving her a rudimentary education and installing that lifelong belief that she was undeserving of the miserable conditions of her childhood and the stunted ambitions of the rural underclass.

The first step on Emma's road to fame was a small and, given her humble background, a traditional one. Aged twelve, she began work as a housemaid for a local surgeon. It was an ill-fated appointment lasting only a few months, as Emma was inefficient and

MARTYN DOWNER is an art historian and writer. A former director of Sotheby's, he is author of several books including *Nelson's Purse: The Extraordinary Story of Nelson's Lost Treasures* (Smithsonian Institute Press, 2004), an account of his discovery of a large trove of papers and artefacts belonging to Admiral Lord Nelson. He lives near Cambridge, England.

already resentful of her servile position. In 1777, like many girls before and since, she headed for the bright lights of London hoping to slough off her gritty Northern childhood and emerge into a sparkling new world of opportunity. Of course, reality failed to match the dream and within hours of arrival, Emma found herself back in domestic service. After a short period she was dismissed again, vowing never to return to the drudgery of housework. Instead she headed for the stage, or at least the theatre, securing a position as maid to the wardrobe mistress at Drury Lane. Here, amid the hubbub of back-stage life, she could observe the leading actors of the age portray the fantasy life she herself craved. The abrupt end to this appointment, in December 1778, tipped Emma back onto her own resources and probably (but not necessarily) into a short life as a prostitute on the streets of London. Already self-reliant and hardened beyond her years, Emma gained a cynical understanding of the needs and weaknesses of men—and of how to manipulate them. Newly self-styled Emily Lyon, her beauty attracted the attentions not only of clients but painters trawling the West End for cheap models. Emma posed for two of the greatest: Sir Joshua Reynolds and George Romney, the latter falling in love with his subject and depicting her in a series of vivid and alluring oil studies.

In 1779, salvation of a kind arrived in the colourful form of a quack doctor called James Graham who recruited Emma to perform in his bizarre "Temple of Health." Here, aristocrats in desperate search for an heir could take their wives to perform their conjugal duty on the "Celestial Bed," whilst beautiful maidens, Emma foremost among them, performed alluring dances and wafted scent over the lovemaking. It was ludicrous, but for Emma it represented a step upmarket and though typically short-term it gave her *entré* to Madam Kelly's exclusive brothel in Mayfair. Now in luxurious surroundings and promoted as the "Goddess of Health," fourteen-year-old Emma graduated to her new role as a high-class escort girl. So struck with Emma was Sir Harry Featherstonhaugh, a regular at Kelly's, that he negotiated her long-term hire, installing her as his mistress at his country seat in Sussex. At Uppark, with her own apartments and maid, Emma received her first real taste of genteel living. But as her novelty palled for Sir Harry, her sexual allure grew for one of his friends, the serious-minded Charles Greville. Their friendship, then intimacy, was complicated by her giving birth to Sir Harry's daughter in 1782.

The child was put out for adoption and after coming to terms with her, by now, thoroughly disgruntled former lover, Emma sought the protection of Greville. Installed in new lodgings in West London, Emily Lyon was re-invented as Emma Hart, the reformed courtesan. Anxious to improve his catch, Greville trained Emma in the arts, envisaging a lucrative career for her (and him) on the stage. However, the single decision which most propelled her fame was his agreeing to her continued sittings with George Romney. The resulting paintings and prints disseminated her beauty across London, then England.

Ironically, the rising celebrity of his protégé enraged the jealous-minded Greville, whilst his falling income and urgent need for a respectable wife no longer made a mistress affordable or convenient. Fortunately his wealthy, ageing, and recently widowed uncle Sir William Hamilton took close interest in Emma on a visit to London from his post as Envoy Plenipotentiary to Naples. Seizing the chance for escape from an awkward situation, Greville audaciously negotiated the transfer of his mistress from London to Sir William's palazzo in Naples. Emma travelled to Italy in ignorance of her lover's true intent, believing it only a temporary measure to allow him to complete his marriage plans. It took months for her to be learn the bitter truth—that she was merely a chattel to be traded—by which time she had re-established her celebrity in Naples, fast becoming a favourite of the King and Queen, Ferdinand and Maria-Carolina. Acquiescing with growing enthusiasm to her surprising new existence, Emma, who married Sir William in 1791, threw herself into Neapolitan court life. She dabbled (sometimes disastrously) in politics and entertained her husband's guests with her "Attitudes," erotic dances bordering on the burlesque. Then war brought another dramatic turn to her life.

Until 1798, the conflict in Europe, triggered by revolution in France, had largely bypassed the Kingdom of Naples and the Two Sicilies. To avoid invasion, Ferdinand had sought a treaty with Napoleon but, with the fall of Rome in February 1798, this appeared naive and attack on his kingdom imminent. In September, the arrival in the Bay of Naples of a victorious squadron of British warships seemed to offer unexpected deliverance. Led by forty-year-old Admiral Sir Horatio Nelson, already a national hero after earlier naval exploits, the British fleet had just inflicted a crippling blow to Napoleon's ambitions in the Mediterranean with a dramatic victory at the battle of the Nile.

Emma had met Nelson before, on his visit to Naples in 1793. Even then, the close attention the two, both married, had paid each other caused tongues to wag. Now, fêted throughout Europe, the admiral's appeal had grown for her whilst his ships offered escape from approaching calamity. Wounded and exhausted, Nelson willingly submitted to Emma's care. He allowed their friendship to develop into a full-scale affair whilst his strategic judgement was swayed by a vainglorious attempt by King Ferdinand to recapture Rome. Heavily defeated, king and courts, including the Hamiltons, were forced to flee to Sicily in December 1798 under Nelson's escort. Holed up in Palermo and *in extremis*, Emma and Nelson fell in love, setting their faces scandalously against convention and deciding the final course of both their lives.

Restored to his throne following a rebellion in June 1799, King Ferdinand, shamefully assisted by Nelson, set about brutally punishing his Jacobin enemies with a round of vicious reprisals. The bloodletting complete, the Hamiltons, with Nelson in tow, departed for England trailing notoriety, the affair between Emma and Nelson now common knowledge and with Emma showing signs of pregnancy. Their greeting in London in November 1800 was mixed. The populace loudly proclaimed the Hero of the Nile whilst Court and Society deplored the brazenness of his conduct in so shamelessly and publicly conducting an affair with a married woman of such scandalous reputation. The reaction of Lady Nelson was muted but, as was recently revealed in her heartfelt letters to Nelson's agent Alexander Davison, highly pained. She could do little, however, to stop the whirlwind of her husband's feelings for Emma and, despite several attempts, failed to prevent him setting up house with Emma after Sir William Hamilton died in 1803. At Merton Place, Emma and Nelson with their daughter Horatia enjoyed two brief years of happiness living as man and wife. Then late one autumn evening in 1805, Nelson departed on his last mission, never to return.

Emma's extreme distress on hearing of her lover's death at Trafalgar was predictable. Her own future was not. Both Sir William and Nelson made handsome provision for her in their wills and she could have lived comfortably for the rest of her life. But impetuous generosity and increasingly intemperate habits caused by grief, her failing beauty, and declining health, both hastened by the indifference of government and her erstwhile friends, precipitated a rapid and disastrous decline. The house was sold, her possessions dispersed and eventually Emma submitted herself to the sanctuary of a debtors prison. In 1814 she engineered an escape from her creditors by sailing to France where she died six months later on 15 January 1815. After such an extravagant, dazzling life Emma was interred with simple ceremony in public ground outside Calais, all trace of her physical remains soon lost. It is a strangely fitting end for the beautiful girl from the Wirral who mesmerised the world, as if her life had been a feverish dream existing only in the minds of the men who loved her and the artists who captured her for eternity.

## Jean Kislak's Remarkable Connection to Emma Hamilton

BY FLORA FRASER

JEAN KISLAK and I met, at her instigation, at a London hotel in the 1980s, shortly after she read the first biography I wrote, a book that was published in the States as *Emma, Lady Hamilton* (1987). I had been drawn to Emma some years before, oddly enough after studying Greek and Roman vases at Oxford. Emma's husband Sir William Hamilton was an early collector of these artefacts and appreciated Emma for her beauty and grace that rivalled those of the figures on the vases.

The copy Jean read was from the earlier English edition, titled *Beloved Emma*, and, in an inventory of Jean's Hamiltoniana collection, the book duly appears alongside many greater treasures, marked "Inscribed by the author." Inscribed in the course of a very jolly lunch, I might add, at the Hyde Park Hotel, now the Mandarin Oriental, with views of London parkland. I took an immediate liking to Jean. Who could not? I liked her strength as much as her clear gaze and her exquisite politeness, and that strength became obvious early on in our acquaintance.

With hindsight, I think Jean contacted me because she felt that, in *Beloved Emma*, I had done justice to Emma within the context of literature. I certainly felt, as a writer, that the work was now done, that I had made Emma live again as she had once done, a free spirit loving both her aristocratic husband and Admiral Horatio Nelson. And I felt a free spirit too, ready to move on to writing about a different subject. Jean, however, was not ready for me to move on so fast. She wanted me to help her to pick up the baton with Emma. She saw her work as beginning. As curator and collector, through her work with her husband Jay on his early American collection, she knew, as I did not then, the value of the palpable, the tangible, the souvenir.

I think Jean already knew, while we were at lunch years ago, that she could make a rich and wonderful collection based around Emma and her different guises as model to Romney, and wife to Sir William Hamilton, and as half of a world-famous love affair. But Jean also quickly focused on a subject that I had not taken so much to heart. There was no marker showing where Emma had died and

FLORA FRASER lives in London and has written, among other books, *Beloved Emma: The Life of Emma, Lady Hamilton* (1987), *The Unruly Queen: The Life of Queen Caroline* (1996), *Princesses: The Daughters of George III* (2004), and *Pauline Bonaparte: Venus of Empire* (2008). She founded the Elizabeth Longford Prize and Grants for Historical Biography in affectionate memory of her grandmother in 2003, and from 1999 to 2008 was a trustee of the London National Portrait Gallery. She is currently writing a book, *Portrait of a Marriage: The Washingtons*, scheduled for publication in 2012.

been buried, in Calais, France, in 1815, shortly after she had fled her British creditors. The grave had been not far off a pauper's burial in the first place, and war damage and population shifts had meant that neither the house where Emma died nor the grave was left standing.

As pudding was being served, Jean said in sepulchral tones, "Emma needs us. She wants to rest in peace." I stared, utterly baffled. Jean smiled, knowing what I was thinking. What she went on to propose was far-fetched, to say the least. We were to mark the site of Emma's death and burial with a monument in her honour. I thought of the difficult research trips to Calais I had already made in the course of writing my book. I thought of the French bureaucracy, with whom I was apparently to negotiate on Jean's behalf. Jean spoke of her ideas for a design and an inscription for the monument. And I found myself saying, "Yes, of course, so when shall we start?"

Over the next several years Jean and I located a site in the Parc Richelieu, close to where Emma had died, which would be suitable for the monument she envisioned. I liked the location. There were men playing boules and ladies walking poodles and I felt it would have appealed to Emma, who was so interested in other people. We had many meetings with French officials in the great city hall of Calais, where I acted as Jean's translator and she sat, implacably chic and courteous. Approval for the project was granted by the mayor, and in turn Jean approved architects, designers, and engravers for the monument.

At last the great day came in April 1994. A brass band came marching into the Parc Richelieu. Members of the American and British diplomatic corps and members of the distinguished society, The 1805 Club, stood together with the usual inhabitants of the park who stopped playing boules to watch. Together, the mayor and Jean unveiled the monument, and afterwards we all enjoyed a Champagne reception at city hall. More than 300 people attended a memorial service for Emma, held at the historic cathedral only partially restored after its wartime destruction. As I left to catch my train, Jean murmured to me, "Emma is at rest."

Jean and I have remained close over the years, visiting with each other in London and America. I was aware that she was building an Emma Hamilton collection, and that it included celebrated portraits of Emma by Romney. I was pleased to learn that she was acquiring many letters that collector Alfred Morrison had transcribed in the later nineteenth century. In 2002 we discussed the discovery of a cache of manuscripts and other materials. By then, I realized that Jean had long since become the master and I the pupil in Hamiltonian studies.

Today, if not complete, Jean's work is nearly done. Historical manuscripts that were thought lost forever, portraits, landscapes, books of great value, even Emma's daughter's cot—these are some of the riches that Jean has amassed over the years that give palpable life to Emma Hamilton and her world, as my biography alone could never do.

CALAIS MONUMENT.
The 1805 Club, which
conserves and maintains
monuments and memorials
to Nelson and the Geor-
gian sailing Navy, provided
the ball made of sandstone
from the Wirral Peninsula,
the place of Emma's birth.


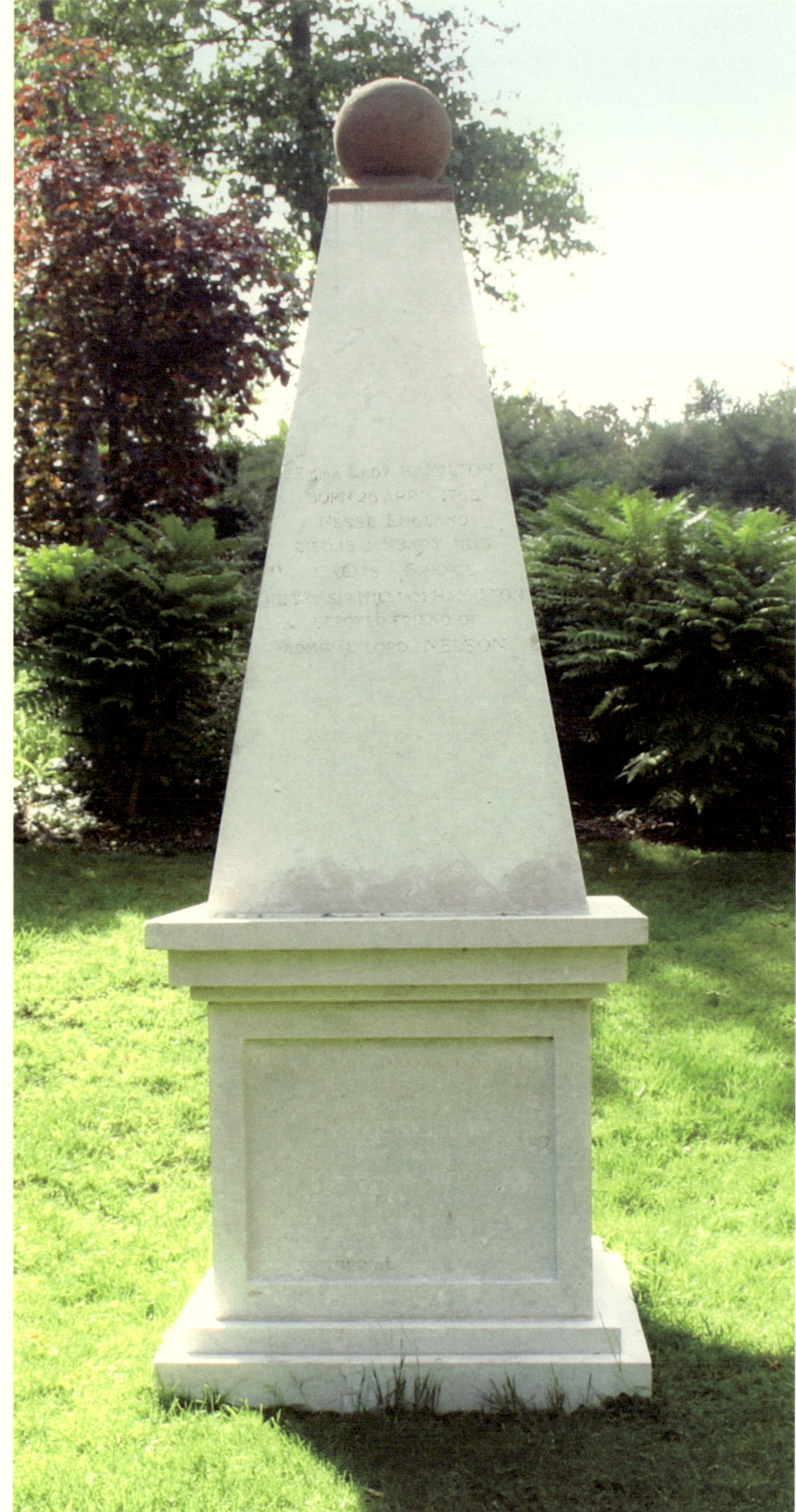

## The Calais Monument

BY MICHAEL NASH

IN 1994 a long overdue monument commemorating the passing of a remarkable woman was erected in Calais, thanks to the generosity and devotion of an American admirer.

Emma, Lady Hamilton died and was buried in France, a country that had been at war with England since 1793. She had slipped back to obscurity and poverty as quickly as she had risen to fame and wealth, all but forgotten. British officers in France after the First World War erected a monument to her memory at the house where she died, but this was destroyed by German bombs during the Second World War.

In the early 1990s I was introduced to Jean Kislak by Flora Fraser. I had first met Flora in the mid-1980s whilst assisting her in researching Emma's origins in Cheshire and North Wales, as Flora was writing her celebrated biography, *Beloved Emma*. Together, Jean, Flora, and I made a couple of trips across the English Channel endeavouring to trace the final resting place of Emma, Lady Hamilton.

Having exhausted all avenues, we came to the conclusion that Emma's bones were probably scattered on two sites: firstly, in the area near the centre of town where her body had been removed shortly after burial; secondly, in a new cemetery north of the town, after graves were unceremoniously dug up later in the nineteenth century to make way for a theatre. Today, when the ground is disturbed around the theatre, bones are frequently unearthed. There was an inscribed headstone marking Emma's grave but this had been broken and later lost altogether. It must be remembered that Calais was almost completely destroyed during the last war.

Therefore it was decided that the best possible site for a memorial was in the Parc Richelieu, as it was here that Emma was first laid to rest. In 1816 it was decided to move the graves to make way for a timber yard, so although her bones no longer lie there, perhaps her spirit still lingers.

At this time I was chairman of the newly-formed 1805 Club, an organization founded in 1990 to restore Nelson-related graves and monuments, so for us this was an ideal project. In addition to assisting in the research, I had the idea of including a piece of local stone from Emma's birthplace—the Wirral Peninsula

MICHAEL NASH is vice president of The 1805 Club, dedicated to the preservation of the memorials of the Georgian sailing Navy. He is associated with Marine & Cannon Books, a specialist in rare antiquarian books, manuscripts, and engravings. He lives in Wirral, England, not far from the place of Emma's birth.

in Cheshire—as not only the symbolism appealed, but also aesthetically the red sandstone made a striking contrast to the local French white stone used for the main part of the monument. Acting on behalf of The 1805 Club, I was able to persuade a local stonemason working on a sandstone wall not far from where I live to let me have a large suitable stone. I then arranged shipment to Calais where the French stonemason fashioned it into the fine red ball that can be seen today atop Jean's splendid memorial to Lady Hamilton. The finished monument is a fitting tribute to a woman who had dazzled society with her beauty, and scandalized Europe with her notorious affair with the Hero of the Nile.

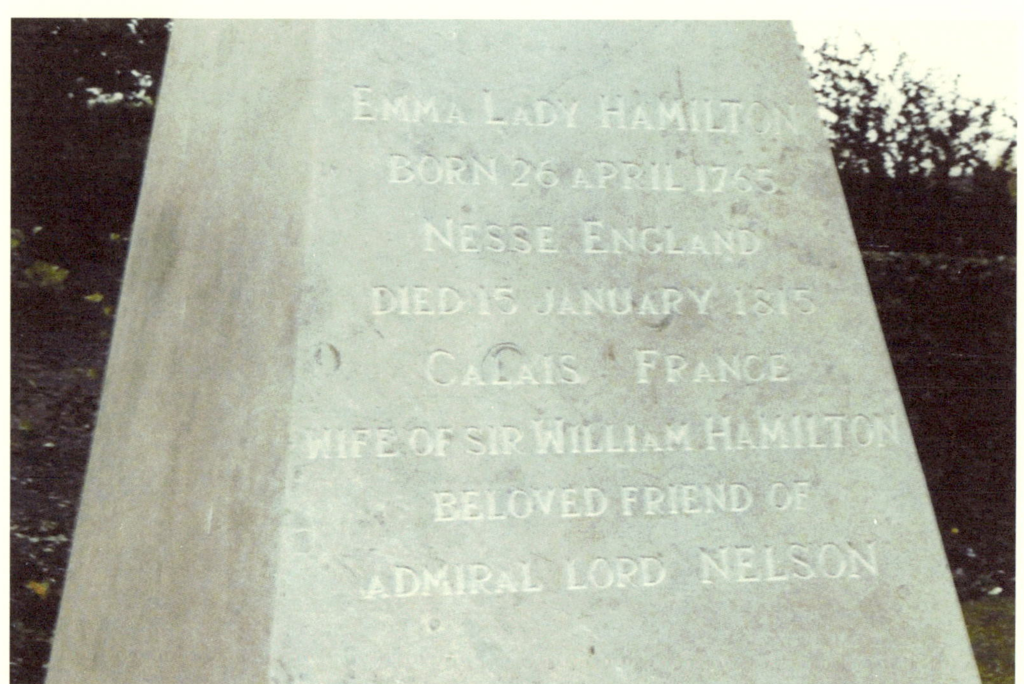

# A Collector

BY JEAN KISLAK

IT IS GREAT FUN, an intellectual challenge, to begin a collection of anything. Your interests can take you to places you never dreamed of going and you can meet many fascinating people connected with your quest.

Like many collectors, I am often asked about the source of my inspiration—about how this particular collection, with its focus on Emma, Lady Hamilton, came to be, and about how I happened to embark on this pursuit. I am not sure when I *became* a collector. I am one of those people who apparently was *born* a collector.

As a child, I enjoyed acquiring paper dolls, signed movie-star photos, confederate stamps, shooter marbles, and all sorts of items that children seem to have an affinity toward. I loved the effort of searching out a wonderful object and learning all about that particular item.

As an adult, working as a corporate art consultant, my interests were again varied—pre-Columbian art, ceramics, Greek art, Egyptian art, and contemporary prints and oils all appealed to me. Twenty-three years ago, I was reading an auction catalogue concerning letters written by historical figures, and a sad, desperate letter written by Emma Hamilton to a friend in 1813, complaining about her finances and health, caught my attention.

Emma, Lady Hamilton, was the most celebrated English beauty of the eighteenth century—described by Goethe as a masterpiece of the great artist, Nature—and lover of Admiral Horatio Nelson, England's greatest naval hero. She had all the exciting elements necessary to whet my appetite. Of course, I had to purchase that letter. Thus began my Emma Hamilton collection.

As a child, I had seen the Alexander Korda movie, *That Hamilton Woman,* a romanticized version starring Laurence Olivier and Vivien Leigh. The movie was reputedly the favorite film of Winston Churchill, who viewed it more than one hundred times and even gave it as a present to Joseph Stalin at Yalta.

Once the collection started, I searched everywhere for things related to Emma. I found every book available. I talked to historians and museum curators. I visited auction houses, antique shops, and art galleries. I travelled to London, Stockholm, Paris, and New

York to look at pictures, letters, manuscripts, and decorative objects—anything about Emma that I could find. Just as she had Admiral Nelson, the artist George Romney, and Churchill, Emma captivated me.

Today, delightfully, she still is in my thoughts—and probably always will be.

◄═════►

Over the years, I've heard more than a few *bon mots* in pursuit of items for my collection, including the following:

COLLECTOR OF THE OTHER EMMA HAMILTON: *I was told you were collecting Emma Hamilton … Saw her on T.V. last night—she was dancing—my, but she is getting fat! But she did fairly well for someone of her age.*

THE AUCTION HOUSE: *You must fly over to London today. A locket of Emma's hair is coming up for auction. You know, she had red hair, dyed of course.*

THE EUROPEAN BOOK DEALER: *Ah, I have some unpublished manuscripts for you to see—racy stuff between Emma and Nelson. You know, of course, she wrecked his life, but so what—it's been over two hundred years.*

# THE ENCHANTRESS

*Emma, Lady Hamilton*

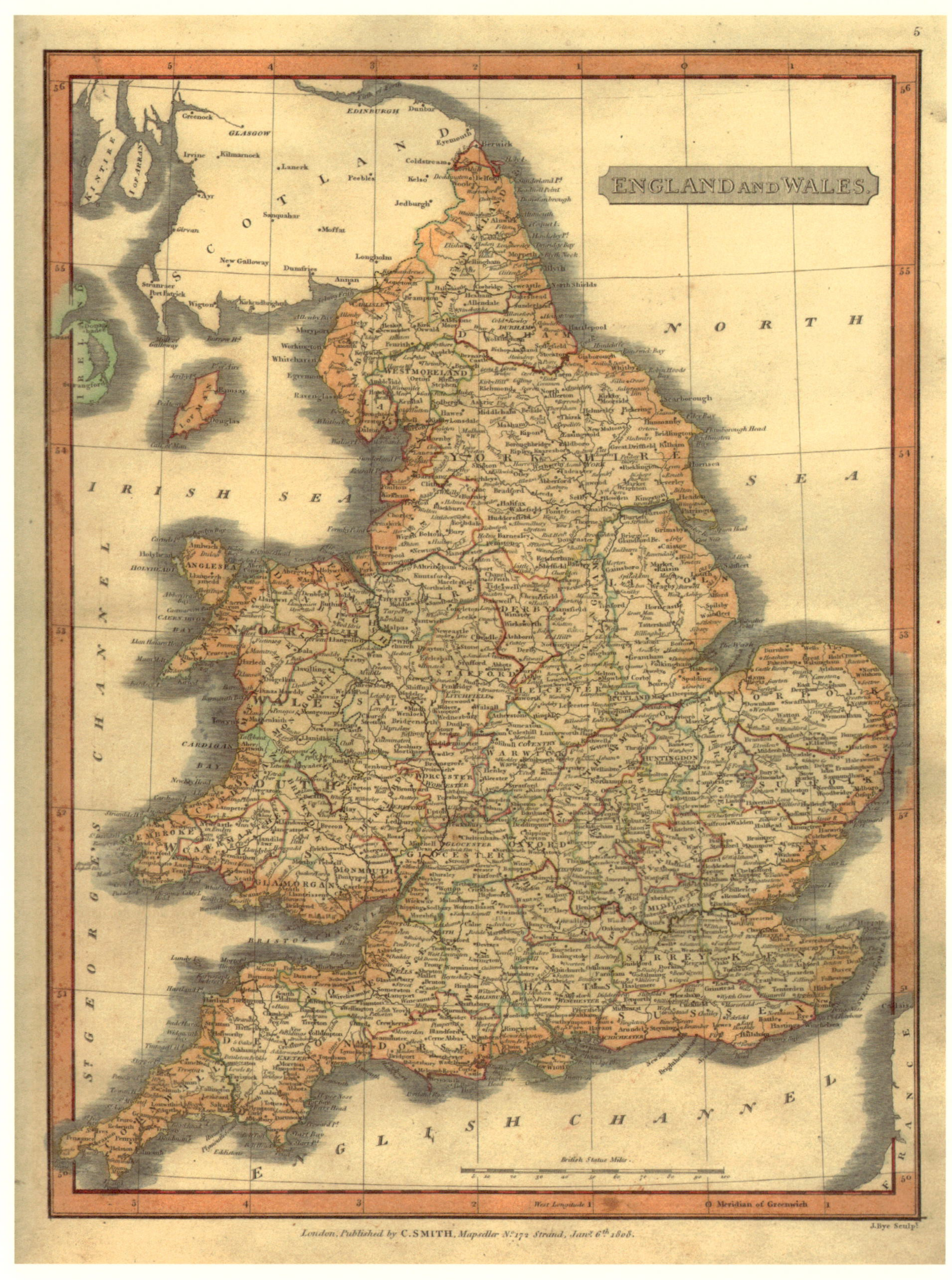



ENGLAND AND WALES. Charles Smith, *Smith's New English Atlas: Being a Complete Set of County Maps, Divided into Hundreds, on which are Delineated all the Direct and Cross Roads.* London: C. Smith, 1808. (2010.102.00.0001)

# I

## *The Road to London*

IN THE SPRING of 1764, Mary Kidd left her home in Hawarden in Wales and travelled across the Dee estuary to Great Neston, near Liverpool, England, to help her brother and his wife after the birth of their first child. There she met Henry Lyon, a blacksmith working for the Ness Colliery. After a whirlwind courtship, they were married on 11 June. Mary and Henry's baby, the future Emma, Lady Hamilton, was born on 26 April 1765, a Friday, and baptized Amy Lyon on 12 May. Two months after her birth, Henry died. Engaged, wed, a mother and a widow, Mary Kidd experienced a lifetime of events in little more than a year. She returned to Hawarden to live with her mother, Sarah Kidd.

WALES [facsimile].
From John Speed (1542–1629), *The Theatre of the Empire of Great Britaine*. London: George Humble, 1627. (2010.105.00.0001)

The compass rose on this map bears the arms of the Prince of Wales. The two side panels show the twelve county towns of Wales; the diocesan cities of Bangor, St. Asaph, Llandaff, and St. David's are depicted in the corners.

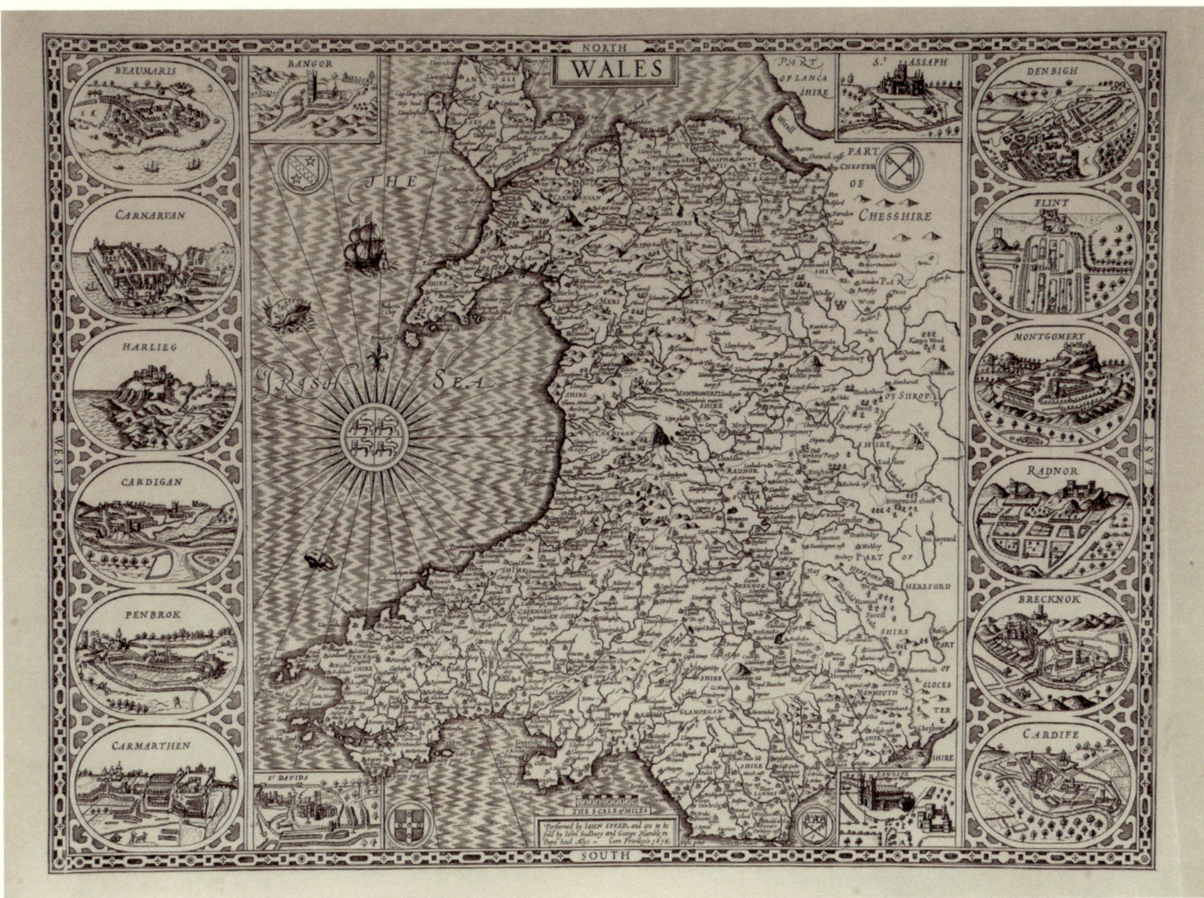

The miniature map of Flintshire was created by John
Seller, royal hydrographer
and mathematical instru-
ment maker to King Charles
II and James II. It is from
Seller's most famous series
of maps of the counties of
England and Wales, the *An-
glia Contracta, or a Description of the Kingdom of England
and Principality of Wales*, first
printed in 1695. This example is from the Francis Grose
edition of 1787, *The Antiquities of England and Wales*.

The Dee estuary forms
the boundary between the
Wirral Peninsula in England
and Flintshire in Wales. The
first mine was opened in 1759
by Sir John Stanley and employed almost 200 men. By
1855 the mines had closed
after silting of the estuary
made it difficult to move coal
in bulk.

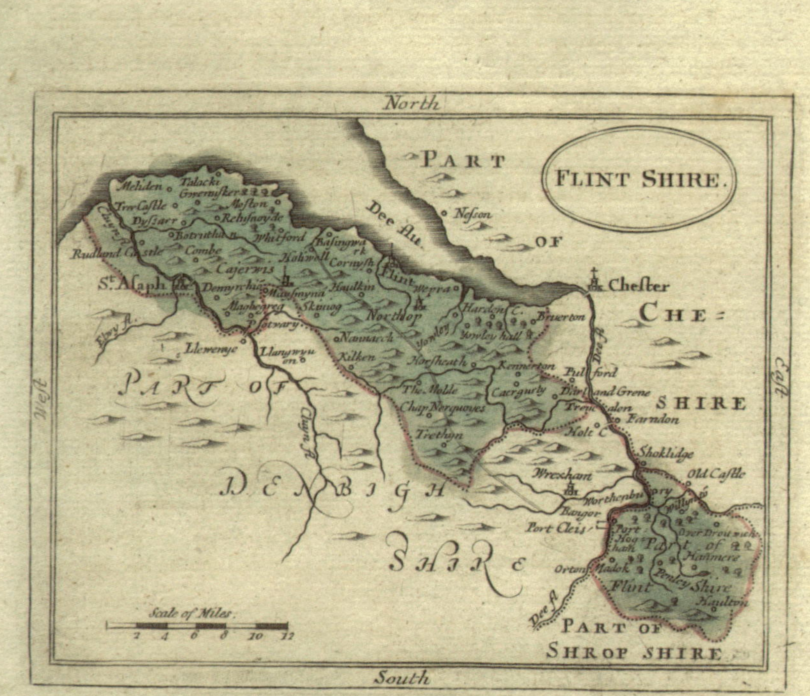


# F L I N T S H I R E

IS a maritime county, which under the Romans was part of the country of the Ordo-
vices. It is in the province of Canterbury, and partly in the diocese of St. Asaph, and
partly in that of Chester. It is bounded on the North by the estuary of the river Dee;
on the South by Denbighshire; on the East by Cheshire; and on the South by Cheshire
and part of Denbighshire; and the Irish Sea on the West. It is the least of all the counties in Wales, containing 160,000 square acres, being but 33 miles in length, nine in
breadth, and 70 in circumference, having 32,400 inhabitants, is divided into five hundreds, and contains 28 parishes, with one city, St. Asaph, and three market towns, viz.
Flint, Caerwis, and Hollywell. Its rivers are the Dee, Clwyd, Wheeler, Sevion, Elwy,
Fliddion, Tagidog, and Alen. Its products are mill-stones, pasture, corn, cattle, butter,
honey, coal, and lead. It sends two Members to Parliament, and pays one part of the
land-tax. Its principal places are Air Point and Flint Castle, the Dee's Mouth and
Clwyd's Mouth; several remarkable hills, Common Wood and St. Winifred's Well.
The air of this county is cold, but healthy; the soil, as it is not so mountainous as in

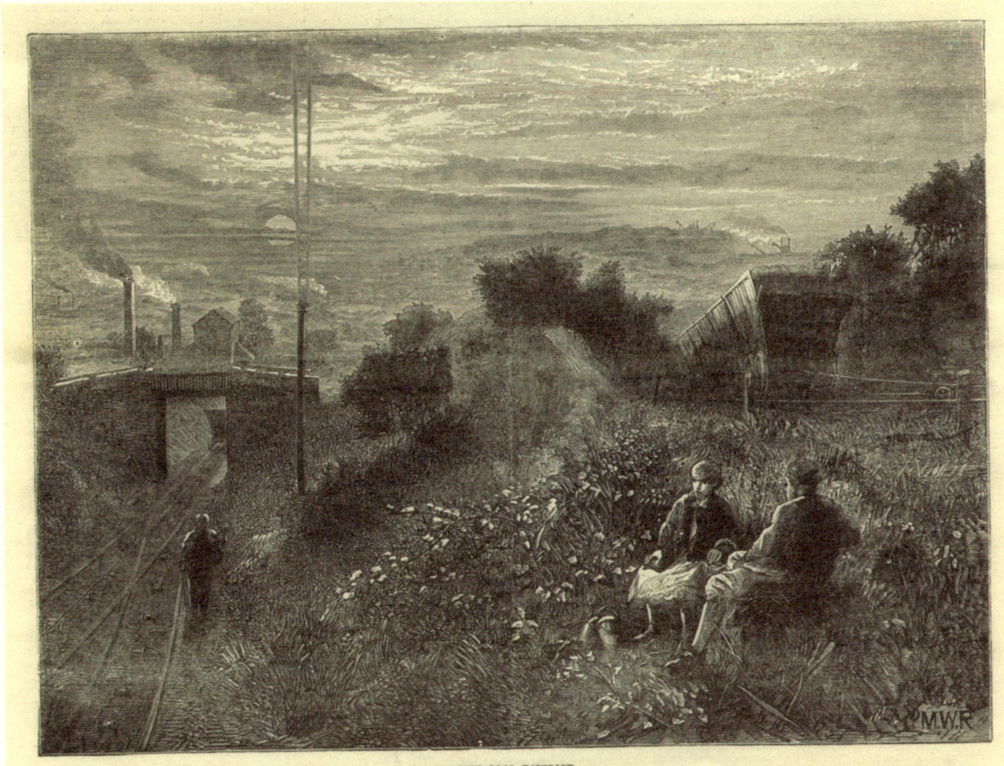


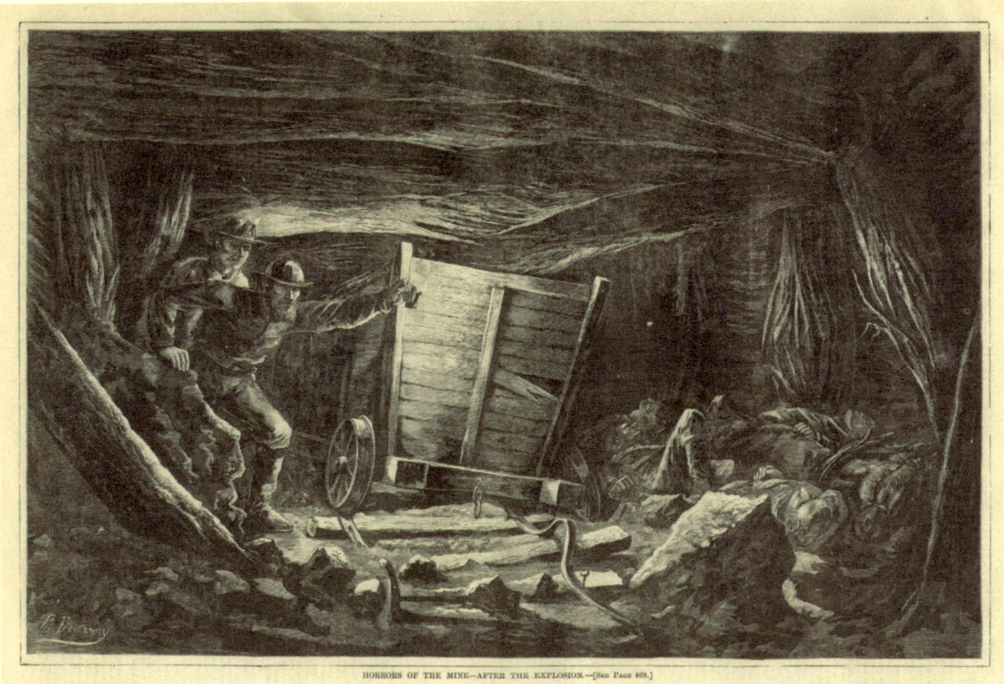


PITS AND PITMEN: THE COAL DISTRICT. *The Graphic*, 2 February. London, 1871. (2010.099.00.0001)

HORRORS OF THE MINE—AFTER THE EXPLOSION. *Harper's Weekly*, 5 May. New York: Harper & Brothers, 1873. (2010.098.00.0001)

CHESTER, HAWARDEN,
NORTHOP, DENBIGH, TO
CONWAY. John Owen and
Emanuel Bowen (1693–1767),
*Britannia Depicta, or Ogilby
Improv'd.* London: Thomas
Bowles, 1720, pl. 57. Texts pre-
pared by Owen, with cartogra-
phy and engraving by Bowen.
(2010.103.00.0001)

The map describes a route
from Chester to Conway in
Wales. It starts in the lower left
corner and goes up the page in
a series of columns ending at
the top right of the page. Hawarden is located in the center
of the far left column. Progress
along the route is indicated by
mileage markers, little dots
roughly equally spaced along
the center of the major road.
The highly detailed map de-
picts useful landmarks, including hills, bridges, rivers and
streams, windmills, churches,
and wells. Cities, towns, and
villages are named along the
way and side roads are marked
with their destinations.

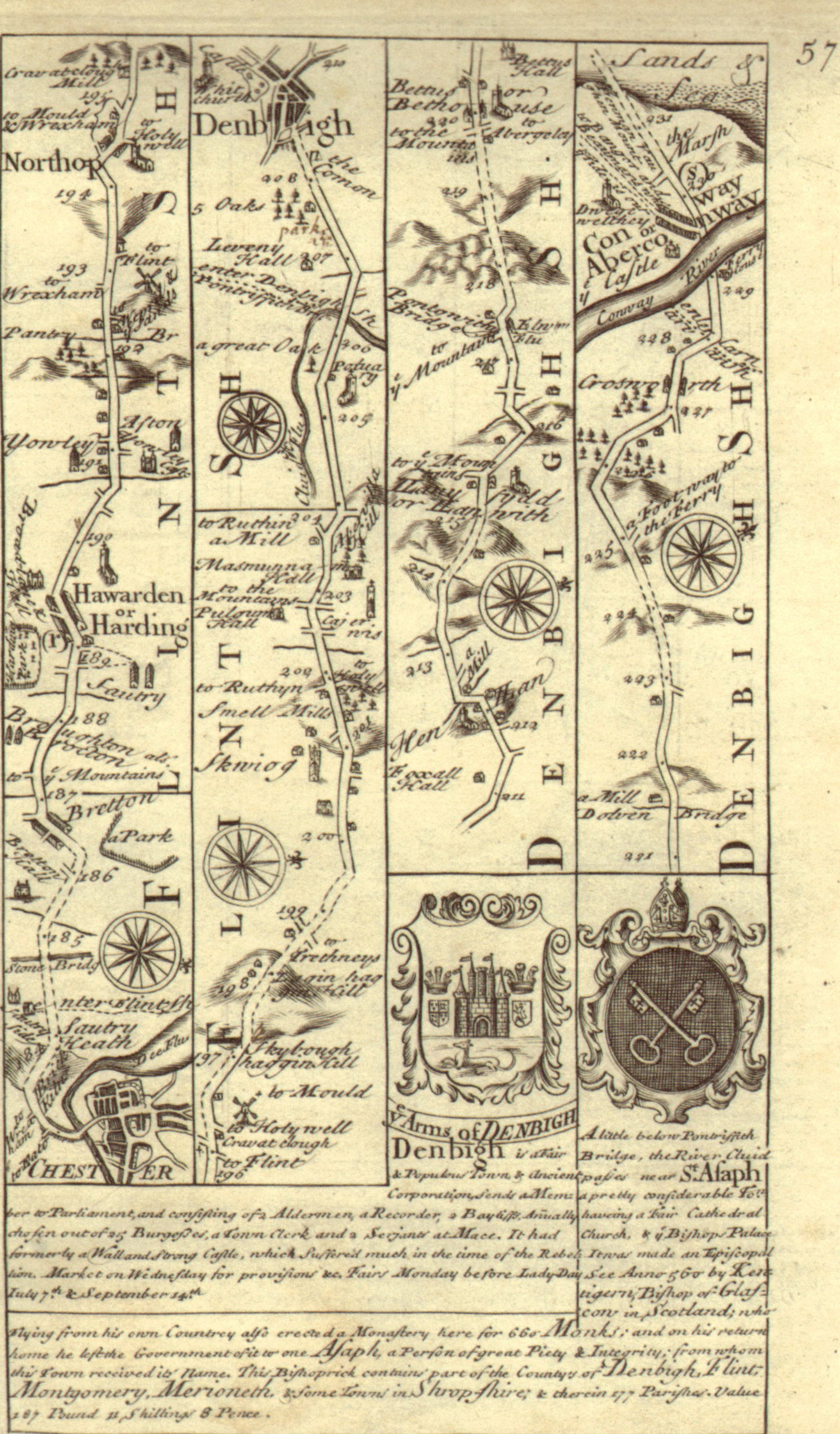

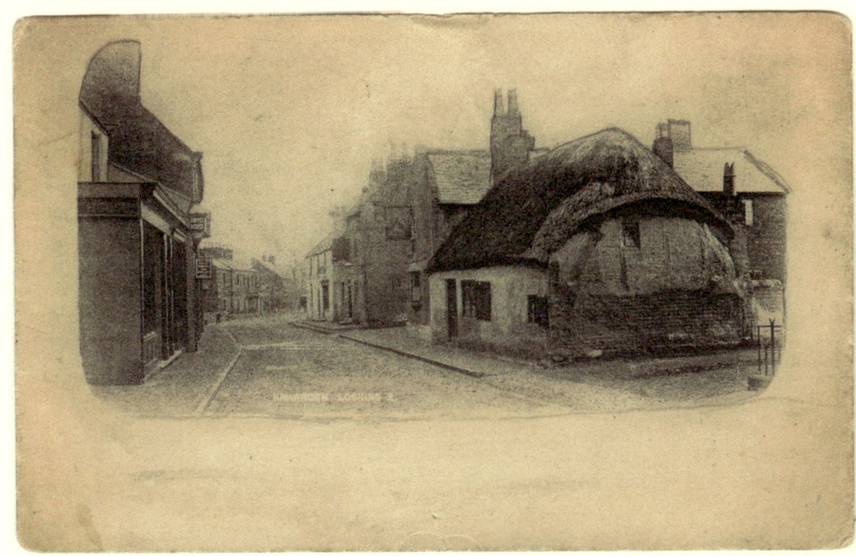

EMMA'S GRANDMOTHER'S HOME in Hawarden was demolished in 1890.

*Hawarden, a very considerable village, situated on the road leading to Chester, near the river Dee, and has still the ruins of a strong castle, although it does not appear by whom it was built ... The air of this county is extremely cold, but so healthy, that many of the inhabitants live to a great age ...*

Nathaniel Spencer (pseud.) Robert Sanders (ca. 1727–1783), *The Complete English Traveller, or a New Survey and Description of England and Wales.* London: J. Cooke, 1772.

The details of Emma's early life are obscure. By the summer of 1777, her mother had left Hawarden for London and Emma, at the age of twelve, was on her own, working as a maid in the home of Dr. Honoratus Leigh Thomas. After a short time she was fired and left Hawarden, never to return. Emma (still known as Amy) made the 180-mile journey to London, where she found employment in the home of another doctor, Richard Budd, a surgeon in Blackfriars, in the southeast part of the city.

FORE-EDGE PAINTING. "The entrances to London at Highgate and Islington." Junius, *Stat Nominus Umbra: A New Edition.* London: Vernon & Hood, 1805. Two volumes. (2010.091.02.0002)

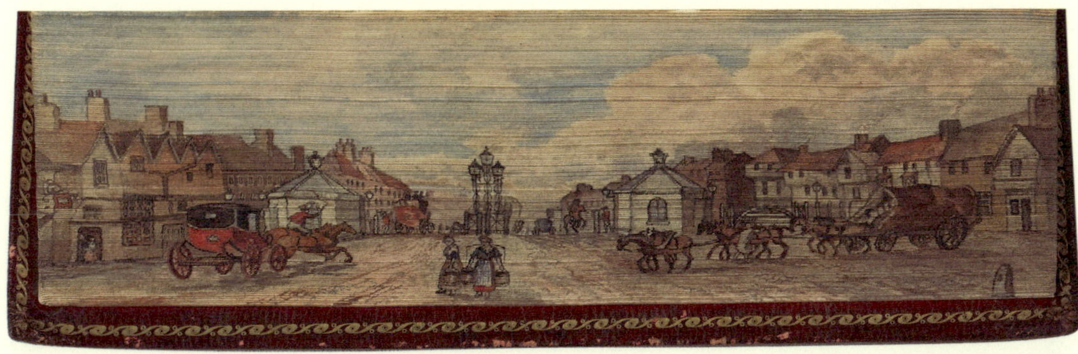

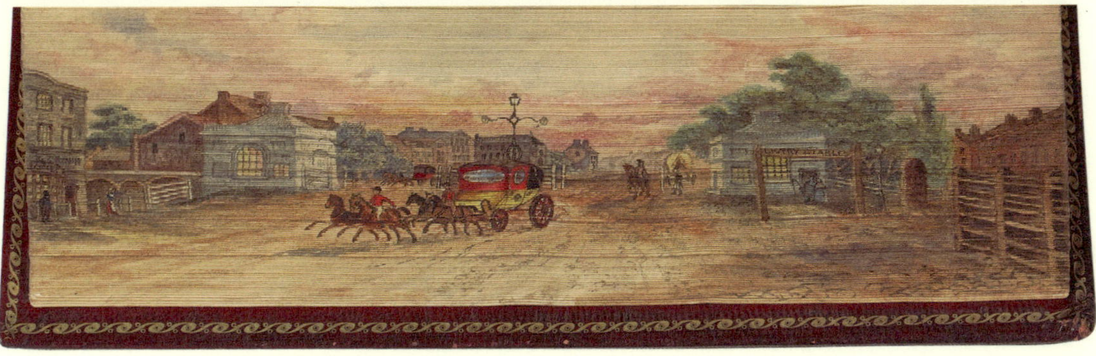

An aspiring young actress named Jane Powell was also in service to the Budds. Emma and Jane became fast friends and Jane introduced Emma to the theatre world in Covent Garden. Their adventurous explorations of city life soon led Mrs. Budd to turn the two girls out. Emma went to live with her mother and found work as dresser and maid at the Drury Lane Theatre in Covent Garden.

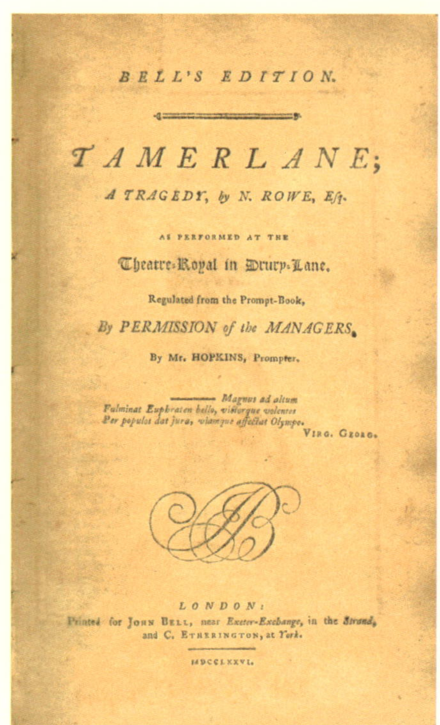

N. ROWE. *Tamerlane; A Tragedy, as Performed at the Theatre Royal in Drury Lane.* London: John Bell, 1776. (2010.110.00.0001)

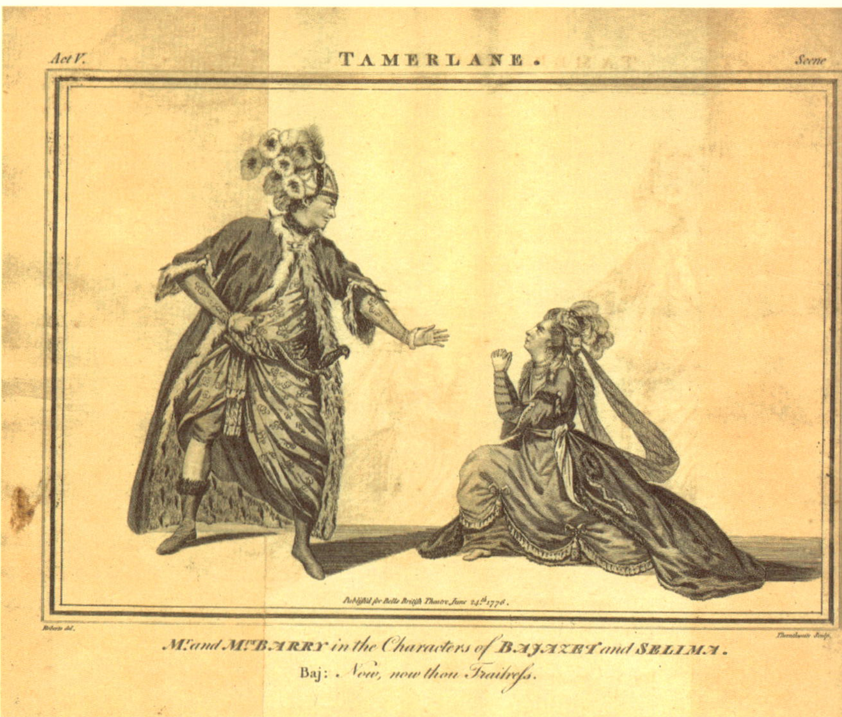


About this time the young and beautiful Emma began to pose for artists. She was eventually painted by many prominent artists, including Joshua Reynolds, Thomas Lawrence, John Hoppner, Gavin Hamilton, Benjamin West, Angelica Kauffmann, Richard Cosway, and Élisabeth-Louise Vigée Le Brun. But it was George Romney who would immortalize her.

In 1779, fourteen-year-old Emma was discovered by the quack doctor and sexologist, James Graham. Graham presented young women as "Goddesses of Youth and Health" in his Temple of Health and Hymen. Emma was one of Graham's earliest goddesses. She posed lightly clad among the marble statues as the goddess Hygieia and sold Graham's pamphlets and potions. The establishment's greatest attraction was a "Great Celestial State Bed" that delivered mild shocks that supposedly aided conception. Infertile couples paid high prices to try it.

Sir

As I understand by Mess.ʳˢ Adam that you have been so obliging as to give your Consent to my making a Trap door in the floor of the front Parlour in the house I now occupy, I hereby engage that the Alteration shall be made under the inspection of Mess.ʳˢ Adam to see that no material Injury is done to the principal Timbers, And also engage, at my Expence, to reinstate the floor or other damage that may have been occasioned by the intended alteration, to yours and Mess.ʳˢ Adam's Satisfaction, before I quit the House, — I am

Sir

Adelphi, 23.ᵈ December
    1779

Your most Obedient Servant

Ja.ˢ Graham

To John Henderson Esq.ʳ

JAMES GRAHAM. Autograph letter, signed: to John Henderson. 23 December 1779. 1 page, 4ᵗᵒ. (2005.023.00.0001)

This letter acknowledges an agreement with the owner for a trap door to be installed in the parlor of his "Temple of Health." One can only imagine what was elevated from—or disappeared into—this device.

Here, Emma modeled, danced, and learned to attract the attention of men. She soon became a minor celebrity. Shortly after leaving Graham's "Temple," Emma met Sir Harry Featherstonhaugh and began her first serious relationship. Sir Harry took her as his mistress and moved her to Uppark, his country estate, where she acted as hostess and entertainer for friends who came to hunt and carouse. Emma spent more than a year at Uppark, but when she became pregnant, in 1781, Sir Harry sent her away and she returned to stay with friends in Cheshire.

## *Charles Greville*

*Image Opposite*: THE HON. CHARLES FRANCIS GREVILLE, by George Romney (1734–1802). Half-length, in a brown coat and white necktie, ca. 1780s. Oil on canvas. 76.2 × 64.7 cm. (2005.007.00.0001)

The Greville family was introduced to Romney in 1768, and were his first aristocratic patrons. He completed a portrait of Georgiana, Lady Greville, after her marriage to George, Lord Greville (Charles's elder brother) in 1771. The present work seems to have been executed in the 1780s: there are sittings recorded in Romney's 1781–88 Diaries for "Grenville" (*sic*) on 22 June 1781, 30 March, and 22 April 1782. There are further sittings recorded under "Greville" on 27 November and 4 December 1781; 16 April and 15 May 1782, and for "Mr Greville" on 23 April, 22 June, 2 and 15 May 1787.

In desperation, Emma wrote to Sir Harry's friend, Charles Greville, pleading to be rescued. Agreeing on condition that she mend her ways, he responded on 10 January 1782, "*I will forget your faults and bad conduct … if I shall find that you have learnt by your experience to value yourself & endeavor to preserve your Friends by good conduct & affection,*" continuing, "*take another name, by degrees I would get you a new set of acquaintance …*"

Greville brought Emma to London and installed her in a rented house along with her mother (who also took a new name, Mrs. Mary Cadogan). In early March the baby, known as Emma Carew, was born and soon dispatched to the care of her great-grandmother, Sarah Kidd, in Hawarden.

Thenceforth, Amy Lyon would be Mrs. Emma Hart, and would wear the sober dress of a maid. "[*S*]*oon after she became acquainted with Mr. Greville, he took her to Ranelagh, where she attracted so much notice, that she perceived it gave him pain; she, therefore, of her own accord, put off her gay attire, and assumed the garb of a lady's maid, in which she ever after appeared, and never again went to any public place.*" (John Romney, *Memoirs of the life and works of George Romney*, 1830).

Thus began her four-year sojourn with Greville.

Born in 1741, Charles Francis Greville was a younger son of Francis Greville, Earl of Warwick, and a nephew of Sir William Hamilton. When his father died in 1773, his brother inherited the lands and title and Charles inherited his father's seat in the House of Commons and an income of £500 a year.

Over time, Charles Greville served the government in various capacities, including member of the Board of Trade, vice chamberlain to the royal household, and Lord of the Admiralty. He

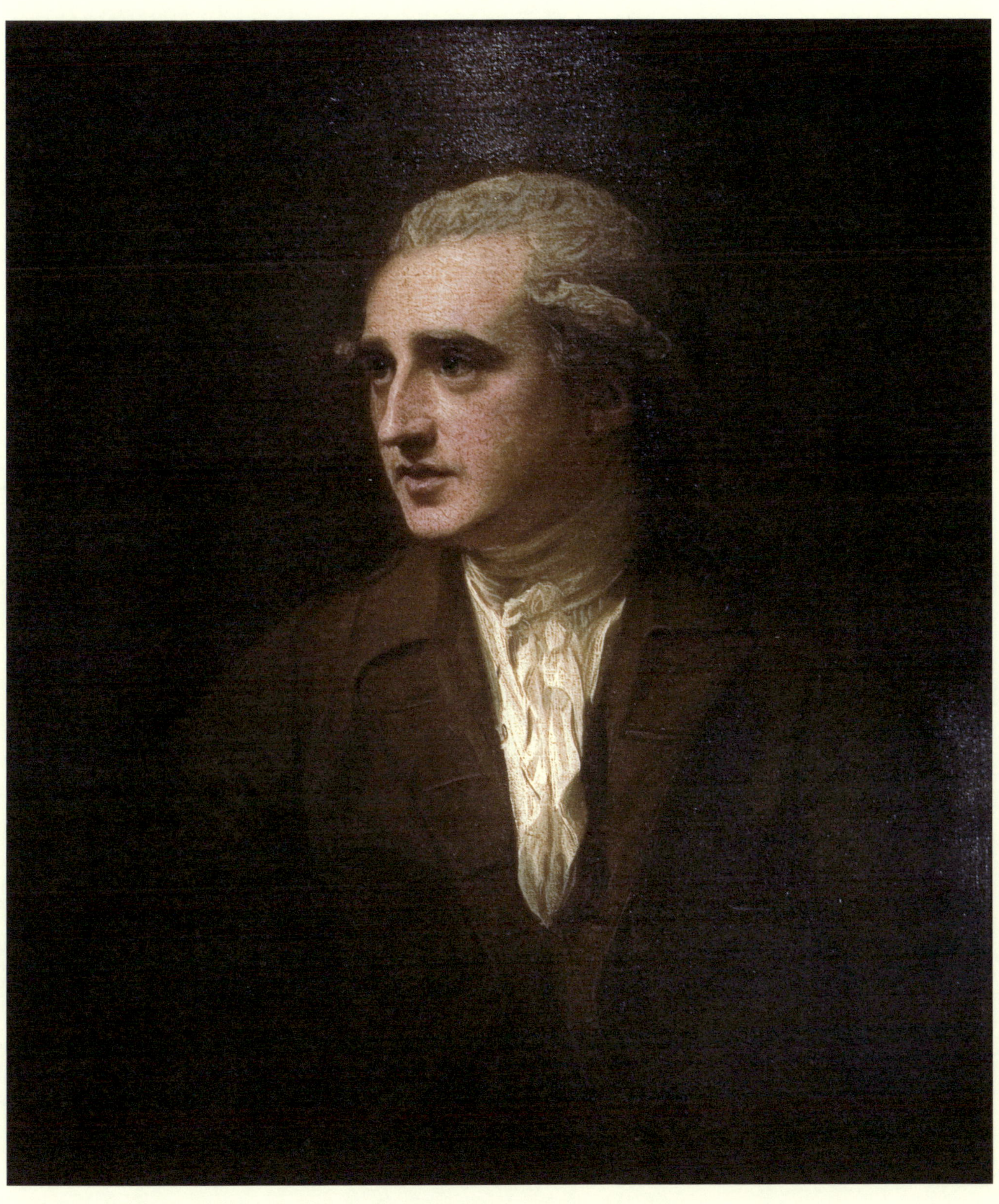

moved in the highest circles and, like his uncle, was a Fellow of the Royal Society for the Improvement of Natural Knowledge and the Society of Dilettanti, an elite group of aristocratic travellers committed to the study of antiquity and the enjoyment of life—wine, women, wit, and revelry.

Greville always maintained a close relationship with Sir William. They corresponded often, trading views on politics, their collections, and the state of Greville's finances, which were always

CHARLES GREVILLE. Autograph letter, signed: to William Hamilton. London, August or September, 1775. 4 pages, folio. (1990.035.10.0002)

In this chatty letter, Greville writes to thank his uncle for hospitality and kindness in Naples, and touches on subjects of mutual interest: wine, paintings, and acquaintances, concluding, *I flatter myself that in many ways I am like you for I find a difficulty in separating the ideas I've collected from you from those which I have presented …*

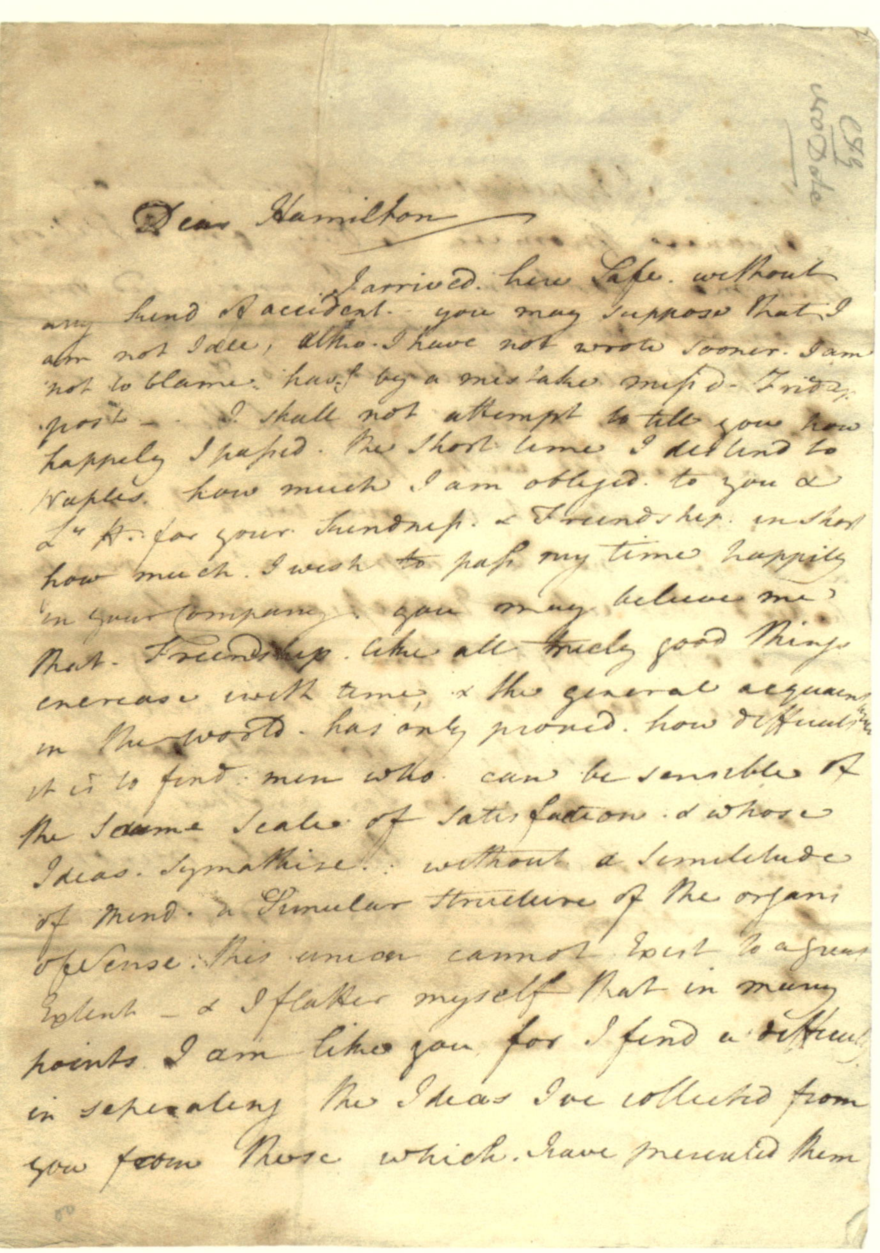

tenuous. Despite a chronic lack of money, Greville amassed an important mineralogical collection comprising more than 15,000 specimens that was purchased for the British Museum after his death.

Emma and Charles lived separately from 1782 until 1784, when Greville sold his home and moved into the house he rented for Emma and her mother on Edgware Road in the decidedly unfashionable East London.

WILLIAM HAMILTON. Autograph letter, signed: to Charles Greville. Naples, 3 August 1779. 5 pages, folio. (1990.035.03.0002)

Sir William wrote to Greville, commenting on the outbreak of war with France and Spain: *We are playing a very high game & at this moment the stake is very great indeed, but if we escape this campaign I have no doubt but that we shall make France and Spain regret their rash measures.*

The Armada of 1779 was an exceptionally large joint French and Spanish fleet intended to facilitate an invasion of England, as part of the wider conflict sparked by the American Revolution. The invasion never materialized.

| Nov'br # | Money Paid &c | L | S | D |
|---|---|---|---|---|
| 1 | Coach — | 0 | 1 | 0 |
| | Bakers Bill — | 0 | 4 | 11 |
| | Butter Bill — | 0 | 5 | 0 |
| | Milk — | 0 | 2 | 3 |
| | Gardener — | 0 | 2 | 0 |
| 2 | Butcher — | 0 | 2 | 6 |
| | 1 sack of Coals — | 0 | 3 | 6 |
| | Oysters — | 0 | 0 | 8 |
| | porter — | 0 | 0 | 2 |
| | Eggs — | 0 | 0 | 4 |
| | Handkerchifs — | 1 | 10 | 0 |
| | stockings — | 2 | 10 | 0 |
| 3 | Mrs Hackwood — | 4 | 12 | 6 |
| | widgeins — | 0 | 2 | 6 |
| | Coals — | 0 | 3 | 6 |
| 4 | Muton — | 0 | 2 | 0 |
| | Fowl — | 0 | 2 | 4 |
| 6 | Coals — | 0 | 3 | 6 |
| 7 | oysters — | 0 | 0 | 6 |
| | | £10 | 9 | 2 |

| Nov'br # | Money Paid &c | L | S | D |
|---|---|---|---|---|
| 7 | muton — | 0 | 3 | 0 |
| | candles — | 0 | 2 | 9 |
| | mold candles — | 0 | 1 | 6/ |
| | storch — | 0 | 1 | 0 |
| | Blue — | 0 | 0 | 6 |
| | soap — | 0 | 2 | 0 |
| 8 | a pint of Porter — | 0 | 0 | 2 |
| | 2 Rabbits — | 0 | 1 | 3 |
| | Beef stakes — | 0 | 0 | 8 |
| | Coals — | 0 | 3 | 6 |
| | Butter Bill — | 0 | 4 | 9 |
| 9 | Bakers Bill — | 0 | 4 | 11 |
| | Milk — | 0 | 2 | 3 |
| | Gardener — | 0 | 2 | 0 |
| 10 | wrighting paper wax &c — | 0 | 2 | 6 |
| | Cooch — | 0 | 2 | 0 |
| | a fowl — | 0 | 2 | 0 |
| | Black lead — | 0 | 0 | 2 |
| | pins & thread — | £1 | 17 | 8 |

EMMA HART [Emma, Lady Hamilton] (1765–1815). Autograph manuscript. 18½ pages, 4to. Detailing payments made from 27 October 1784 to 21 February 1785 and, at the back, payments received from 29 October 1784 to 7 February 1785. (1990.035.00.0003)

The ledger, above, details payments made and received from 27 October 1784 to 21 February 1785. The accounts show how frugally the couple lived. Only three payments for amounts more than one pound are recorded—for stockings, the butcher, and the brewer—and none over the Christmas period. Eggs were constantly bought, oysters occasionally, and "orranges" only for Christmas.

Constantly short of funds, Greville sought to marry wealth but never succeeded. In 1788, he purchased a house in Paddington, then a suburban district of London, where he pursued his interests in mineralogy and horticulture, introducing many new species to England. He died there in 1809, a few weeks shy of his sixtieth birthday.

## Romney & Emma: Reciprocal Muses

### BY ALEX KIDSON

WHEN the young Fanny Burney sat for her portrait to the pastellist Catherine Read in February 1775, and was asked by the artist to adopt "an attitude," she burst out laughing, writing later in her diary that she could not imagine what Miss Read meant. Twelve years later, when Johann Wolfgang von Goethe paid a visit to Sir William Hamilton in Naples and witnessed a performance of "Attitudes" by the young lady in the house, he wrote of the experience as of the discovery of a new art form.

"We witnessed," he wrote, "that which has been dreamt of by thousands of artists—carried out on the spot and in rapid succession ... One thing is for sure—the pleasure is *unique*!" At the heart of this change of sensibility—one of European dimensions—lay the visits Sir William's mistress had paid a few years previously to the London studio of the artist George Romney. As has been recognised at least since the publication in 1835 of the *Memoirs* of Elisabeth Vigée Le Brun, it was the experience of modelling for a succession of Romney's fancy pictures—females from classical mythology, allegory, and literature old and new—that instilled in Emma the self-confidence, the physical skill, and the mental adroitness to invent a new artistic phenomenon.

How—beneath the surface of received wisdom, beyond the Hollywood cliché of a lonely middle-aged painter's infatuation for a teenaged girl—did this happen? Emma certainly did not become Romney's muse overnight. In the spring of 1782, when the artist's friend Charles Greville first brought his new mistress to sit for her portrait (*Emma as Nature*, now in the Frick Collection—see p. 25), her visits were limited in scope and duration. They were terminated even before Romney could finish a second picture (*Emma as Circe*, at Waddesdon) in which, in some sort of compact with Greville—and as if in private competition with Sir Joshua Reynolds—he distilled Emma's role as Greville's enchantress. Nearly eighteen months were to pass before Romney saw Emma again.

And yet in the experience of working on the *Circe*, in her flowing white Grecian robe, and with her exaggeratedly theatrical pose and expression, a seed was sown. Two decades of rivalry with Reynolds had wedded Romney to a view of portraiture as the capturing of something momentary, something heightened—the very opposite of the technique of public, "historical" distillation

ALEX KIDSON studied history at Oxford University, and from 1982 until 2008 he was Curator of British Art at the Walker Art Gallery, Liverpool. He curated the bi-centenary Romney exhibition held in Liverpool, London and Los Angeles in 2002 and is currently writing a complete catalogue of Romney's paintings.

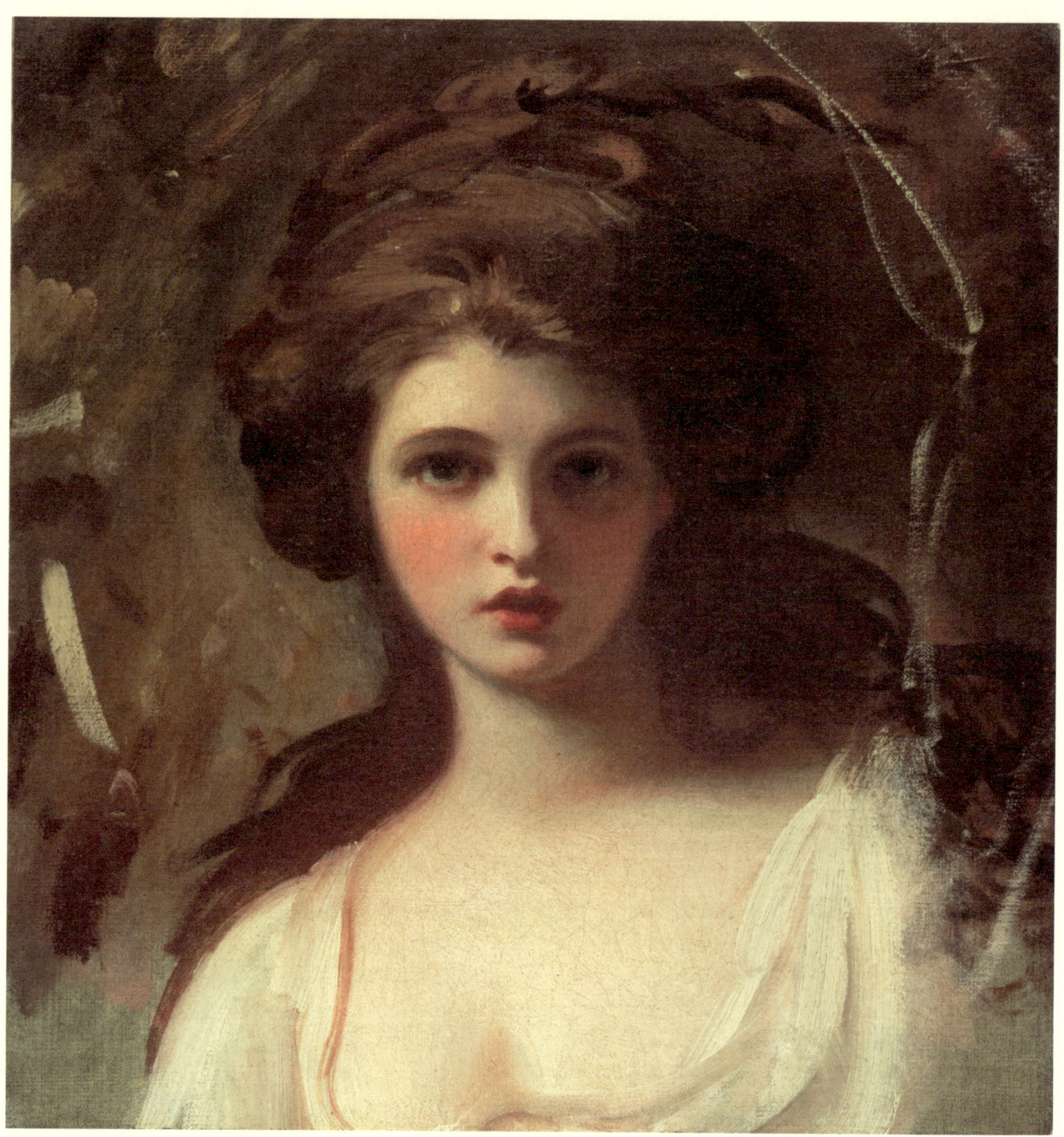



of character practised by Reynolds, and much closer to today's idea of a great photograph. The sittings for the *Circe* included one in which Romney painted an oil sketch that captured the expression of the enchantress on the wing and enshrined a directness and spontaneity of feeling as though of some beautiful film still. Here was a model whose ability to assume, hold, and remember difficult poses and strong, legible expressions—unlike his day-to-day clients—fired Romney to paint in the way he really wanted.

16

Emma returned to Romney's studio at the end of 1783 at the request of Greville's uncle, Sir William Hamilton, who was visiting London from Naples and ordered a picture of her as a classical bacchante. (She sat for Reynolds concurrently in the same role.) As with the *Circe*, that picture and its sequel, the *Spinstress* that Greville himself commissioned as an essay in contrast, were too concerned with mining art-historical precedent, too much like set-pieces, to allow Romney to explore the deeper creative implications that Emma's first visits had raised.

Romney's mid-1780s small painting of Emma with her head in a white cloak, from the Kislak collection, is probably an early idea for the *Spinstress*. The magnificent *Emma as Sensibility*, also in the Kislak collection, came from the next phase of Emma's creative engagement with Romney, starting in the autumn of 1784, when the pattern of her visits to his studio changed.

By now, Greville was more relaxed and positively encouraging about Emma going out into public spaces. Her visits to Romney's studio had gradually become regular weekly or bi-weekly events, a way of keeping her occupied; for Emma herself, they were the nearest she got to the "polite" world of high society, trips out of her Edgware Road cottage that she looked forward to as the most charged events of her life. With the *Spinstress* out of the way, her sessions with Romney soon became more experimental. By the middle of November 1784, more and more of her visits were his only appointment of the day, as though he had begun to need space around them to handle the different creative demands they made. There are indeed strong signs that he deliberately scaled his society portraiture back, taking as few clients as possible in order to devote more time to his special model.

Romney began a string of new subjects from her—besides the *Sensibility*—*Alope*, another *Bacchante*, *Cassandra*, the figure of Comedy nursing the infant Shakespeare, a *Gipsy*, *Medea*, *Saint Cecilia*, *Serena* (from his friend William Hayley's popular poem *The Triumphs of Temper*), a *Sibyl*, and last but not least, *Miranda*, from Shakespeare's *The Tempest*—plus portraits of Emma in real life, studies, and *têtes d'expression*. It was evidently in this period that Emma's talent for slipping from one role into another, as she would do in the Attitudes, was honed, and her absorption into Romney's highly personal aesthetic, part austerely classical, part proto-Romantic, was accomplished.

It is unclear how long into 1785 this phase of Romney's and Emma's creative partnership—for such it had surely become—lasted. Romney's sitter-book for that year is lost, though it is tempting to imagine that Romney's rather priggish son destroyed it as evidence of his father's growing obsession. But, by the spring of 1786, in the weeks before Emma's departure for Naples, the pattern of her visits to his studio had reverted to that of their early days: evidence that some sort of watershed had been reached and a resolution attained—

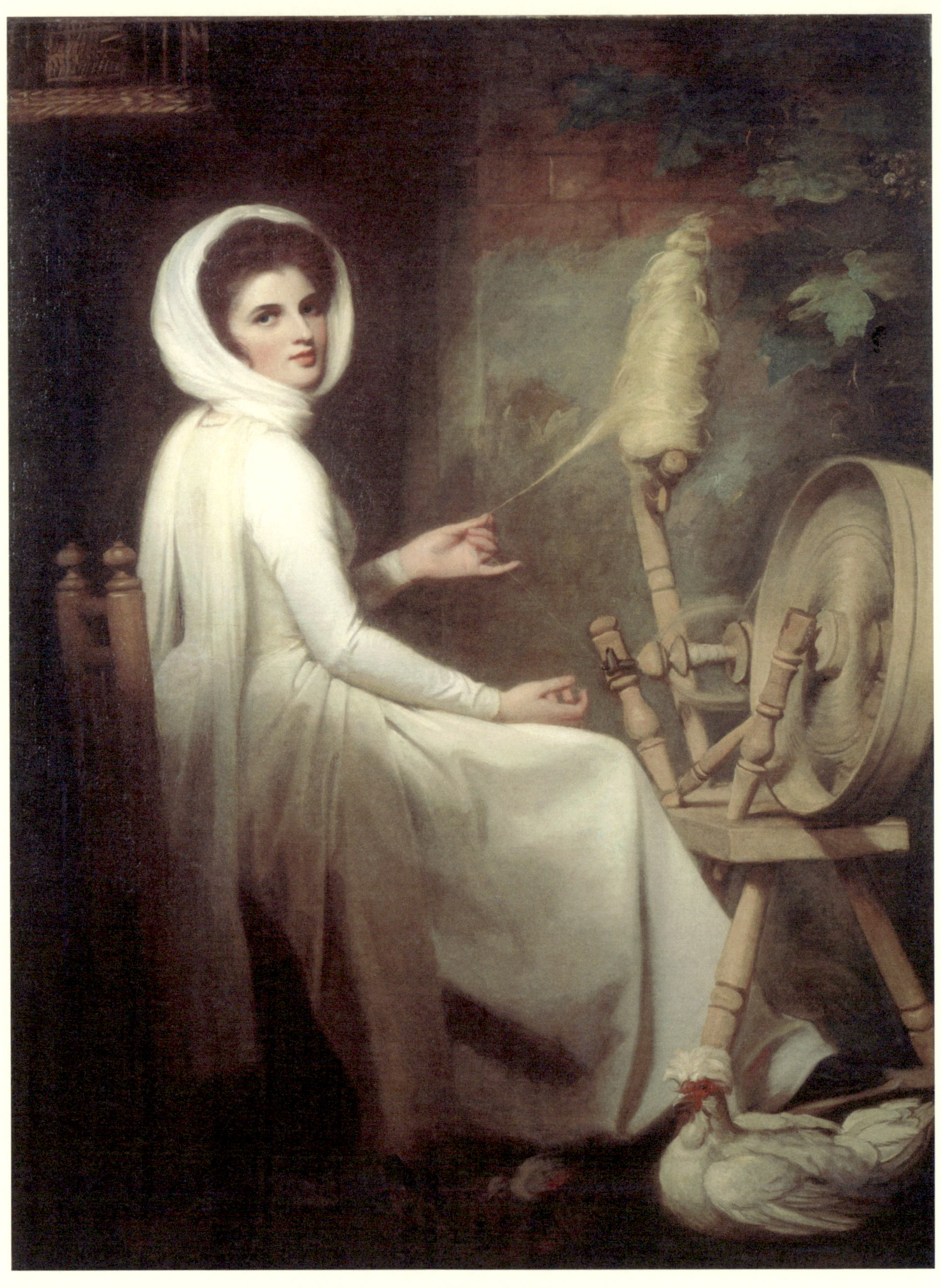

THE SPINSTRESS, Emma Hart at the Spinning Wheel, 1782–86, by George Romney (1734–1802). Oil on canvas. 172.7 × 127 cm. © Kenwood House, The Iveagh Bequest, London.

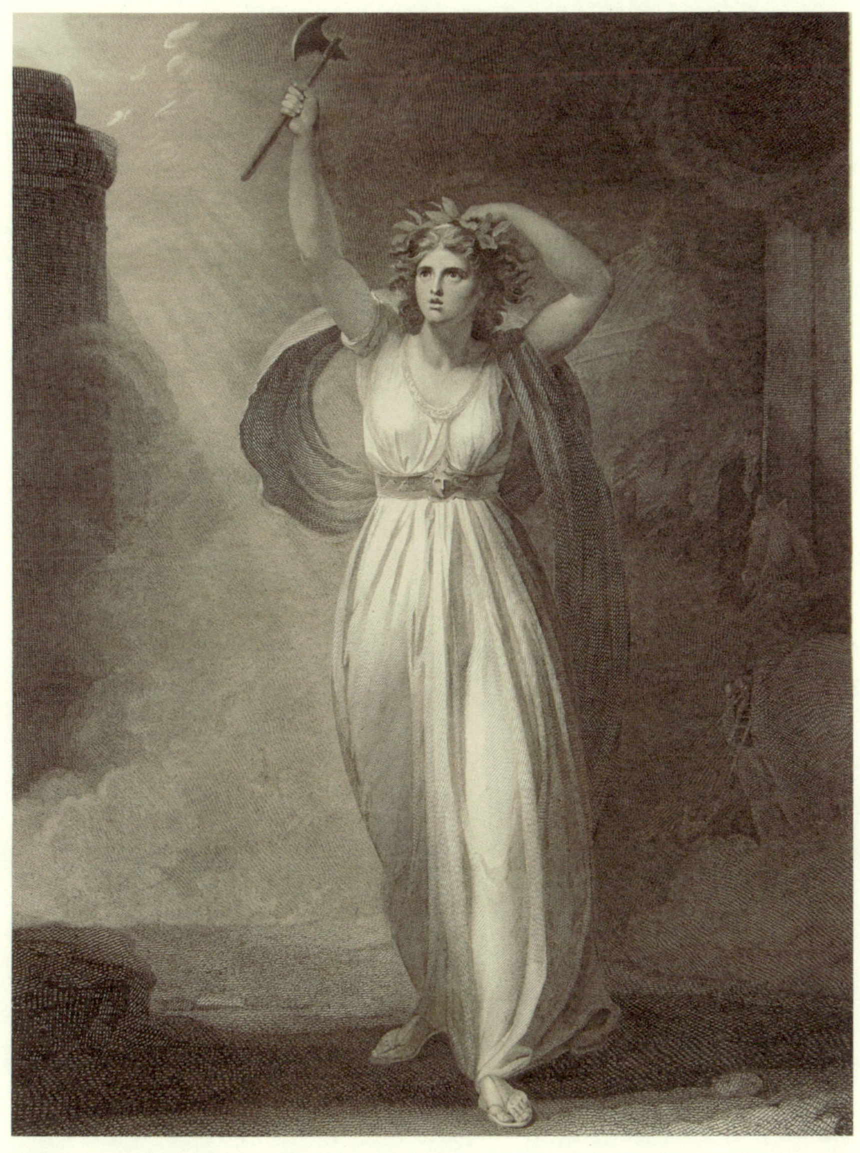



as though Romney could teach Emma no more. It is possible that
Emma had already begun performing her Attitudes before she left
London, since in one of her first letters to Greville from Naples
she mentions the term without gloss, evidently expecting him to
understand.

By the time she returned to London with Sir William Hamilton in 1791, Emma was already something of a celebrity. Romney
could no longer count on her to be his model; the most that he
could hope was that she would give him enough sittings to finish the *Cassandra*, the grand pendant to the *Circe* which had been
left incomplete on her departure for Naples in 1786. In fact, the
six weeks between 8 June and 20 July 1791 witnessed the most

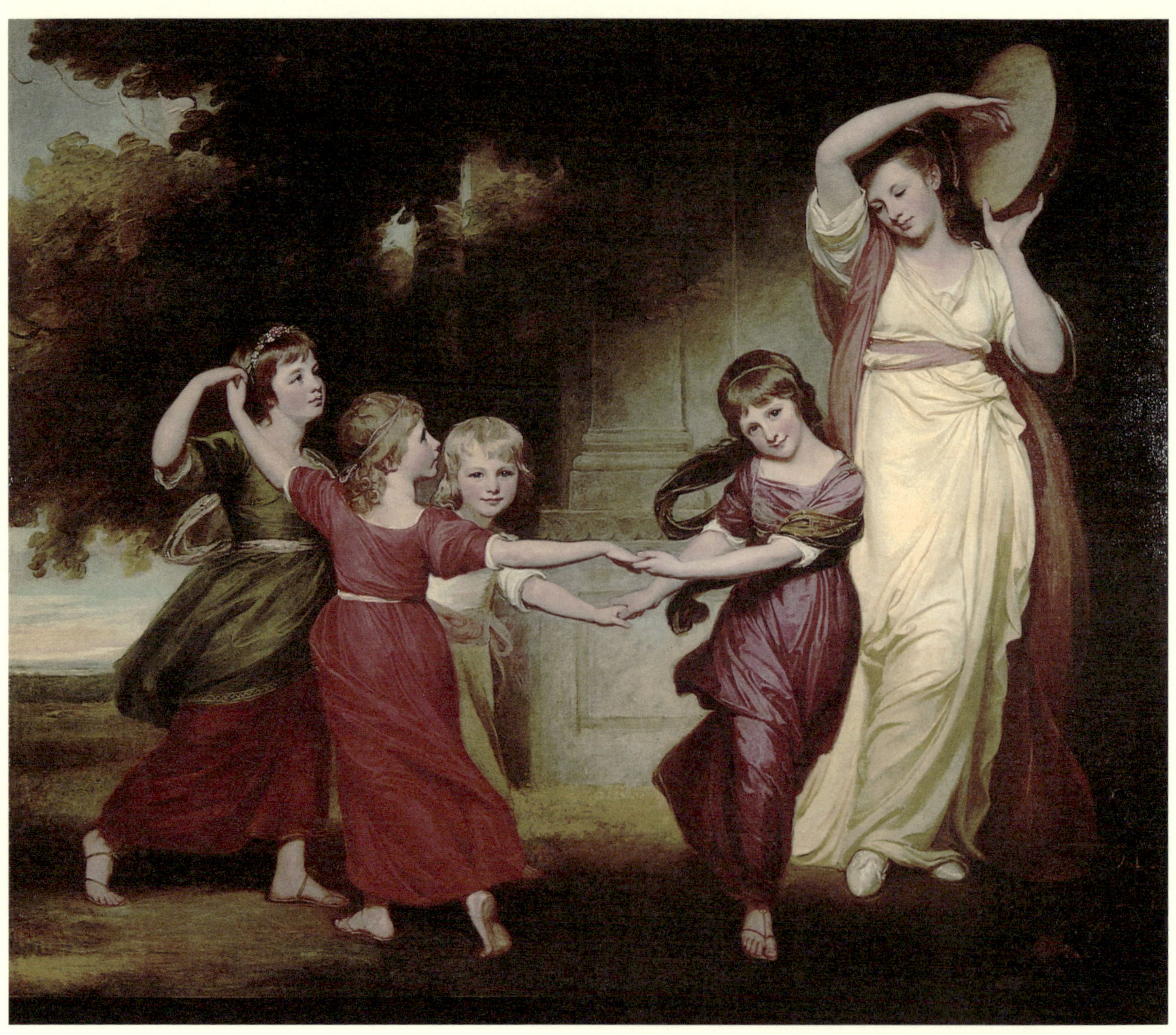



intense bout of modelling for Romney that Emma ever undertook. Many new subjects were begun, including a *Magdalen* and an *Iphigenia*, two of the roles in which Emma is portrayed in the twelve illustrations of the Attitudes by Friedrich Rehberg published in 1794, which suggests that Emma proposed these subjects to Romney rather than the other way around.

The emphasis in the Attitudes on classical and religious figures, as witnessed in Rehberg's illustrations, probably reflected the input of Sir William Hamilton himself and at a superficial glance only a small minority of their subjects are ones painted by Romney. But on closer inspection the poses depicted by Rehberg, even if used by Emma for different characters, often derive, as if interchangeably, from Romney paintings—and not

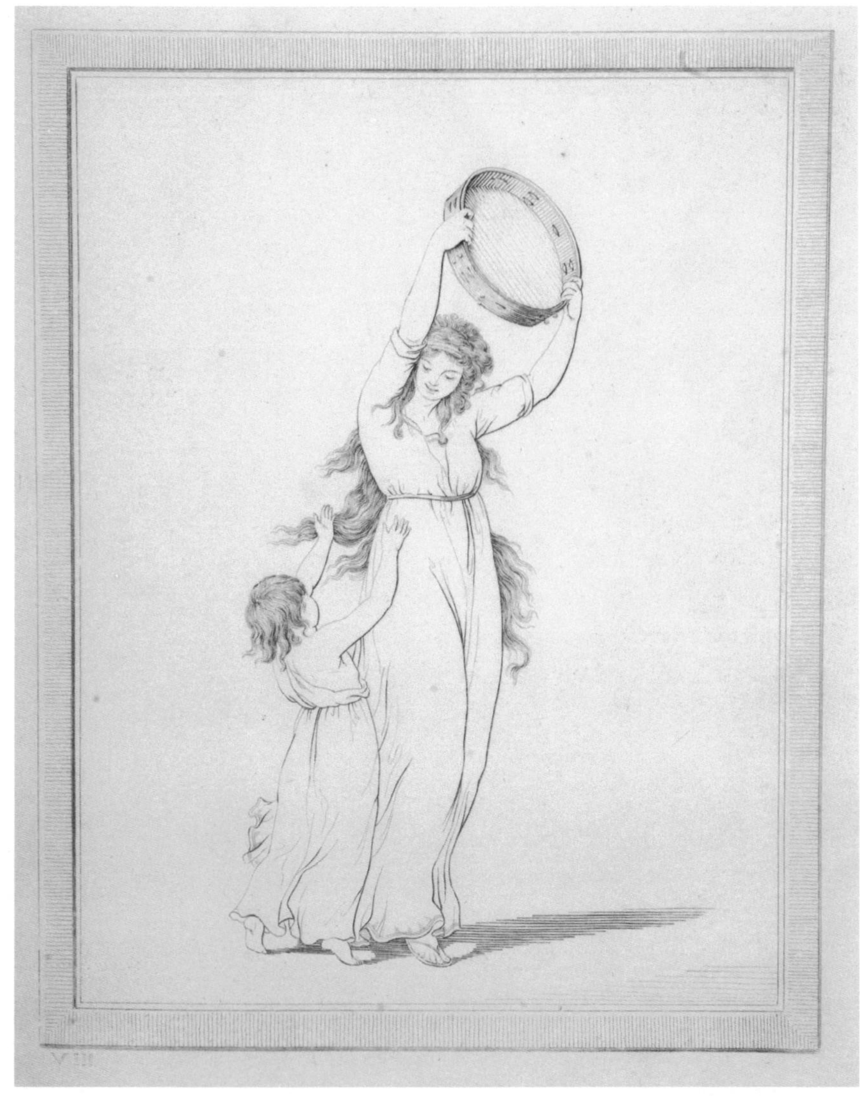



FRIEDRICH REHBERG (1758–1835), *Drawings Faithfully Copied from Nature at Naples, and with Permission Dedicated To the Right Honourable Sir William Hamilton, His Britannic Majesty's Envoy Extraordinary and Plenipotentiary at the Court of Naples, by his most humble Servant Frederick Rehberg* [London]: 1794, pl. VIII. (1991.295.00.0005)

just of paintings of Emma herself but also paintings of other female sitters, which Emma would have seen or heard about in Romney's studio. The close similarity between the pose of Emma's *Nymph*, with her tambourine, and Lady Anne Leveson-Gower, in Romney's earlier masterpiece *The Leveson-Gower Family*, for example, leaves no doubt that Romney taught Emma as well as painted her. There could hardly be a finer demonstration of the essential unity of the two artists' creative worlds.

—ALEX KIDSON

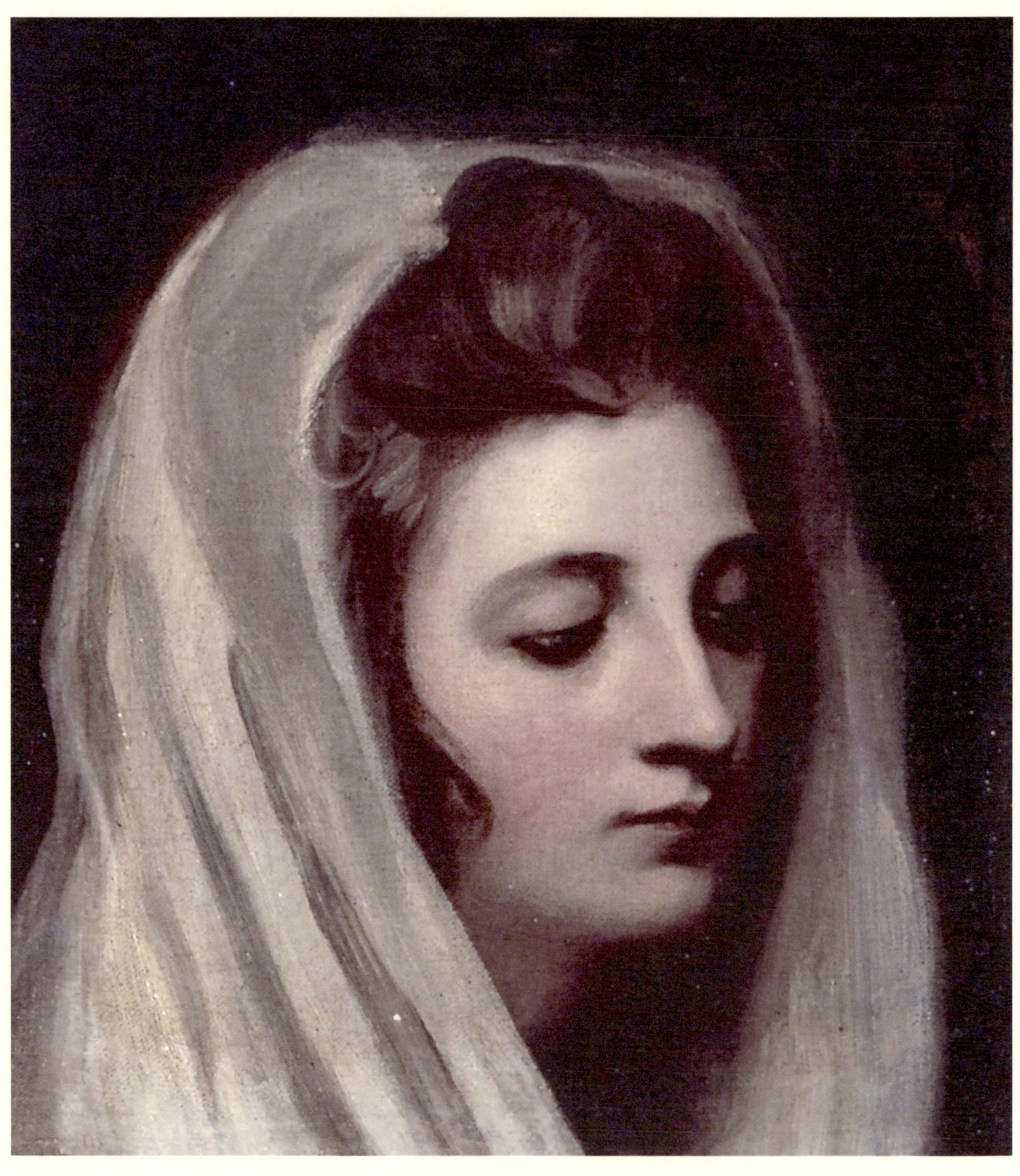

EMMA HART in a white cloak, ca. 1788, by George Romney (1734–1802). Oil on canvas. 36.5 × 32 cm. (1992.009.00.0001)

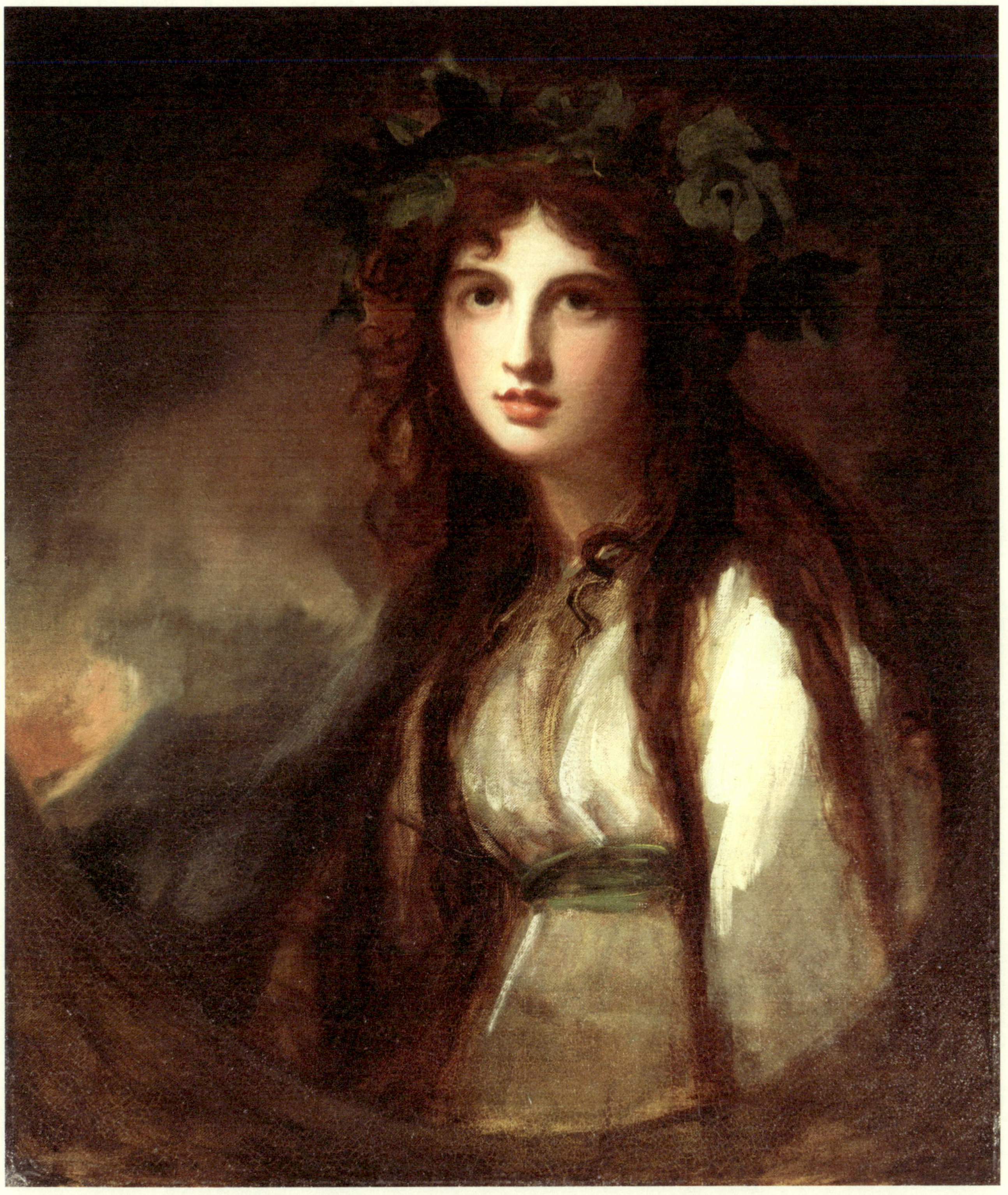

PORTRAIT OF EMMA HART as a bacchante, ca. 1784–1786, by George Romney (1734–1802). Oil on canvas. 76.2 × 63.5 cm. In a painted oval. Half length, in a white dress with a blue sash and a crown of laurel leaves, against a background showing Vesuvius erupting. (1993.004.00.0001)

It is intriguing to note that this painting was bought by William Randolph Hearst in 1928 and given to his mistress, Marion Davies.

*Image Opposite*: EMMA HART AS *Nature,* by George Romney (1734–1802). Mezzotint engraving by John Raphael Smith, 1784, after Romney's painting. 26.7 × 22 cm. (2003.200.00.0001)

The painting is now conserved in the Frick Collection, New York.

---

CHARLES GREVILLE brought Emma to sit for a portrait by George Romney on 12 March 1782, soon after the birth of her child. Later correspondence suggests that Greville had an unfulfilled scheme to sell Romney portraits of her at a profit. *"In the beginning of 1782 Lady Hamilton, who then passed under the name of Mrs. Hart, first sat to Mr. Romney. She was brought by the Honourable Charles Greville to sit for a three-quarters portrait. It was that beautiful one, so full of naivete, in which she is represented with a little spaniel lap dog under her arm."* (John Romney, *Memoirs of the life and works of George Romney,* 1830). The portrait *Nature* became one of the most popular paintings in Romney's studio. A print was soon produced and sold in shops throughout London.

Inspired by Emma's beauty and acting talent, Romney sketched her in emotions from surprise to joy to rage, then turned the sketches into paintings showing characters as diverse as St. Cecilia and Medea.

Romney's daybooks record more that 100 sittings between 1782 and 1784 and Emma's relationship with Romney continued unabated until Emma left England for Naples in 1786. Undoubtedly there were many more sittings, but the daybook for 1785 is lost.

◄═══►

Among the most celebrated of Romney's many portraits of Emma is the personification of *Sensibility,* which was inspired by one of Emma's favorite poems, William Hayley's *The Triumphs of Temper.* William Hayley (1745–1820), writer and poet, was patron not only to Romney—for whom he wrote *A Poetical Epistle to an Eminent Painter* (1778) and *The Life of George Romney* (1809)—but also to John Flaxman and William Blake. Blake illustrated Hayley's *Life of Cowper* as well as *Life of Romney.* The circumstances of how *Sensibility*'s composition came about are explained by Hayley, *"During my visit to Romney … I happened to find him one morning contemplating by himself a recently colored head on a small canvas."* Hayley suggested that the same head should be drawn on a larger canvas, with the figure extending its hand to a mimosa plant to illustrate his poem: *"I like your suggestion,"* replied the painter, *"and will enlarge my canvas immediately,"* and *"without loss of time I will hasten to an eminent nurseryman of Hammersmith, and bring you the most beautiful plant I can find that may suit your purpose"* (William Hayley, *Life of George Romney,* 1809). Emma Hamilton could not have actually posed for the picture, however, as she had already been living in Italy for a year. Mimosa (*Mimosa pudica*) is a species of "sensitive" plants that so fascinated eighteenth-century scientists

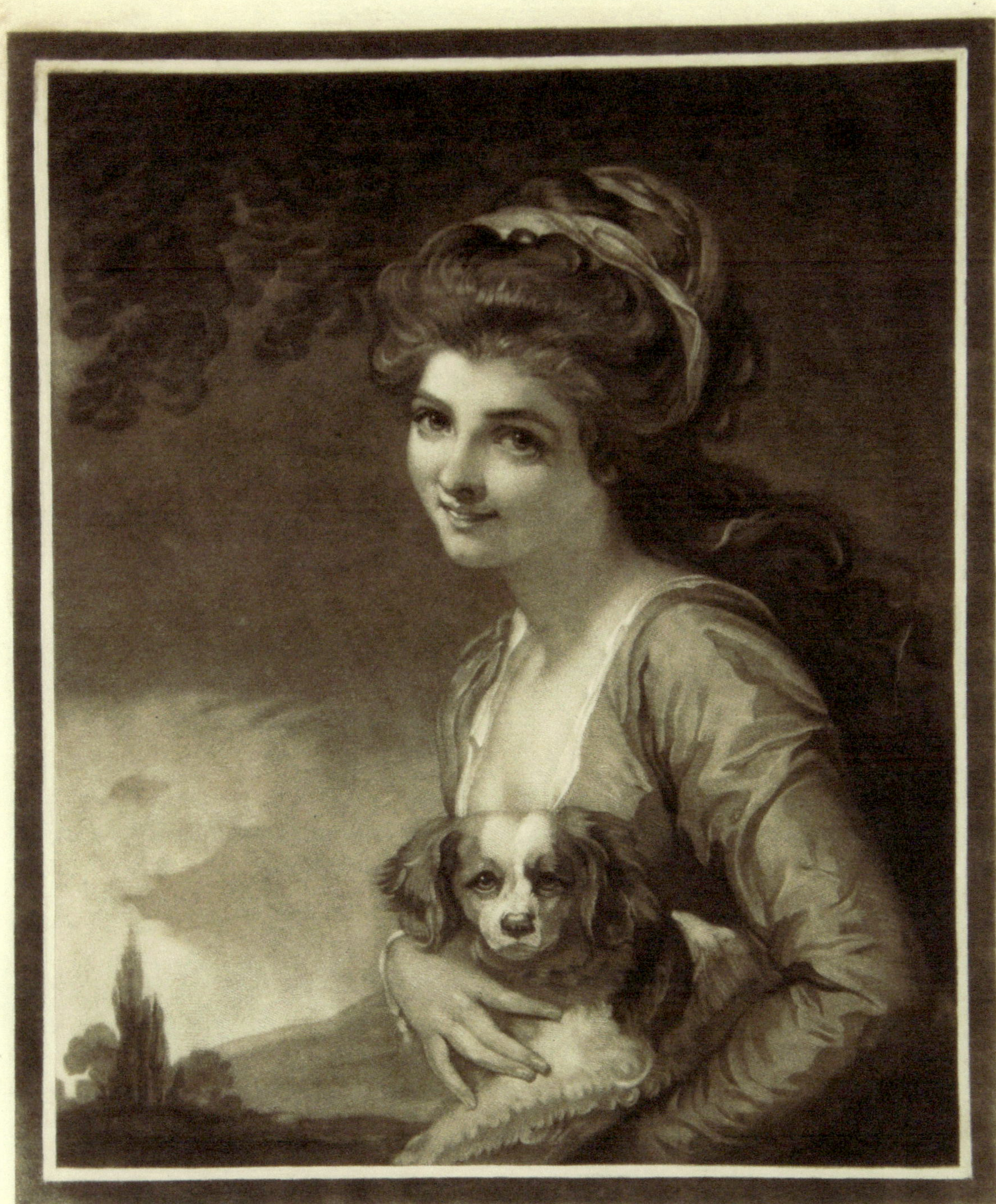

Painted by G? Romney

Engrav'd by I.R. Smith.
Mezzotinto Engraver to his Royal
Highness the Prince of Wales.

NATURE

WILLIAM HAYLEY (1745–1820), *The Triumphs of Temper; A Poem, in Six Cantos*. Chichester: Cadell and Davies, 1803. (2009.078.00.0001)

This edition includes six original designs by Maria Flaxman engraved by William Blake.

The engravings of female figures in the early editions of Hayley's *Triumphs of Temper* are thought to be of Emma herself. The first edition was published in London by J. Dodsley, 1781. (2009.079.00.0001)

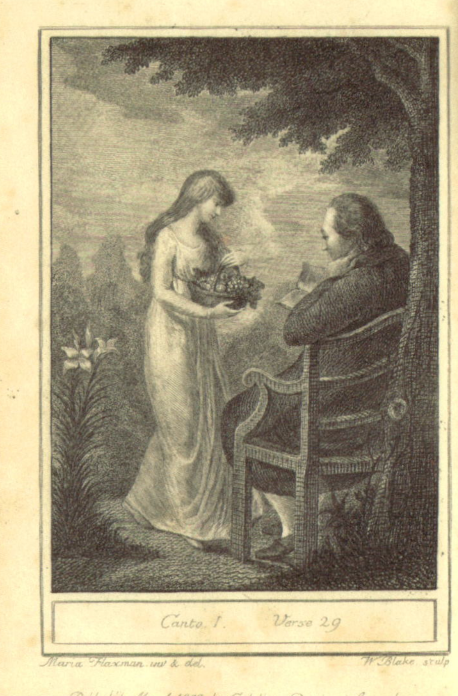



and dilettantes, as they seemed to bridge the vegetable and animal kingdoms. The newly discovered American plant sensitive, the Venus Flytrap, was first illustrated by John Ellis, naturalist and fellow of the Royal Society, in 1770, and he sent specimens of the plant to Carolus Linnaeus, who called it a "miraculum naturae." Hayley's lines that served as the inspiration for Romney's *Sensiblity* are as follows:

> *For Sensibility is sovereign here.*
> *Thou seest her train of sprightly damsels sport,*
> *Where the soft spirit holds her rural court;*
>
> *…*
>
> *Of vivid youth, and pleasure's purple flame,*
> *Gilds her accomplish'd work—the female frame!*
> *With rich luxuriance tender, sweetly wild,*
> *And just between the woman and the child.*
> *Her fair left arm around a vase she flings,*
> *From which the tender plant Mimosa springs;*
> *Towards its leaves, o'er which she fondly bends,*
> *The youthful fair her vacant hand extends*
> *With gentle motion, anxious to survey*

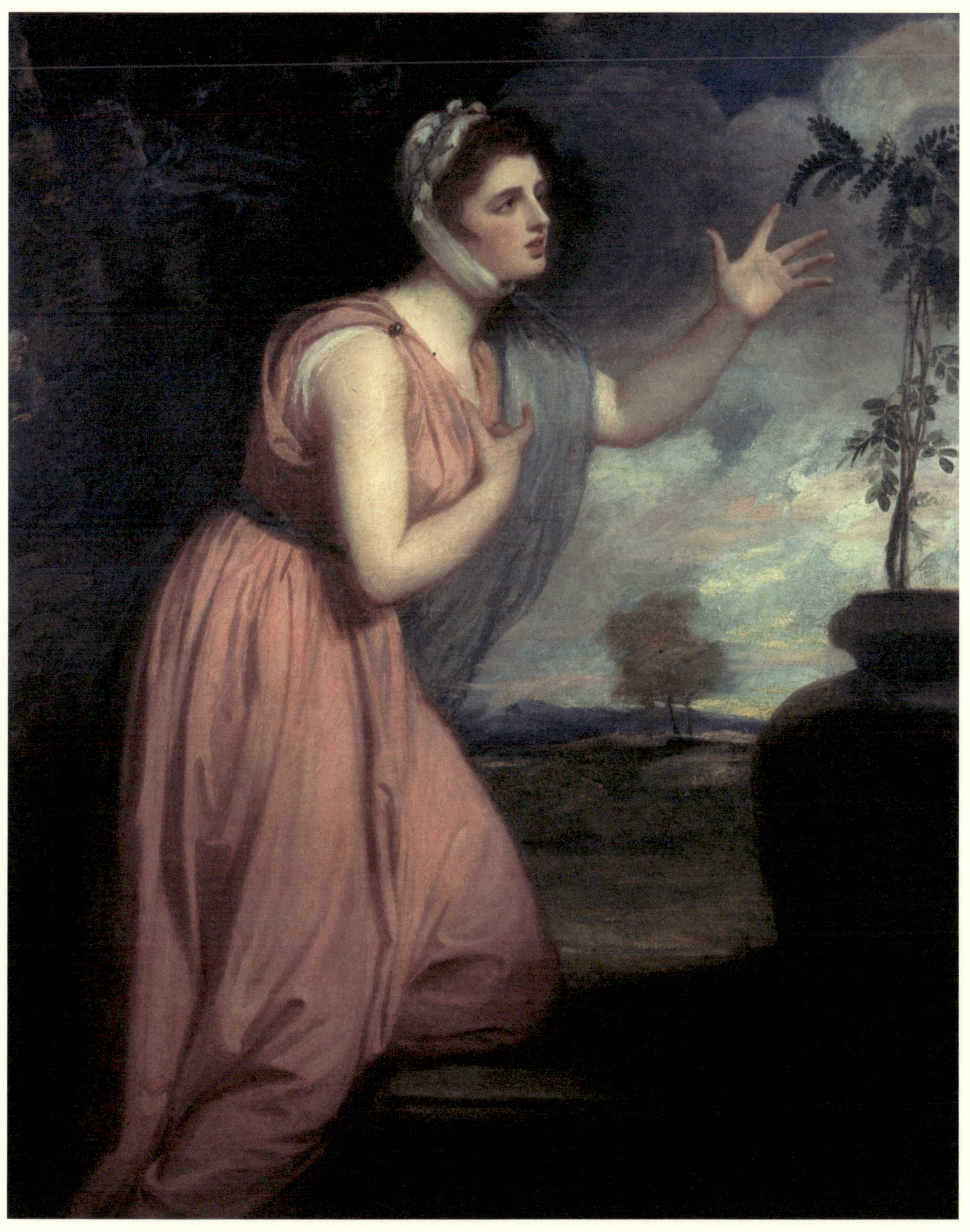

Portrait of Emma Hart as *Sensibility*, ca. 1787, by George Romney (1734–1802).
Oil on canvas. 150 × 121.5 cm. Full length, standing in a landscape. (1989.015.00.0001)

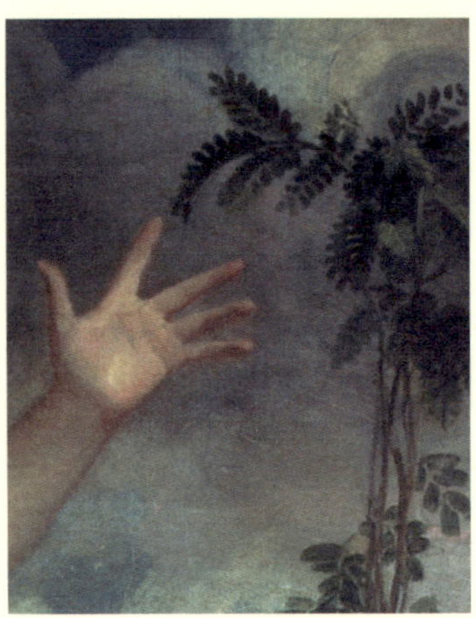

*How far the feeling fibres own her sway;*
*The leaves, as conscious of their queen's command,*
*Successive fall at her approaching hand!*

The mimosa, subject to Sensibility's "sway," obediently and rapidly closes its leaves upon being touched.

William Hayley's *The Triumphs of Temper* was very popular, running through as many as fourteen editions and provoking the scorn of Lord Byron (*English Bards and Scotch Reviewers: A Satire*, 1809):

*Behold!—ye tarts!—one moment spare the text—*
*Hayley's last work, and worst—until his next;*
*Whether he spin poor couplets into plays,*
*Or damn the dead with purgatorial praise,*
*His style in youth or age is still the same,*
*For ever feeble and for ever tame.*
*Triumphant first see 'Temper's Triumphs' shine!*
*At least I'm sure they triumph'd over mine.*

Romney was a brilliant draftsman whose spontaneous drawings influenced many younger contemporaries including John Flaxman and William Blake. Even today his drawings retain their freshness and spontaneity.

At the height of his career as a portraitist Romney was more in demand than Sir Joshua Reynolds or Thomas Gainsborough, and during the last fifteen years of his working life, he produced a sequence of "fancy subjects" derived from classical literature and Shakespeare that are among the most imaginative of the period.

At his death in 1802, his reputation was at its lowest ebb, and his association with Emma, Lady Hamilton, contributed to the eclipse of his reputation during the Victorian era.

The 1807 sale of 119 lots of pictures and sketches that were left in his studio produced a meager few hundreds of pounds. It is curious to note that Christie's falsely called him "George Romney R.A."—a peculiar error given that he had died so recently and that he was well known in artistic circles for his inveterate hostility to the Royal Academy, which never invited him to join.

A

# Catalogue

OF

## THE SELECT AND RESERVED COLLECTION

OF

# PAINTINGS,

OF

*That eminent and very celebrated Artist,*

## GEORGE ROMNEY, ESQ. R. A.

DECEASED:

CONSISTING OF

### The most admired Productions of his Pencil;

PARTICULARLY

His large Copy from the TRANSFIGURATION of RAFFAELLE; Sir ISAAC NEWTON making
Experiments on the PRISM; KING LEAR; the DYING DAMSEL, in the Ballad, " *'Twas when
the Seas were roaring*;" Miss WALLIS as MIRTH and MELANCHOLY; and many other Fancy
Pieces, and Portraits of celebrated Characters.

## WHICH

WILL BE SOLD BY AUCTION

# BY MR. CHRISTIE,

AT HIS GREAT ROOM, PALL MALL,

## ON MONDAY APRIL 27, 1807,

AT TWELVE O'CLOCK.

To be Viewed Two Days preceding the Sale (Sunday excepted). Catalogues may be
in Pall Mall.

*A Catalogue of the Select and Reserved Collection of Paintings of That eminent and very celebrated
Artist, George Romney, Esq. R.A., Deceased: Consisting of The most admired Productions of his
Pencil … [London: Christie's], 1807. (1989.026.00.0001)*

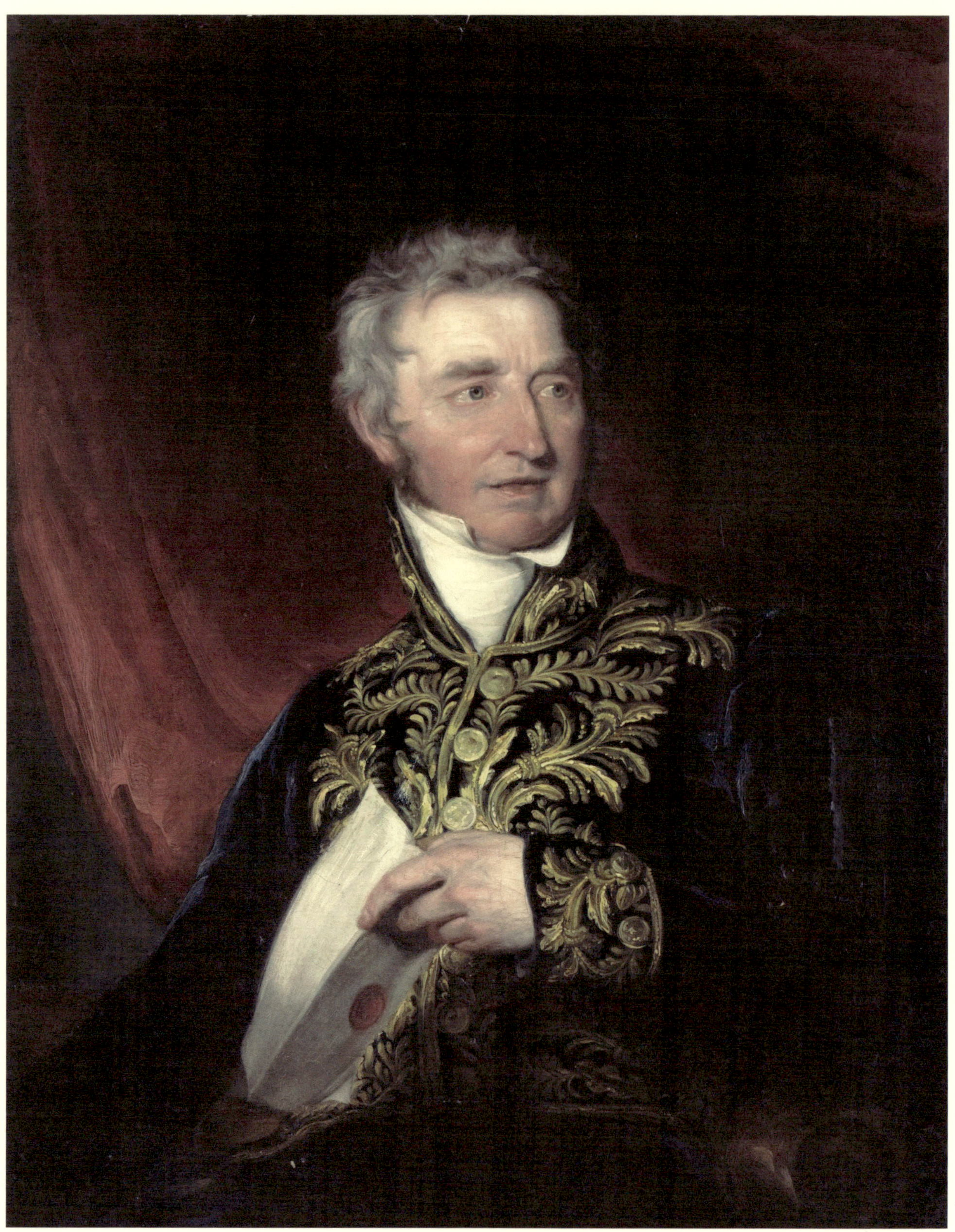

## Sir William Hamilton

Sir William Hamilton was born on 12 January 1731. Officially, he was the fourth son of Lord Archibald Hamilton, governor of Jamaica, and Lady Jane Hamilton, daughter of James Hamilton, Sixth Earl of Abercorn. Lady Jane was also the mistress of Frederick, Prince of Wales, the father of King George III. It was rumored that William was Frederick's illegitimate son and William did little to discourage the rumor, referring to the king as his "foster brother." If this was true, William's fate was to be cuckolded by his wife, Emma, as Lord Archibald was by Sir William's mother, Lady Jane.

After attending Westminster School, Hamilton was commissioned into the Third Foot Guards in 1747. He left the army in 1758 after his marriage to Catherine Barlow, a wealthy Scottish heiress. Hamilton then served as a Member of Parliament until 1764, when George III appointed him Britain's envoy to the Court of Naples.

Sir William's birth and upbringing allowed him entry to the highest circles. He mixed freely with lords and libertines, scientists and scholars. With his nephew, Charles Greville, he was a member of both the Royal Society for the Improvement of Natural Knowledge and the Society of Dilettanti.

In Naples, Lady Catherine's wealth enabled Sir William to pursue his varied scientific and historical interests. He was an avid collector and dealer in antiquities and art—paintings by Holbein, Titian, Rubens, Canaletto, Tintoretto, and Romney all passed through his hands. After his collection of Greek vases was acquired by the British Museum, and he set about assembling another: *"My new collection of vases will throw great light upon the ancient history, fabulous history & mithology of the Greeks, but they are a treasure for artists. It is now beyond a doubt that they are Grecian & not Etruscan. I wish Wedgewood had this collection two years in his possession, he wou'd profit much by them..."* The obsessive collector was also concerned with appearances, *"I have surely laid out more than £2000 in antiquities ... but I am delicate as to the manner of selling, as I shou'd hate to be looked upon as a dealer..."* (Autograph letter, signed: from Sir William Hamilton to Charles Greville. Naples, 21 September 1790 [1990.035.04.0002]).

In all, he collected more than a thousand vases and numerous terracotta, glass, and bronze antiquities, which filled his homes.

The Portland Vase, now in the British Museum, a Roman cameo

*Image Opposite*: SIR WILLIAM HAMILTON, ca. 1801, by Sir William Beechey (1753–1839). Half-length, wearing diplomatic uniform, with decorative gold frogging, holding a letter in his left hand. Oil on canvas. 90 × 70.5 cm. (2008.026.00.0001)

This portrait was commissioned by Lord Nelson, who wrote to Beechey on 28 December 1801, explaining: *"I wish Sir William Hamilton to sit to you for his picture a half length the same as my Fathers ..."*

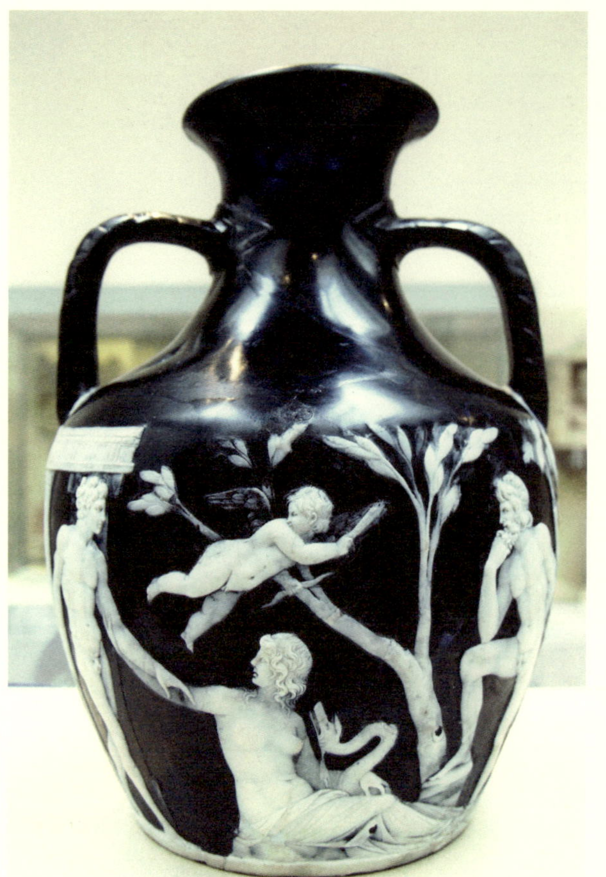

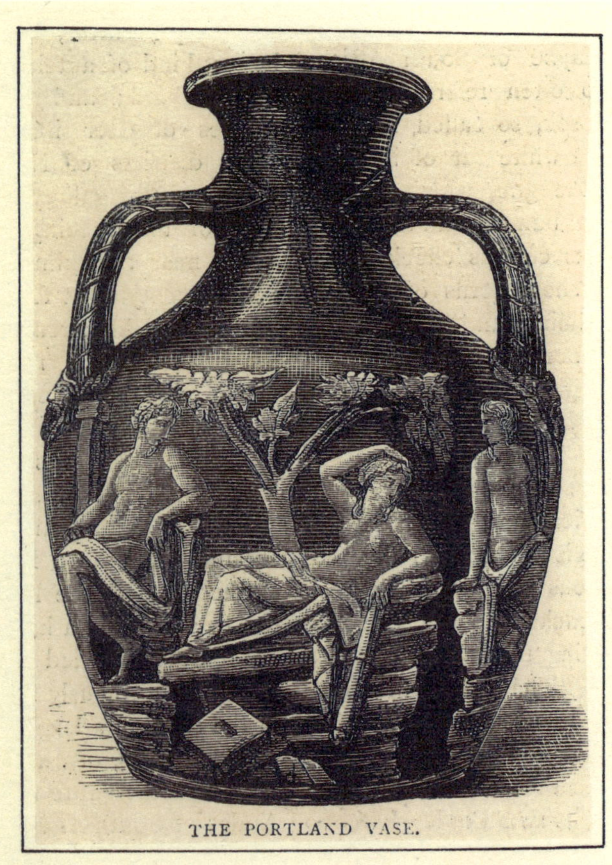


THE PORTLAND VASE.
Roman cameo cut-glass vase,
first century B.C.E. Victoria &
Albert Museum.

THE PORTLAND VASE.
Walter Sichel (1855–1933),
*Emma Lady Hamilton: From
New and Original Sources
and Documents…* London:
Archibald Constable, 1905.
(1992.004.00.0002)

cut-glass vessel created in the first century B.C.E., is the most famous. The subject is a mythological theme of love and marriage.
It is not known where and when the vase was found. Its earliest
record dates to 1601, when it was in the collection of Cardinal
del Monte in Italy. After his death it went to the Barberini family
where it remained for 150 years. In 1778, it was purchased by Sir
William Hamilton, who sold it to Margaret, Duchess of Portland,
in 1784. In 1786 her son lent it to Josiah Wedgwood, who made it
famous and inspired many modern glass and porcelain makers. It
was deposited in the British Museum by the fourth Duke of Portland in 1810 and finally purchased by the Museum in 1945.

The Attic red-figure krater, once in the collection of Sir William Hamilton, was discovered near Naples in 1789 and is attrib-
uted to Painter of Athens. Apollo crowned for his victory over
Marsyas by Nike stands on a pedestal, playing the kithara. The
god is flanked on the right by a youth wearing a Phrygian cap,
and Ares and Athena wearing Corinthian helmets. On the left are

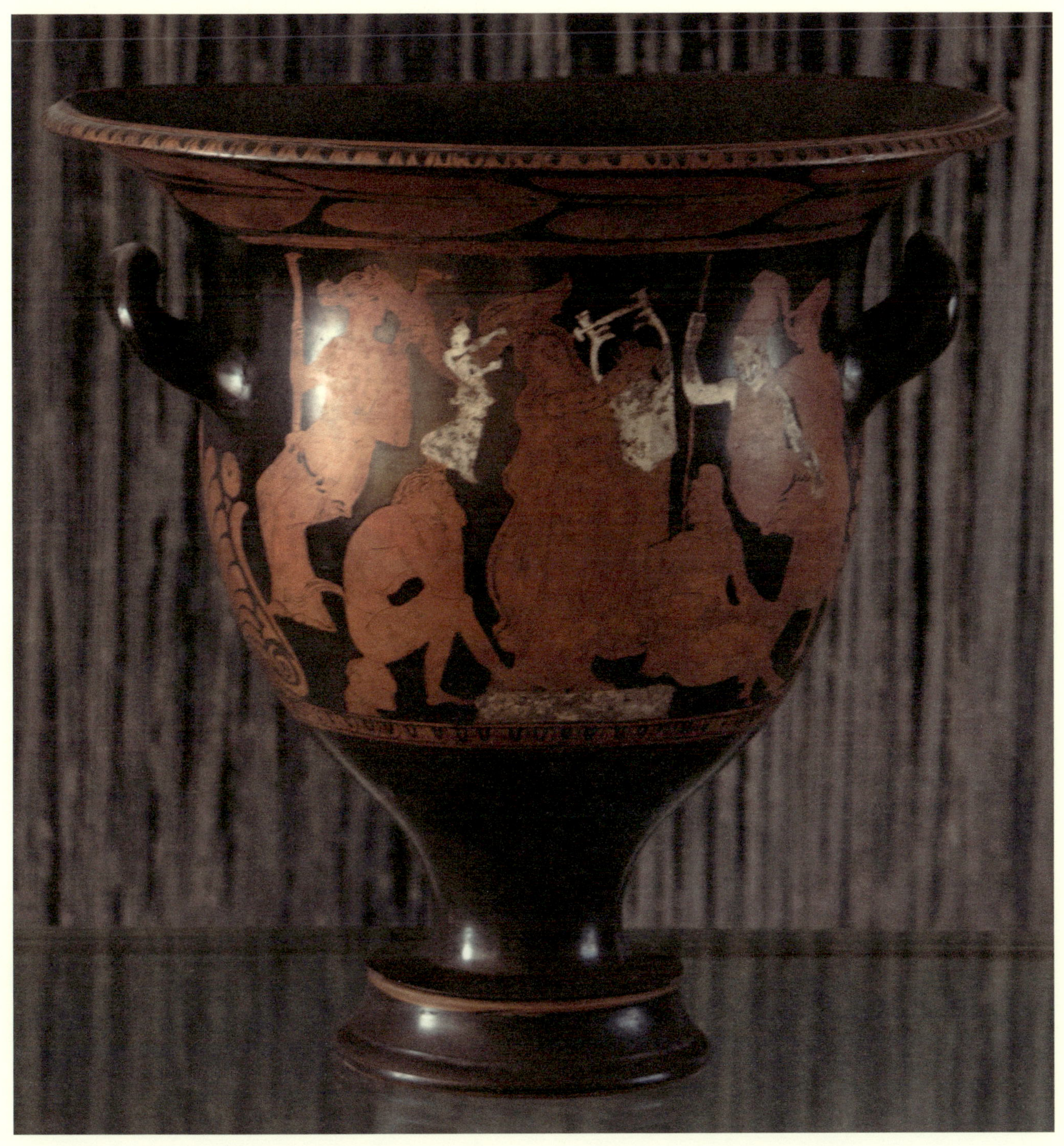

ATTIC RED-FIGURE BELL KRATER. 4th century B.C.E. Formerly in the
Sir William Hamilton Collection and now in the Jean Kislak Collection.
(2005.008.00.0001)

a bearded satyr, probably Marsyas, and Artemis holding torches. The reverse is decorated with three draped youths on either side of a stele surmounted by a disk.

◀═══════▶

When Sir William arrived in Naples in November 1764, he was able to observe the eruptive phase of Vesuvius, which continued until October 1767. He was elected a Fellow of the Royal Society for the Improvement of Natural Knowledge in 1765 and subsequently submitted a series of letters describing the activity of the volcano. These were read aloud at the Society's meetings, published in its *Transactions*, and make up the text of his monumental publication, *Campi Phlegræi: Observations on the Volcanos of the Two Sicilies*.

This sumptuous book—one of the most beautiful produced in the eighteenth century—is also a major scientific work. Hamilton's investigations addressed a fundamental question of eighteenth-century geology—whether volcanoes represented peripheral or central phenomena in the structure and workings of the earth. After careful observations, Hamilton concluded that volcanic activity was central, active throughout earth's history and that the effects of this activity were positive in reshaping the environment and creating rich soils.

Fabris' exquisite illustrations convey the awesome power of Vesuvius and depict the progression of the eruption with scientific accuracy.

*Below & opposite*: SIR WILLIAM HAMILTON, *Campi Phlegræi: Observations on the Volcanos of the Two Sicilies, as they have been Communicated to the Royal Society*. Naples: [n.p.], 1776. Text in English and French. Map and 59 plates etched and hand-colored by Pietro Fabris, pls. VI and II. (1990.024.00.0001)

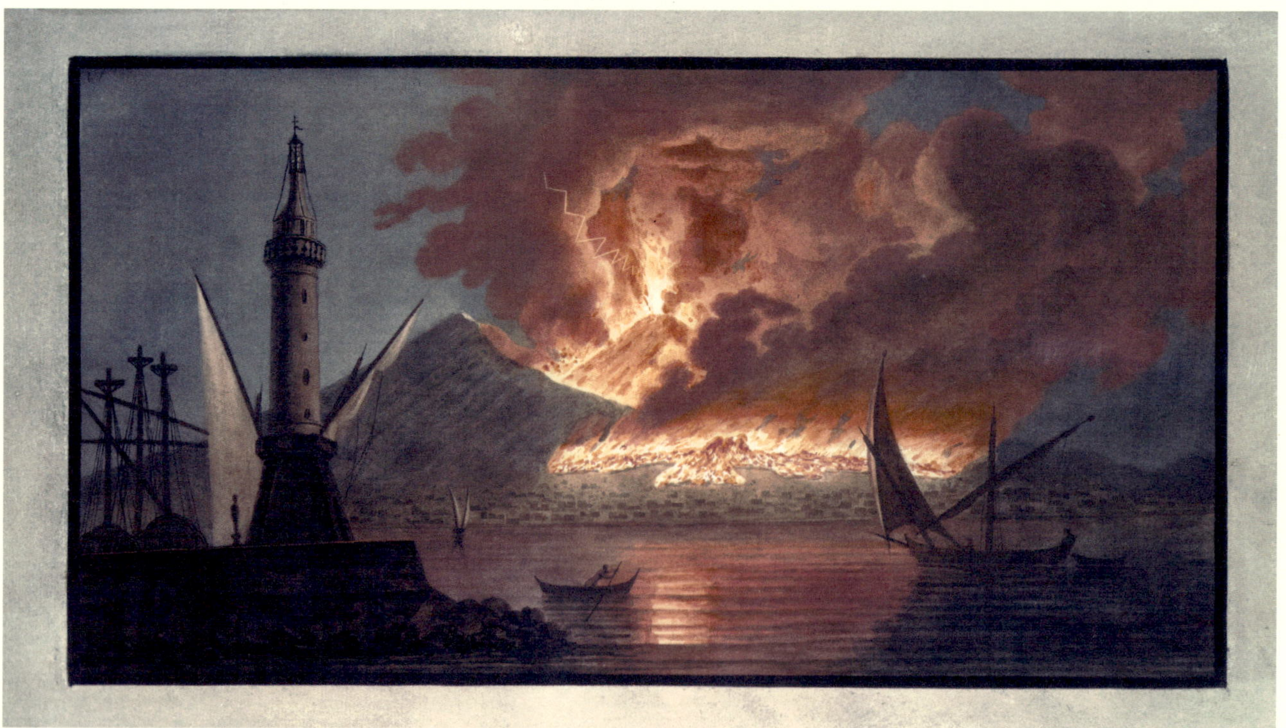

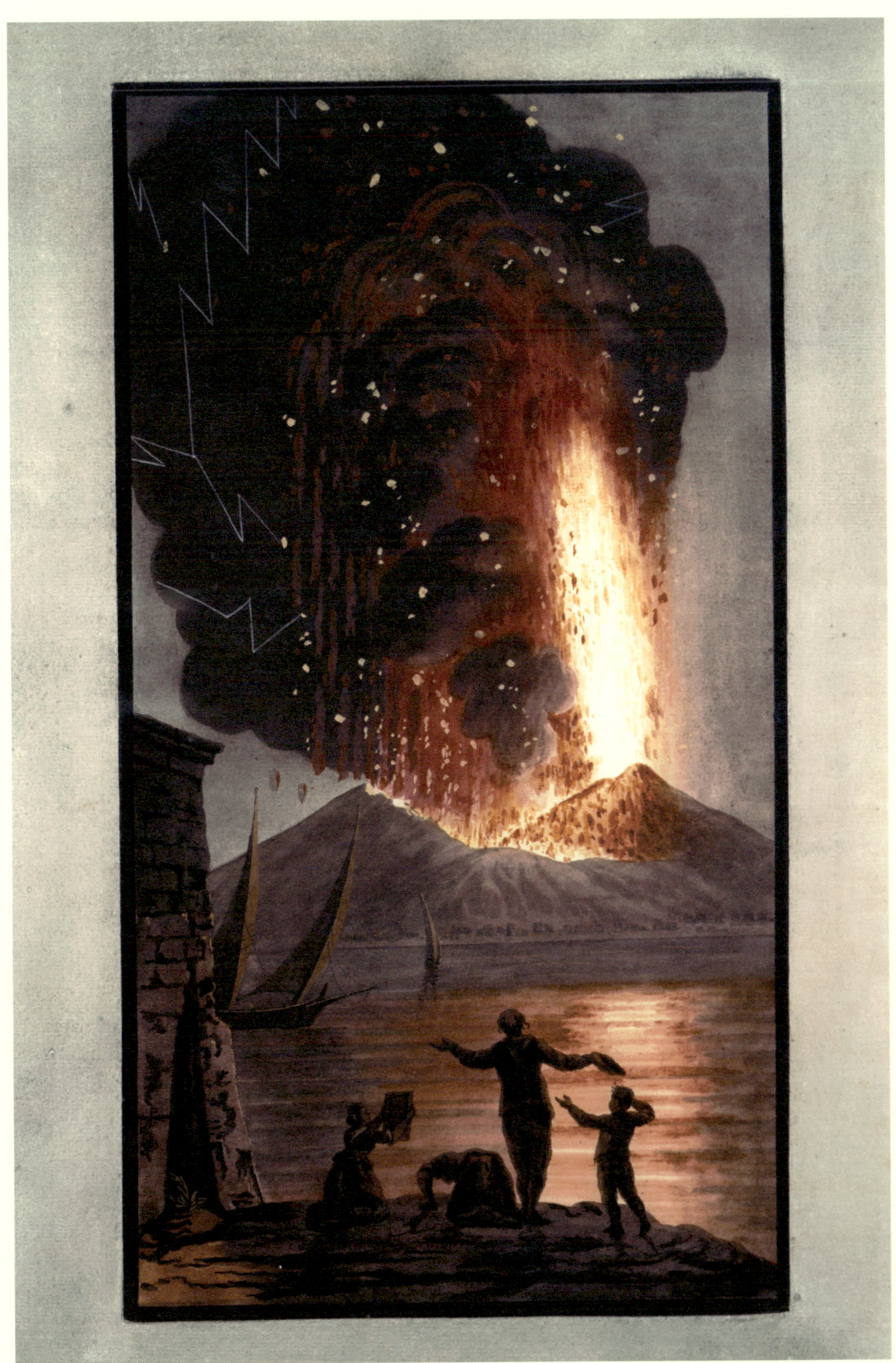

be here in a day or two — The prospect
of possessing so delightful an object
under my roof soon certainly causes
in me some pleasing sensations but
they are accompanied with some
anxious thoughts as to the prudent
management of their business however
I will do as well as I can and
hobble in an out of this pleasant
scrape as decently as I can. You
may be assured that I will comfort
her for the loss of You as well as
I am able but I know from the
small specimen during your absence
from London that I shall have at
times many tears to wipe from those
charming eyes which, if shed for any

# II

*The prospect of possessing
so delightfull an object under my roof soon certainly
causes in me some pleasing sensations*

LADY CATHERINE HAMILTON died childless in August 1782. In August of the following year, Sir William returned to London to deal with her estate. He was introduced to "Mrs. Hart" at the house on Edgware Road that Charles Greville had rented for her. They immediately were attracted to each other. He was taken by her youth and beauty; she was impressed with his sophistication and wealth and enjoyed the lavish attention of the older man. Undoubtedly, each had been prepared by Greville.

Sir William visited Emma almost daily, much to the consternation of his family and associates. Evidently smitten, he commissioned Sir Joshua Reynolds to paint Emma as a bacchante. Displeased with the result, he then commissioned Romney to paint another. Both pictures accompanied Sir William when he returned to Naples in September 1784.

Greville borrowed heavily and was thwarted in his efforts to marry an heiress whose wealth could help him deal with his mounting debts. He was tiring of Emma and hatched a plan to pass her on to Sir William. Polite negotiations ensued over the next year by correspondence and an understanding was reached in late 1785. A *quid pro quo* was arranged—in exchange for Emma, Sir William would stand surety on a bond to settle Greville's debts.

Emma was told a calculated lie: Charles needed to attend to business in Scotland for six months and she would go to Naples for a holiday. Sir William sent

---

*Opposite*: SIR WILLIAM HAMILTON. Autograph letter, signed: to Charles Greville. Naples, 25 April 1786. 3 pages, 4^to. (1990.035.01.0002)

*[I] had an account of the arrival of our friend [Emma] at Geneva the 27th of last month, so that she may be here in a day or two. The prospect of possessing so delightfull an object under my roof soon certainly causes in me some pleasing sensations, but they are accompanied with some anxious thoughts as to the prudent management of this business; however, I will do as well as I can, and hobble in and out of this pleasant scrape as decently as I can. You may be assured that I will comfort her for the loss of you as well as I am able, but I know, from the small specimen during your absence from London, that I shall have at times many tears to wipe from those charming eyes, & which, if shed for any other but yourself, might give me jealousy. Now that you have had, the resolution of taking this necessary step, you will, I dare say, turn your mind seriously to the improving your fortune.*

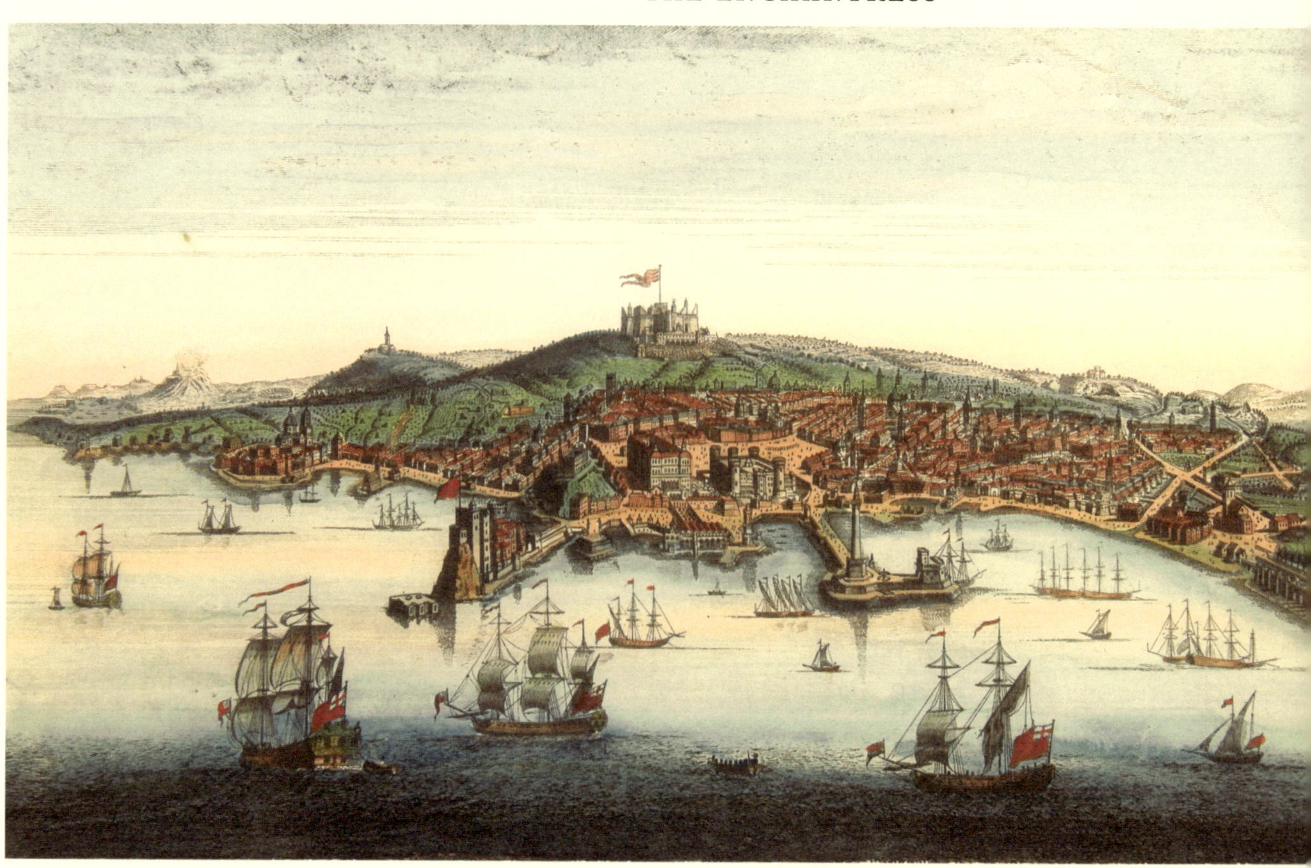



£50 for travel and on 14 March 1786, Emma, her mother, and a companion, Gavin Hamilton, set off for Naples, little knowing that the six month "holiday" would last 13 years.

After weeks of overland travel through Europe, Emma and her mother arrived in Naples on 26 April 1786—her twenty-first birthday. The home of Sir William Hamilton was the entire southern wing of the Palazzo Sessa, which commanded a panoramic view of the harbor with Mount Vesuvius in the distance. Here he entertained lavishly and displayed his vast collections of art and antiquities. Being surrounded by luxury, attended by servants, travelling in sumptuous carriages, and dining with aristocracy must have been a dramatic change from Emma's frugal life with Greville.

During her first months in Naples, Emma was still in love with Greville and refused to consider an intimate relationship with Sir William. She eagerly anticipated Greville's arrival in the fall to fetch her back to England and wrote often. Finally, he told her the truth—he was not ever coming to get her and she should make the best of her situation with Sir William. The shock of his betrayal

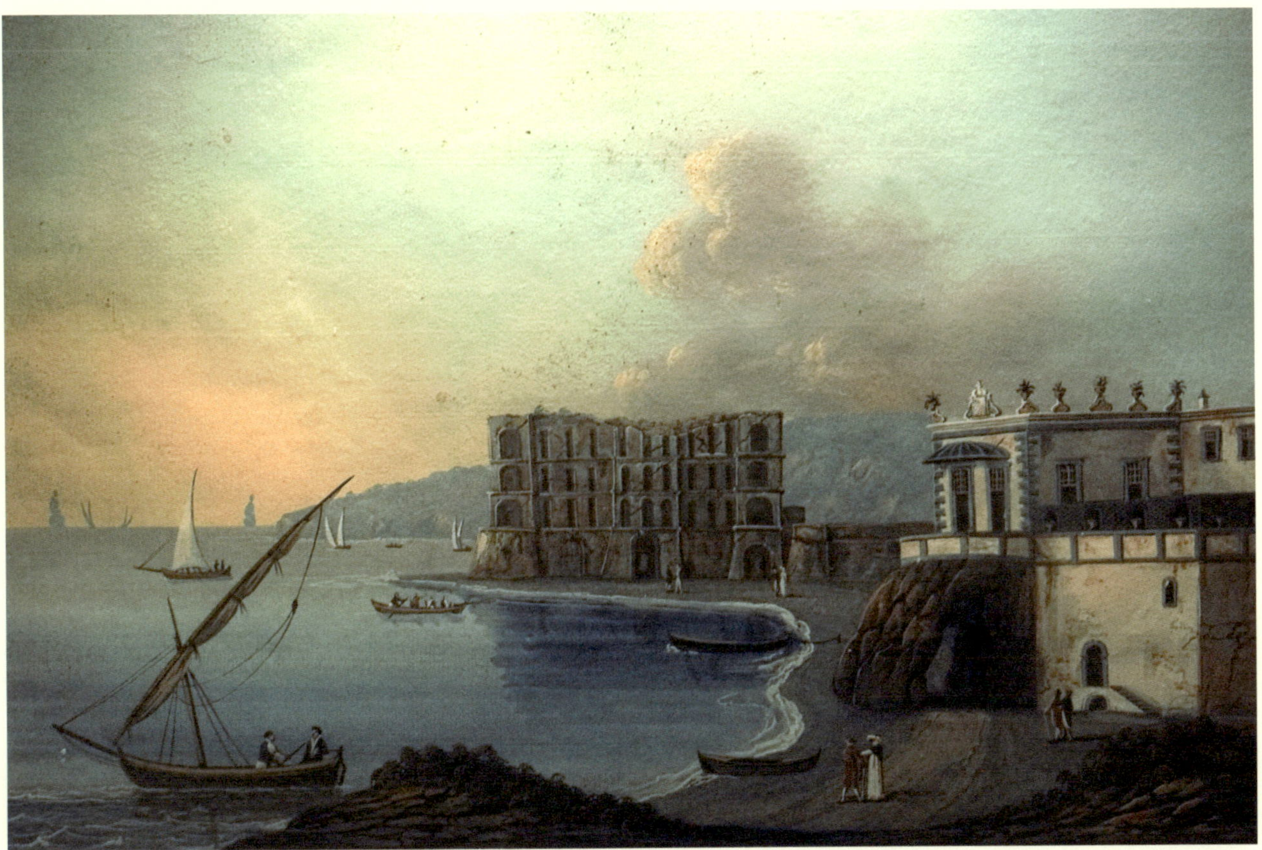

was devastating and caused her to fall out of love. Perhaps she understood that she was being treated as another object to be traded by these two wealthy "cultured" men.

Rising to the challenge, Emma eagerly seized the opportunity to become *"a little more improved"* (Emma Hart to Sir William Hamilton, 3 December 1785). Sir William was delighted and engaged French and Italian language tutors, a dancing master, singing coach, and guitar and harpsichord teachers. He wooed her with lavish attention, praise, and gifts—a fine horse, clothes, and jewelry. He took her to the opera, the theatre, and fine dinners. By fall 1786, Emma and Sir William were lovers—she was his mistress.

Sir William maintained five residences in and around Naples. On summer afternoons from May to September Sir William often went to his bayside "casino" with Emma to dine and sail and escape the heat. Lord Herbert, the son of the Earl of Pembroke, when he visited Naples, made the following entry in his diary:

*August 24ᵗʰ, 1779* [...] *"I dined with Sir William Hamilton and Lady Hamilton at their Cassino (consisting of three rooms and a kitchen) ...*

CASINO D'AMILTON, à posilipo, presso Ferdinando Roberto strada. (Gouache?) 30 × 45.7 cm. (2010.033.00.0001)

*"I wish you was here, bathing in the Sea every morning & dining at my little Casine at Pausilipo & in autumn we shall go to our delightful hill home at Portici."* William Hamilton, autograph letter, signed: to Charles Greville. Naples, 3 August 1779. (1990.035.03.0002)

*[it] is the last house a carriage can arrive at. It is built on small rock and consists of three rooms and a kitchen, with a very diminutive garden. There are two flight of stairs to come up to it. When the weather is fine, a small terrass before the building constitutes the Setting Room, with a large Venetian blind to guard it from the heat of the sun ... The next house in ruins is said to have belonged to Queen Joan* (S. C. Herbert, *Pembroke Papers*. London: 1938–1950. vol. 1, p. 225).

For the next thirteen years Sir William and Emma followed the seasonal movements of the Bourbon court—from the royal palace at Caserta in the spring and fall to Portici or Capri in winter and summer, travelling to Naples only when necessary for official business or a gala event. Caserta is forty kilometers northeast of Naples and the palace was the largest in Europe. Built to rival Versailles, it is situated on 300 acres and has more than 1,200 rooms that required a staff of 3,000. Work began in 1752 and was completed in 1780.

The town of Portici at the foot of Mount Vesuvius was completely destroyed by the eruption of Vesuvius in 1631 and subsequently rebuilt. The Royal Palace was constructed over a ten-year period beginning in 1738, and 122 grand residences, known as the Vesuvian Villas, were built in the surrounding countryside to house the court. During King Ferdinand's reign, the *Palazzo Reale di Portici* was overshadowed by the far grander *La Reggia di Caserta*.

Emma's beauty caught the eye of Ferdinand, King of Naples. Her youth, spontaneity—and relationship with the British envoy—brought her to the attention of Queen Maria Carolina, the thirteenth child of Empress Maria Theresa and Emperor Francis I of Austria, and sister of Queen Marie Antoinette of France and Emperor Joseph II of Austria. Maria Carolina had married Ferdinand as part of an Austrian alliance with Spain. She bore eighteen children, only seven of which survived to adulthood. Ferdinand, a third son not groomed to be ruler, was neither well-bred nor well-educated. He was devoted to sports and hunting and preferred the company of the common people (*lazzaroni*) to the aristocrats at court. Lady Catherine reports on one sporting expedition with Sir William: *"Hamilton is just come from a hunt with the King, where they kill'd five & twenty wild boars, & was at one yesterday where they kill'd three hundred & seventy-six wild ducks; what slaughter!"* (Lady Catherine Hamilton. Autograph letter, signed: to Charles Greville. 30 December 1776 [1990.035.11.0002]).

In contrast, Queen Maria Carolina envisioned the kingdom of Naples becoming a great power, and King Ferdinand was content to leave government in the hands of the queen. Emma's influence in Naples grew as she became a leader of society and a confidant of the queen—they were so close that it was rumored they shared an intimate relationship.

Emma's ambition, indeed her goal, was to marry Sir William and be the ambassadress. Although his letters are full of praise for her, at this time Sir William had no intention to marry:

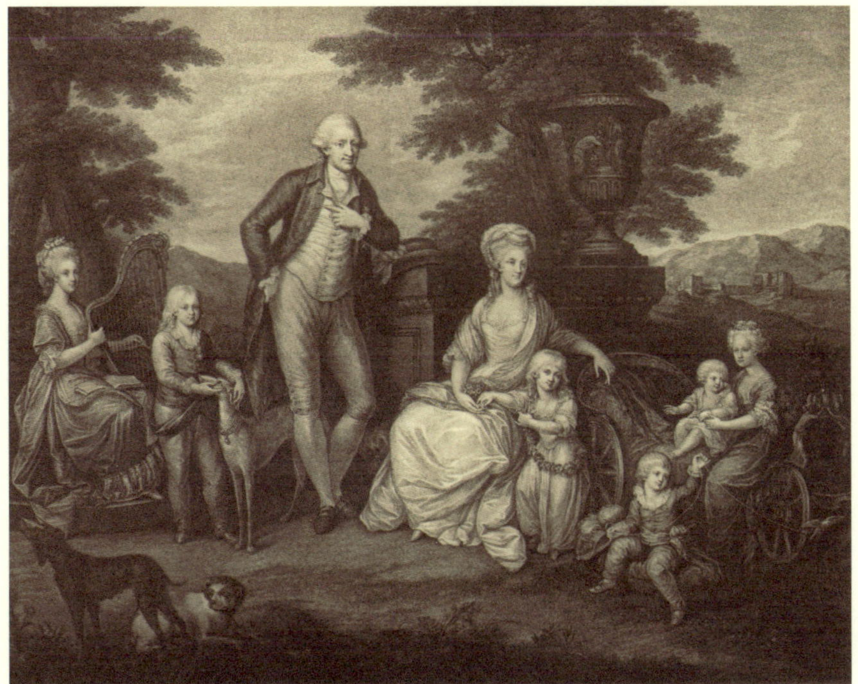

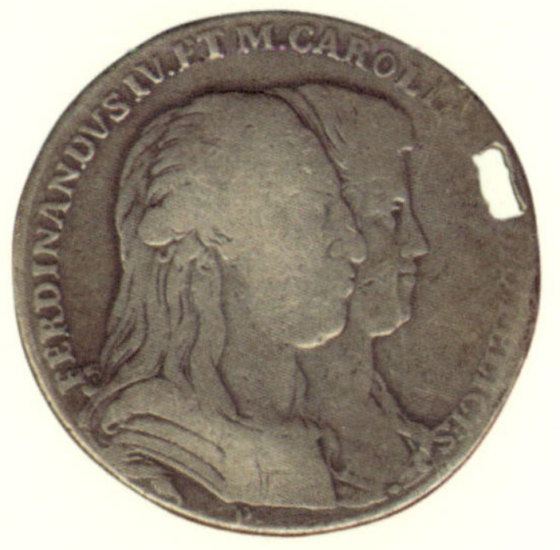

*Left*: THE ROYAL FAMILY. Hilda Gamlin, *Emma Lady Hamilton: An Old Story Re-told.* Liverpool & London: Simpkin, Marshall, Hamilton, Kent & Co., 1891. (2010.081.00.0001)

*Above*: FERDINAND IV "ZO-DIAC" PIASTRA: Naples & Sicily, 1791. *Obverse:* Portraits of Ferdinand & Maria Carolina. (2010.135.00.0001)

*Her conduct is such as to gain universal esteem, & she profits daily in musick and language. I endeavour to lose no time in forming her, & certainly she would be welcome to share with me, on our present footing, all I have during my life, but I fear her views are beyond what I can bring myself to execute; & that when her hopes on that point are over, that she will make herself & me unhappy; but all this entre nous; if ever a separation should be necessary for our mutual happiness, I would settle £150 a year on her, & £50 on her mother, who is a very worthy woman; but all this is only thinking aloud to you, & foreseeing that the difference of 57 & 22 may produce events; but, indeed, hitherto her behaviour is irreproachable, but her temper, as you must know, unequal …I only trouble myself at present with making her accomplished, let what may come of it.*

*I give Emma 200£ a year to keep her & her mother in cloths & washing, and you may imagine every now and then a present of a gown, a ring, a feather, &c., and once indeed she so long'd for diamonds that, having an opportunity of a good bargain of single stones of a good water & tolerable size, I gave her at once 500£ worth. She realy deserves everything, & has gained the love of everybody, &, wou'd you think it, is preached up by the Queen & nobility as a rare example of virtue…*

*Her knowledge of musick will surprise you as it does me, for I did not expect her to apply as she has done. She has grown thinner of late, & is the handsomer for it.***

*SIR WILLIAM HAMILTON to Charles Greville. Naples, 26 May 1789 (*see overleaf*).

**SIR WILLIAM HAMILTON to Charles Greville. Naples, 21 September 1790 (*see overleaf*).

another collection will be made considering the variety of subjects & beauty of the Forms. I have two or three very Extraordinary indeed, but the Museum shall not have them till I can see no more, for they beautify my new appartment — Emma often asks me do you love me? ay but as well as your new appartments? Her conduct is such as to gain universal Esteem and she profits daily in musick & language, I endeavour

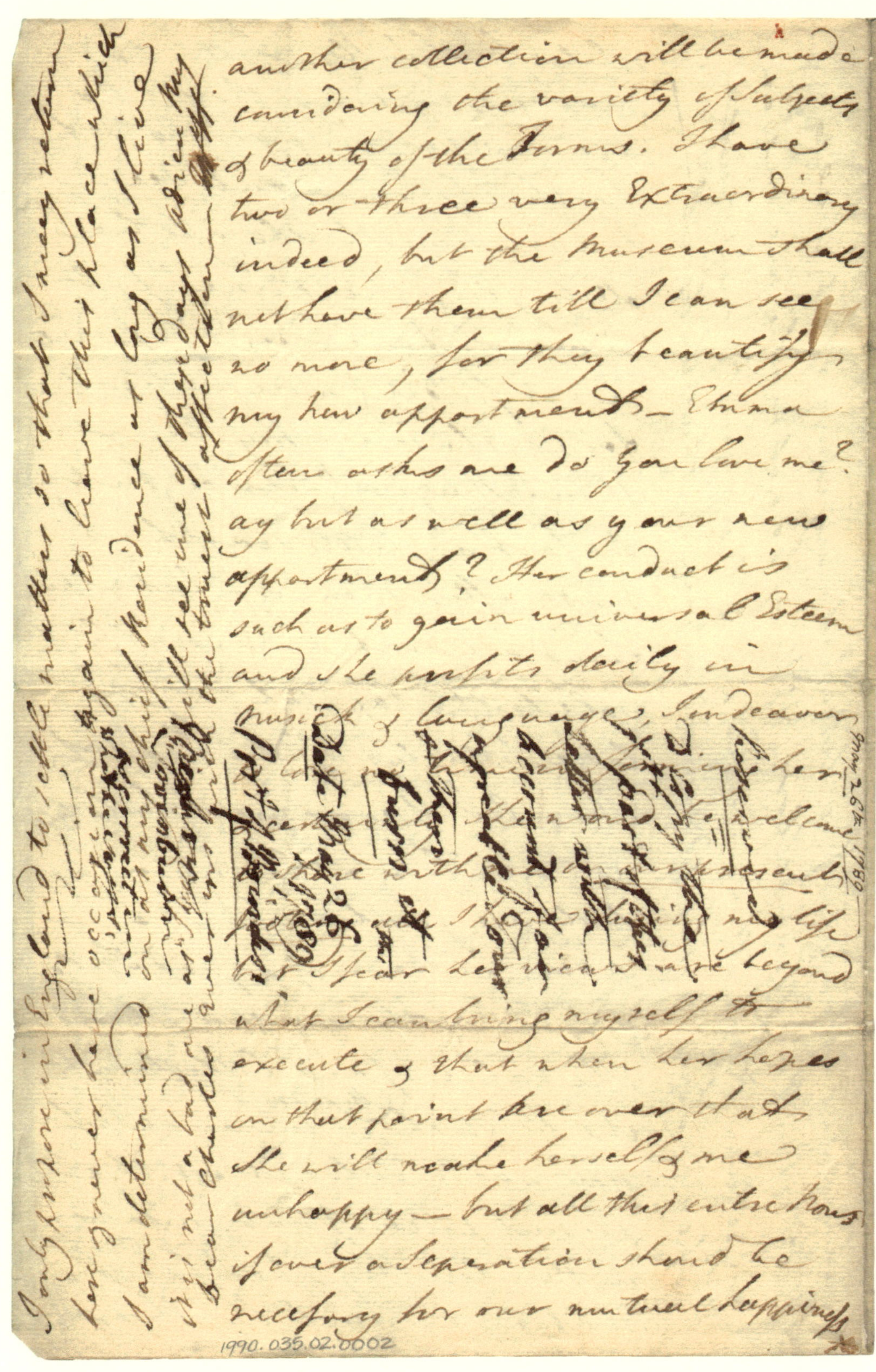

but I fear her views are beyond what I can bring myself to execute & that when her hopes on that point are over that she will make herself & me unhappy — but all this entre nous, if ever a separation should be necessary for our mutual happiness



SIR WILLIAM HAMILTON. Autograph letter, signed: to Charles Greville. Naples, 26 May 1789. 4 pages, folio. (1990.035.02.0002)

my situation, and act as you wou'd
do in the like situation. When I am in
England I hope to settle all my affairs
properly — by degrees I am running
into Ross's debt instead of his being
in mine which he was considerably
when I left England — I am determined
at any rate to pay all my debts, &
one comfort is that I have a sufficient
stock in hand to do it / The fitting up
my new appartments cost me much
more than I thought it wou'd, near
4000 L I give Emma 200 L a year to
keep her & her Mother in cloths &
washing and you may imagine every
now and then a present of a gown or
ring a feather &c and once indeed she
so long'd for diamonds that having an
opportunity of a good bargain of single
stones of a good water & tollerable size
I gave her at once 500 L worth. She realy
deserves every thing & has gained the love
of every body & wou'd you think it is
is preached up by the Queen & nobility a

SIR WILLIAM HAMILTON. Autograph letter, signed: to Charles Greville. Naples, 21 September 1790. 4 pages, folio. (1990.035.04.000)

In his diary for the 28th January, 1790, the Comte d'Espinchal described a dance performance by Emma:

*Mrs. Hart, a tall and splendid Englishwoman with the face of an angel, who has for some years been living with Sir William Hamilton, the English minister, and is thought to be secretly married to him, also sang at this concert with infinite taste ... I derived the greatest pleasure from watching a very unconventional and very voluptuous dance called the tarantella, which much resembles the Spanish fandango. It was marvellously danced by some extremely pretty young Neapolitan bourgeoises called Amici; but Mrs. Hart endowed it with a degree of grace and voluptuousness that would have set any man's senses aflame, however cold and insusceptible he might be.*

—JOSEPH THOMAS, COMTE D'ESPINCHAL,
*Journal d'emigration.* Translated by Mrs. Rodolph Stawell.
London: Chapman and Hall, 1912, pp. 72–73.

[ANONYMOUS]. *La Tarantella.*
(2000.096.00.0012)

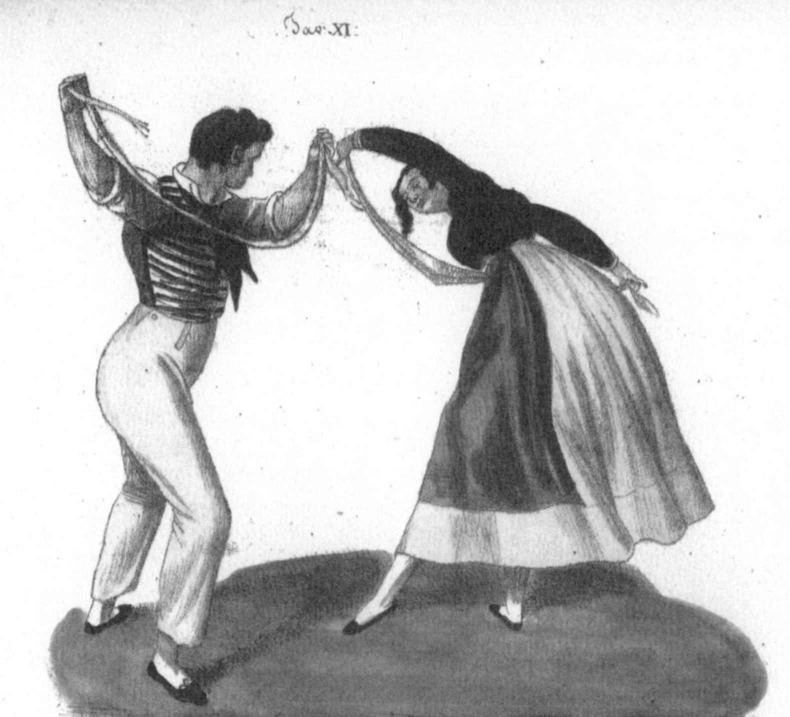

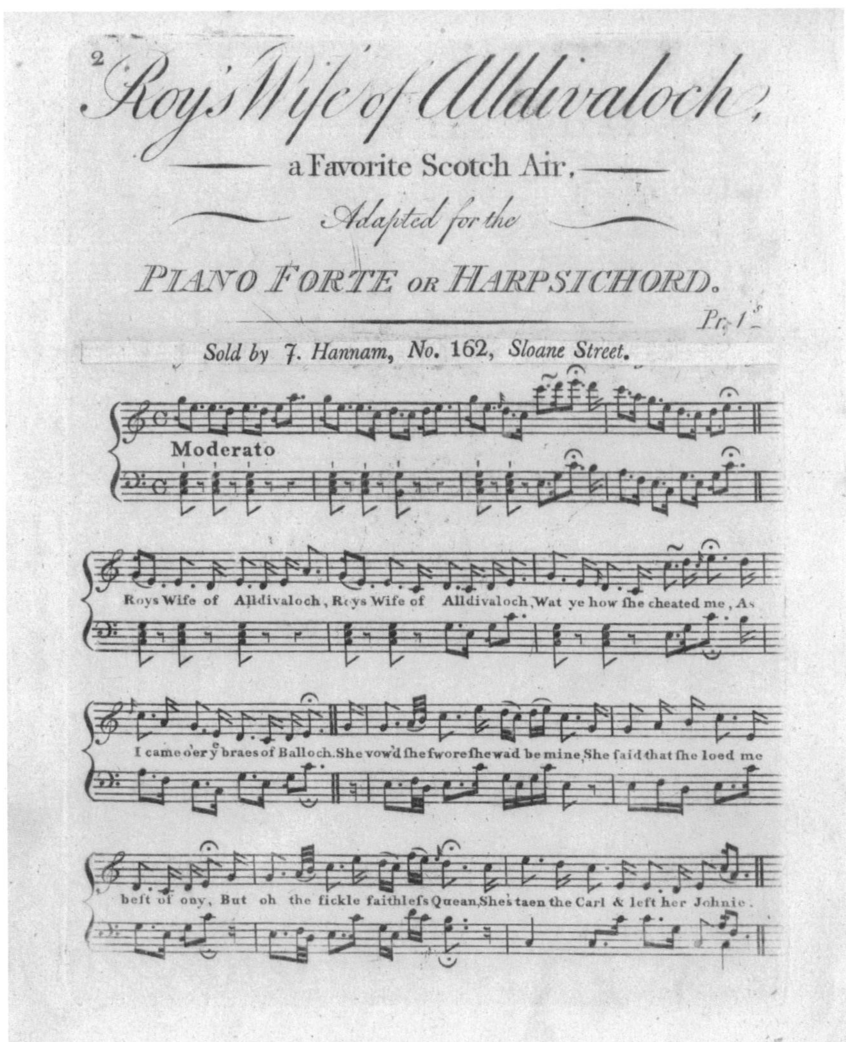


*Roy's Wife of Alldivaloch, a Favorite Scotch Air, Adapted for the Piano Forte or Harpsichord.* [London: J. Hannam, (n.d.)]. (2010.071.00.001)

Signed and dated "Lady Hamilto[n] / July 19th 180[7? 9?]."

The French painter Louise-Élisabeth Vigée Le Brun, who was exiled by the French Revolution (she was the portraitist of Marie Antoinette, among other royals), depicted Emma in several canvases during this period.

*I painted Mrs. Hart as a Bacchante reposing on the sea-shore, and holding in her hand a cup. Her lovely face was very animated ... she had an enormous quantity of beautiful chestnut hair, which when loose covered her entirely—thus as a Bacchante she was perfect...*

*Sir William Hamilton had this portrait done for himself; but I must mention that he frequently sold his pictures when he found he could make money on them, which caused the eldest son of our Ambassador at Naples, M. de Talleyrand, to say one day on hearing that Sir William Hamilton was a patron of art: 'Say rather it is art who is his patron.' The truth is that after*

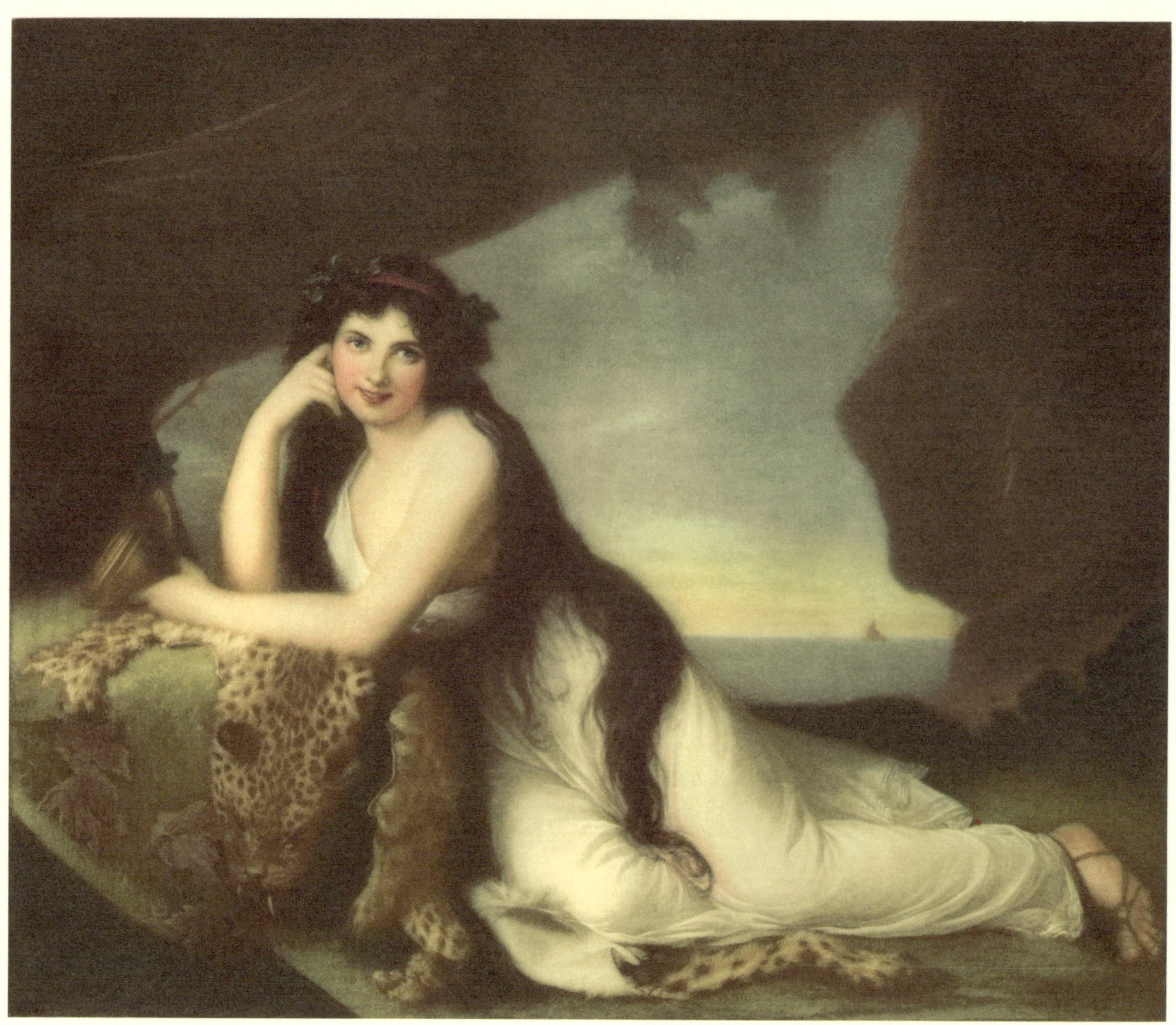



*having bargained a long time for the portrait of his mistress, he got me to do it for a hundred louis, which was 2,400 francs, and that he sold it afterwards in London for three hundred guineas, or in French, money 8,000 francs. Later on when I had again painted Lady Hamilton as a sybil for the Duc de Brissac, I made a copy of the head as a present to Sir William Hamilton, who without hesitation sold it.*

—LOUISE-ÉLISABETH VIGÉE LE BRUN
*Souvenirs of Madame Vigée-Lebrun.* Translated by Morris F. Tyler.
New York: J. J. Little, 1879. Third edition, page 149.

The painting hung in the Palazzo Sessa—along with fourteen other portraits of Emma. It was Nelson's favorite picture of her and he purchased it in 1801 prior to the Hamilton sales at Christie's. Emma included it in the sale of Nelson's estate in 1809 to help pay her debts.

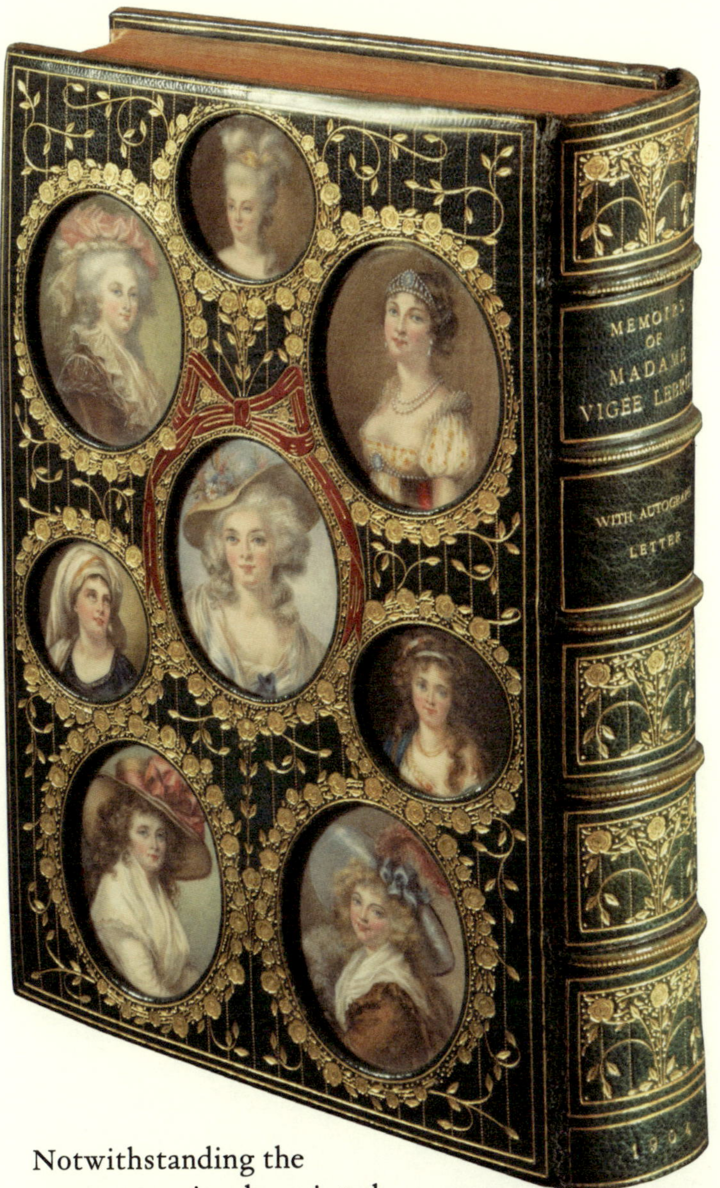



EMMA AS A PERSIAN SIBYL, by Louise-Élisabeth Vigée Le Brun, as shown on the binding by Rivière & Son, London. *The Memoirs of Madame Vigée Lebrun*, translated by Lionel Strachey. London: Grant Richards, 1904.

*Below*: Detail of vignette. (2010.072.00.0001)

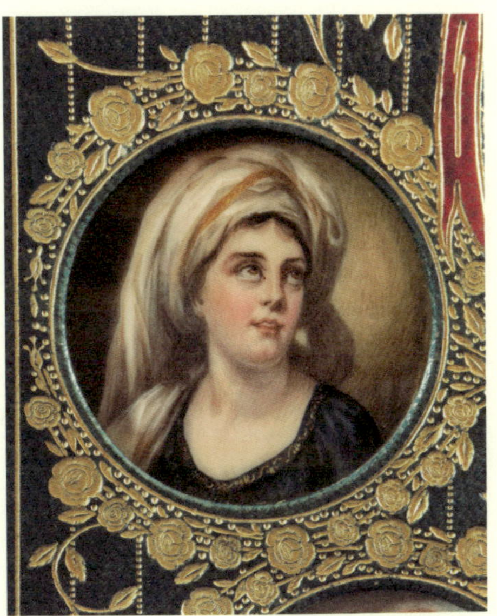

Notwithstanding the many portraits she painted of Emma, Vigée Le Brun was also highly critical of her:

*Lady Hamilton was not at all clever, though she was extremely supercilious and disdainful, so much so that these two defects were conspicuous in all her conversation ... She wanted in style, and dressed very badly when it was a question of every-day dress.*
—*Memoirs of Madame Vigée Lebrun*, page 63.

Vigée Le Brun's portrait of Emma as a Persian sibyl appears on the rear cover of the edition of the *Memoirs* shown above (*center left*), magnificently bound by Rivière & Son, London.

*I remember that when I did my first picture of her, as a sibyl, she was living at Caserta, whither I went every day, desiring to progress quickly with the picture ... The Duchess de Fleury and the Princess de Joseph Monaco were present at the third sitting, which was the last. I had wound a scarf round her head in the shape of a turban, one end hanging down in graceful folds. This head-dress so beautified her that the ladies declared she looked ravishing.*

—*Memoirs of Madame Vigée Le Brun*, page 63.

### Emma Hamilton's Attitudes

*In the attitudes of Lady Hamilton are mirrored the entire palette of female icons, from the furies to the saints, which continues in the work of such contemporary artists such as Cindy Sherman in the black and white photographs of secretaries, house wives and femmes fatales in her 'Untitled Film Stills.'*

—LINDY ANNIS, performance artist, 2004

Emma probably began developing the idea for her "Attitudes," or poses, shortly after arriving in Naples, surrounded by Sir William's antiquities collection and inspired by the vestiges of ancient Rome. Using shawls and props, she presented a succession of emotions and characters in a *tableau vivant* performance that combined her innate talents for acting and dance with her experience as a model for Romney, who often portrayed her as a character from classical antiquity, literature, or history.

Her performances were famous and were witnessed by connoisseurs and grand tourists, including the celebrated author Johann Wolfgang von Goethe:

*Naples, 16 March 1787: Sir Wm. Hamilton who is still living here as English ambassador, has now, after many years of devotion to the arts and the study of nature found the acme of these delights in the person of an English girl of twenty with a beautiful face and perfect figure. He has had a Greek costume made for her which becomes her extremely. Dressed in this, she lets down her hair and, with a few shawls, gives so much variety to her poses, gestures, expressions, etc., that the spectator can hardly believe his eyes. He sees what thousands of artists would have like to express realized before him in movements and surprising transformations—standing, kneeling, sitting, reclining, serious, sad, playful, ecstatic, contrite, alluring, threatening, anxious, one pose follows another without a break. She knows how to arrange the folds of her veil to match each mood, and has a hundred ways of turning it into a headdress. The old knight idolizes her and is enthusiastic about everything she does. In her, he has found all the antiquities, all the profiles of Sicilian coins, even the Apollo Belvedere. This much is certain: as a performance it's like nothing you ever saw before in your life.*

—J.W. GOETHE, *Italian Journey*.
Translated by W. H. Auden. London: Wm. Collins & Co., 1962
[Penguin Classics, 1970], page 208.

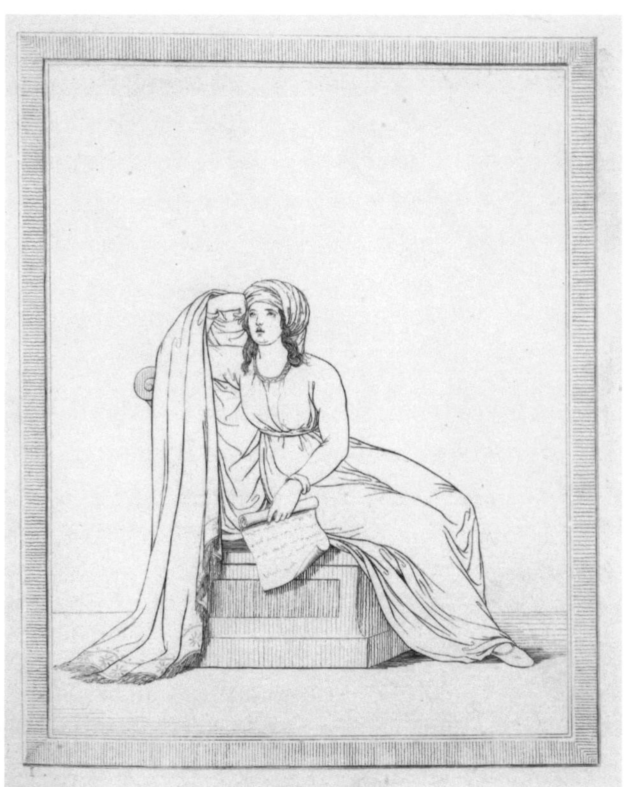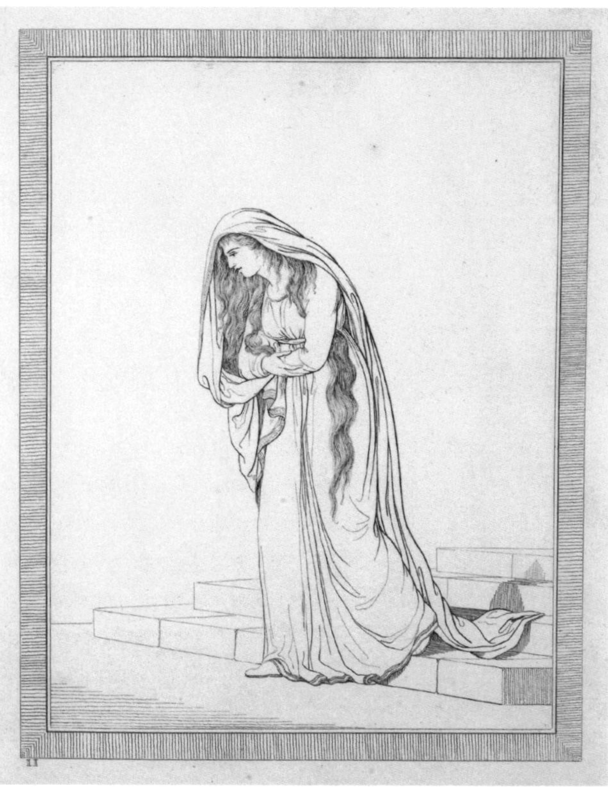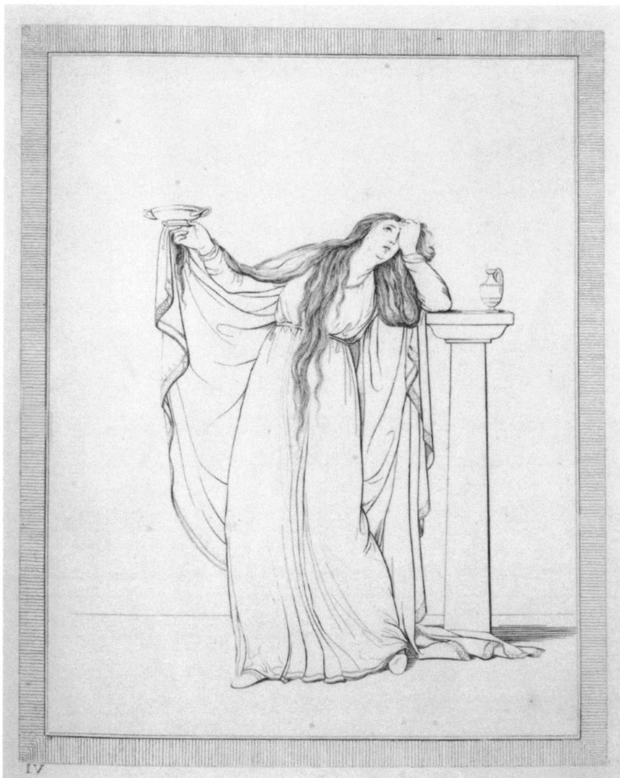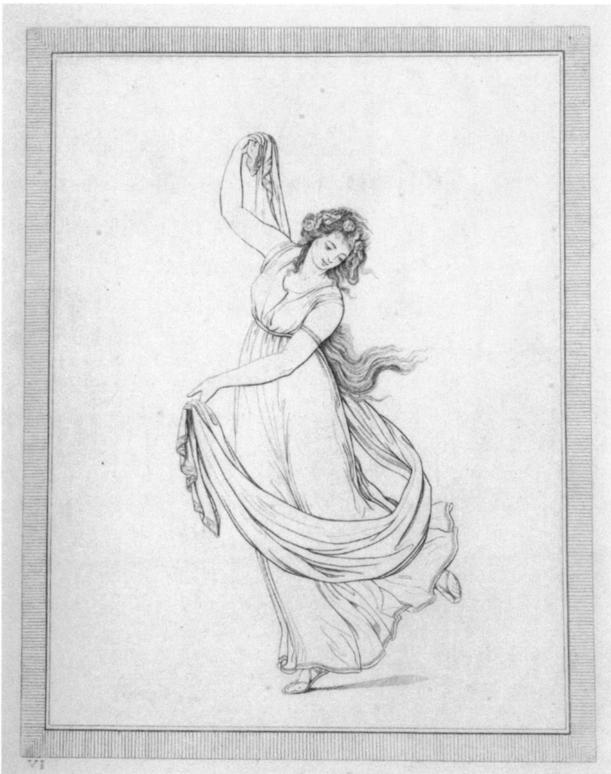

FRIEDRICH REHBERG (1758–1835), *Drawings Faithfully Copied from Nature at Naples, and with Permission Dedicated To the Right Honourable Sir William Hamilton, His Britannic Majesty's Envoy Extraordinary and Plenipotentiary at the Court of Naples, by his Most Humble Servant Frederick Rehberg* [London]: 1794, pls. I, II, IV, VI. (1991.295.00.0005)

Sir William commissioned Frederick Rehberg, historical painter to the court of Prussia, to execute drawings of Emma's "Attitudes." Each of the twelve graceful neo-classical illustrations captures a particular tableau and is among the few visual reminders that remain of Emma as a performance artist.

Prints of Rehberg's drawings became so popular that they were re-issued as a book in 1794.

*Thus accoutred, with the assistance of one or two Etruscan vases and an urn, she takes almost every attitude of the finest antique figures successively and varying in a moment the folds of her shawls, the flow of her hair; and her wonderful countenance is at one instant a Sibyl, then a Fury, a Niobe, a Sophonisba drinking poison, a Bacchante drinking wine, dancing, and playing the tambourine, an Agrippina at the tomb of Germanicus and every different attitude of almost every different passion. You will be more astonished when I tell you that the change of attitude and countenance, from one to another, sometimes totally opposite, is the work of a moment … She sometimes does above two hundred, one after the other, and, acting from the impulse of the moment, scarce ever does them twice the same.*

—LETTER dated 14 February 1796
*The Letters of John B. S. Morritt*
London: John Murray, 1914, p. 281.

As Emma's celebrity spread, performances became social events and invitations were eagerly sought. Even after returning to England in 1800, Emma continued to present her "Attitudes" for many years, adapting the repertoire to suit current taste and interests.

Endlessly creative, Emma invented her own fashion. Inspired by examples of women wearing loose fitting rectangular tunics depicted on the Greco-Roman vases in Sir William's collection, she wore a Grecian-style, high-waisted dress gathered just under the bust over a long, loose skirt that skimmed her body, flat shoes, and crowned with a feathery hat or plumes. Emma's "look" started a fashion trend. Despite the Napoleonic war, classically influenced "Regency" or "Empire" styles became mainstream fashion throughout Europe during the 1790s. The outline is especially flattering to pear shapes wishing to disguise the stomach area or emphasize the bust (qualities that worked to Emma's advantage during her later pregnancy).

---

*Opposite*: AFTERNOON DRESS, *The Ladies' Monthly Museum, or Polite Repository of Amusement and Instruction: Being an Assemblage of what can Tend to please the Fancy, Instruct the mind or Exalt the Character of the British Fair.* September, 1801. London: Vernor and Hood. (2010.100.00.0001)

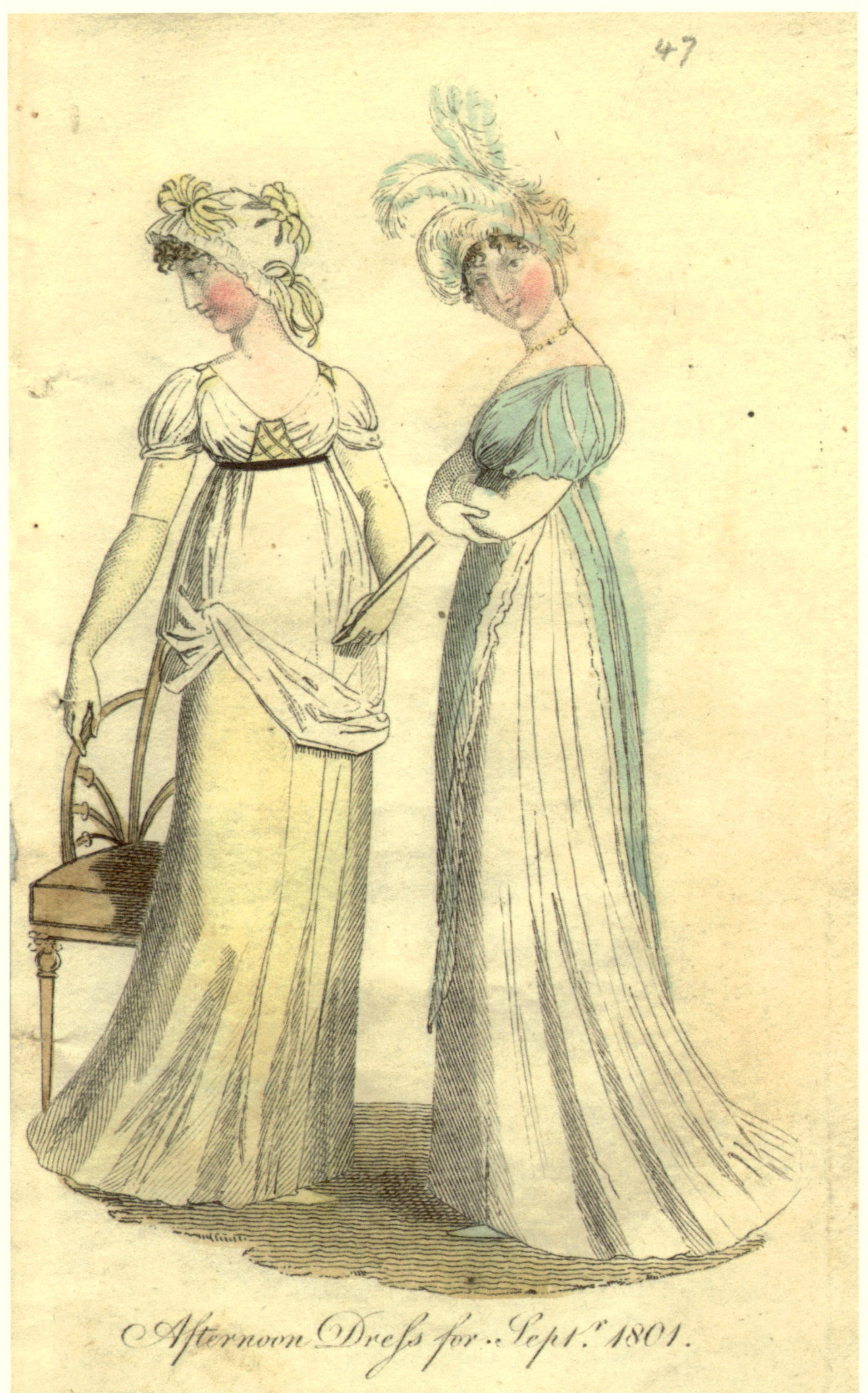

*Afternoon Dress for Sept.r 1801.*

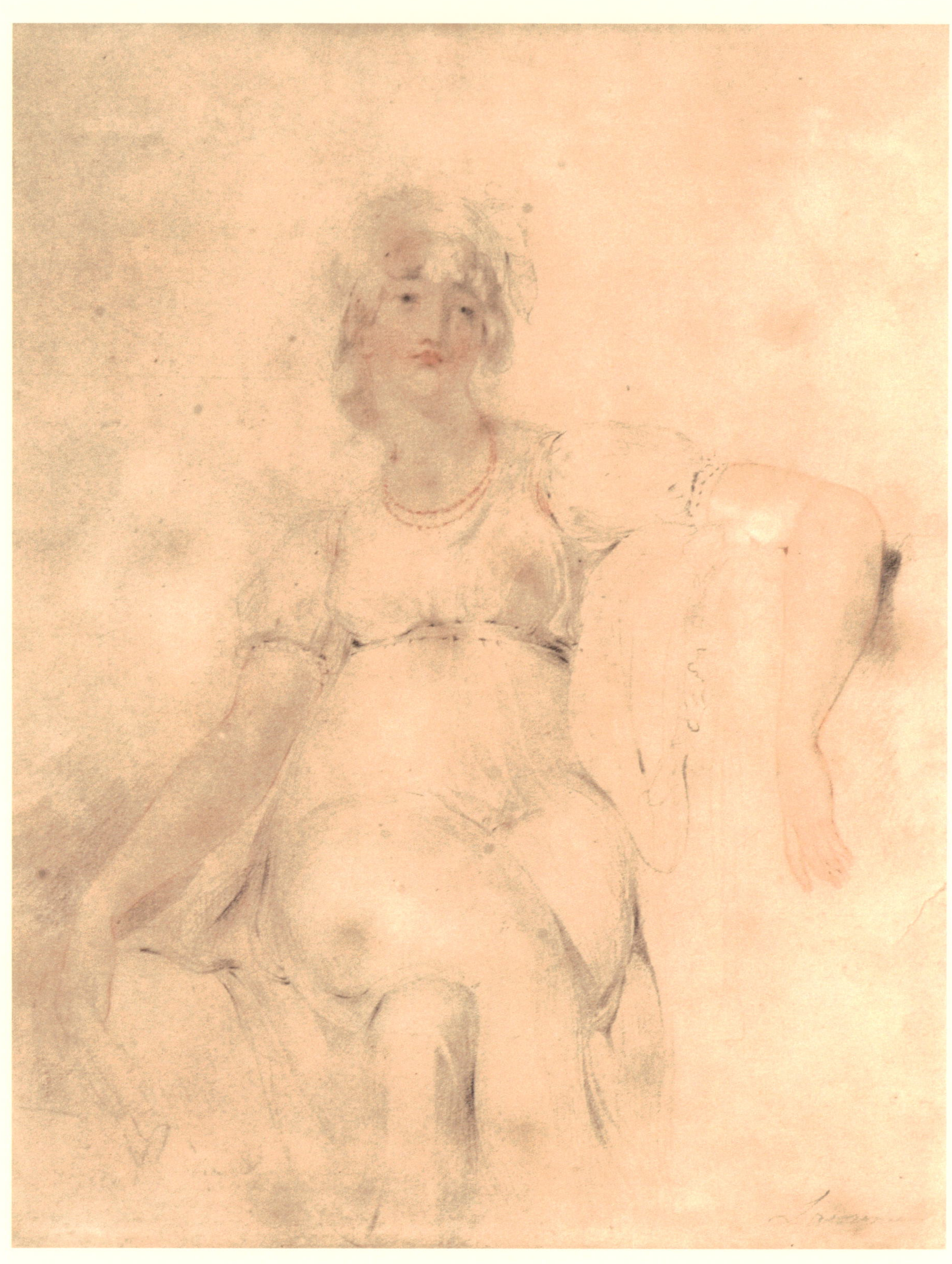

LA PENSEROSA, ca. 1791, by Sir Thomas Lawrence (1769–1830). Red chalk, pencil, and watercolor. 20 × 16.2 cm. (2000.050.00.0001)

# III



*I feel a sort of enchantment every moment I say*
*to myself am I his wife*

AFTER Sir William was passed over for a promotion, he decided to go to England, *"to settle matters so that I may return here* [to Naples] *& never have occasion again to leave this place, which I am determined on as my chief residence as long as I live; it is not a bad one, as I hope you will see one of these days."* (Sir William Hamilton to Charles Greville. Naples, 26 May 1789 [1990.035.02.0002]).

In the spring of 1791 Sir William, Emma, and Mrs. Cadogan travelled overland to London, making stops in Venice and Brussels before arriving on 16 May. Sir William soon left to settle some matters concerning the estate of the deceased Lady Catherine and to visit his properties in Wales.

While Sir William was occupied with business, Emma was much in demand for sittings by artists, resulting in many commissioned paintings, including two for her ardent admirer, the Prince of Wales. Between June and September, she sat thirty-eight times for George Romney alone.

Sir William had decided to marry Emma; although there are no letters expressing his intentions, he told friends that he wished to "make an honest woman" of her. He asked King George III for his consent and on 6 September 1791 they were married. On her wedding day she sat for her last session with Romney. This final portrait presents Emma not as a character, but as herself, as Ambassadress, seated in her wedding dress with Vesuvius in the background.

Amy Lyon, born in Ness, reared in Hawarden, costume dresser in Drury Lane, and mistress Emma Hart, was now Emma, Lady Hamilton, wife of the English envoy to the Court of Naples. The couple made a speedy departure for Naples only two days after the wedding—undoubtedly to avoid the gossip in London.

Shortly, they arrived in Paris. These were stormy days in France. They were present at the Assembly on 14 September when the humiliated Louis XVI was forced to accept a compromise that made him a constitutional monarch and reduced his family to commoners. Marie Antoinette, recently released from prison in the Tuileries, received the Hamiltons at court and gave Emma a letter—perhaps her last—to her sister, Maria Carolina, in Naples.

Continuing on their journey, Emma wrote to Sir William's niece, Mary Dickenson, from Geneva. After expressions of gratitude for being accepted as a correspondent—an indication that she was aware of her once inferior social position—she speaks touchingly of her pride and love for Sir William:

EMMA HAMILTON. Autograph letter, signed: to Mary Dickenson. Geneva, 27 September 1791. 3 pages, 4ᵗᵒ. (1987.005.00.001)

*[A] thousand thanks to you for your kind letter endead I feil as tho I have not deserved it ... & believe me the honer you have done me by coresponding with me & the pleasure is such that I shall seize every opportunity of shewing my gratitude to you for the happiness your dear & instructive Letters gives me ... & believe me before the 6th of sept<sup>br</sup> I was allways unhappy & discontented with myself, ah Madam how much do I owe to your dear uncle I fee every moment my obligations to him & am allways affraid I can never do enough for him since that dear Blessed 6th of sept<sup>br</sup> I feel a Sort of enchantment every moment I say to myself am I his wife & can we never separate more am I Emma Hamilton it seems impossible I can be so happy Surely no person was ever so happy as I am ...*

When they returned to Naples Emma assumed her new position as ambassador's wife, entertaining a constant stream of visitors, supervising elaborate dinner parties, and performing her Attitudes. Upbeat, attentive, and kind, she impressed everyone with her personality and social skills.

Despite their great difference in age, Sir William and Emma were devoted to each other. When Sir William became gravely ill in the summer of 1792, Emma stayed at his side, day and night, to nurse him back to health.

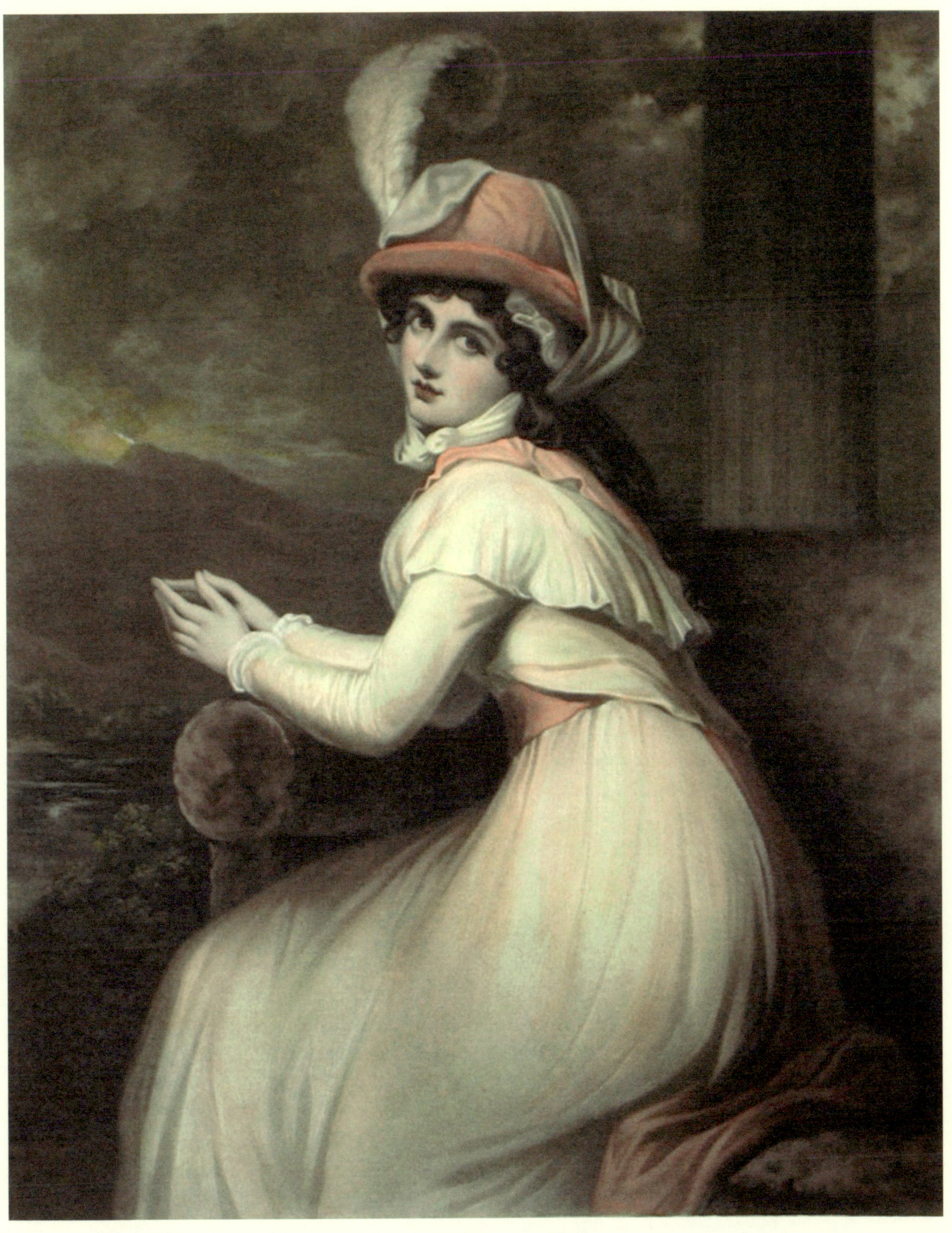

EMMA, LADY HAMILTON, "The Ambassadress." Engraved by Thomas G. Appleton after a picture by George Romney, 1905. Re-strike mezzotint engraving, hand colored. 66 × 53 cm. (2010.154.00.0001)

The Neapolitan court was not initially hostile to the democratic movement in France but felt increasingly threatened as events in France spun out of control. France declared war on Austria in 1792, and then abolished the monarchy. Louis XVI was executed in January 1793, France declared war on England in February, and Marie Antoinette was sent to the guillotine on 16 October. Fearful of invasion and vowing revenge for her sister, Maria Carolina convinced Ferdinand that the kingdom of Naples should join Spain, Holland, Austria, Prussia, and Britain in the coalition against France.

When Admiral Hood, commander of the Mediterranean fleet, wanted Neapolitan support for his troops defending the port of Toulon, then held by French royalists, he sent thirty-five-year-old Horatio Nelson, Captain of the *Agamemnon*.

## *Horatio Nelson*

Horatio Nelson was born on 29 September 1758 in a rectory in Burnham Thorpe, Norfolk, England, the sixth of eleven children of the Reverend Edmund Nelson and his wife Catherine.

He began his naval career in the spring of 1771 at the age of twelve as an ordinary seaman under his maternal uncle, Captain Maurice Suckling, on the H.M.S. *Raisonnable*. Nelson passed his lieutenant's examination and on 10 April 1777 he received an appointment to H.M.S. *Lowestoffe*, under Captain William Locker, sailing for Jamaica to join the war effort against the rebellious American colonies.

In August 1781, at the age of 22, he was given command of the frigate H.M.S. *Albemarle* and assigned to convoy duty in the Baltic. After France entered the war on the American side, Nelson accompanied a convoy to Quebec in 1782, and the *Albemarle* spent the rest of the war cruising the West Indies scouting for French warships. Nelson returned to England in June 1783.

In 1784 he received command of the frigate H.M.S. *Boreas*. From 1784 to 1787, the *Boreas*, a 28-gun frigate, was assigned to the Caribbean to enforce the Navigation Acts that required all imports to British colonies be carried in English ships. The Acts had become a major problem after the end of the American Revolution because American vessels dominated trade in the West Indies. Nelson's manuscript account (*opposite*), duly kept for the Admiralty, begins with his arrival in Barbados in June 1784 and finding the bay "full of Americans."

For three years Nelson was constantly at odds with the local governments and his superior officers, who encouraged him to turn a blind eye to the illegal trade. The situation became critical when the zealous young commander ordered the seizure of four illegally laden American ships in the port of Nevis. Although the ships had obviously violated the Navigation Acts, their captains sued him for illegal seizure. To avoid arrest and imprisonment Nelson spent nearly eight months aboard his frigate. In the ensuing trial the judge eventually upheld the British navy's right to seize the American ships. Entry dated 29 June 1785:

"[A]nd the four masters of said four vessels have been instigated to procure divers writs for the arrest of your Memorialist ... Thus circumstanced your Memorialist is oblige'd to keep himself confined to Your Majesty's ship which added to the unhealthfulness of a West India climate has impair'd your Memorialist's health but he cheerfully submits to those sufferings incurred in Your Majesty's service if they may be allowed to claim Your Majesty's attention."

Judging from the tone of frustration and anger echoed throughout the account, it is no wonder that Nelson fell out of favor with the Admiralty. After an encouraging start, his naval career stalled and he spent the next five years retired in Norfolk at half pay.

HORATIO NELSON (1758–1805). Manuscript: An Account of the Proceedings of Captain Nelson of His Majesty's ship *Boreas*, Relative to the Illegal Trade Carried On Between the Americans & the British West India Islands, ca. 1787. 64 pages. (Kislak Library of Congress Collection MS 1009)

While patrolling the Caribbean, Nelson met and married a young widow, Frances "Fanny" Nisbet. Fanny was born of wealthy parnets on the island of Nevis. After her marriage to Nelson, she subsequently emigrated to England with her son, Josiah.

## Emma & Nelson: The First Encounter

With an increasing French threat, Nelson was finally given command of a ship, the *Agamemnon*, and ordered to join the English fleet in the Mediterranean. He arrived in Naples on 10 September 1793, and suddenly a backwater took on strategic importance. Nelson was hailed as a savior of Italy and was received with state honors. Nelson and Josiah Nisbet, his stepson who served as cabin boy, stayed at the Palazzo Sessa, where Emma and Sir William lavished them with fine food and attention. Within just a few days, Ferdinand made a pledge of support.

Pictured (*opposite*) is the young Horatio Nelson as he may have looked on his first encounter with Emma. Although the portrait was begun in 1777 when Nelson was a lieutenant, it was not finished until 1781 when he returned to England as a captain. It was one of three portraits of promising young officers commissioned by their early commander, Captain William Locker. When Nelson's celebrity after the 1797 Battle of Cape St. Vincent prompted a demand for images of him, Locker lent the portrait to the engraver Robert Shipster, who issued this print.

Nelson, hearing news of a French man-of-war nearby, set sail in hopes of glory. Nelson and Emma would not see one another again for five years.

---

*Opposite*: CAPTAIN HORATIO NELSON, by Robert Shipster. "Horatio Nelson Esqr now Sir Horatio Nelson K.B. Rear Admiral of the Blue Squadron. From an Original Picture in the possession of W. Locker Esqr- Lieut. Govr of Greenwich Hospital Publish R. Shipster, Del et Sculp Pub^d. as the Act directs Aug^t. 14. 1797, by R. Shipster George Street, Woolwich ed 14 August 1797." After a painting by Francis Rigaud, 1777–1781. (2010.131.00.0001)

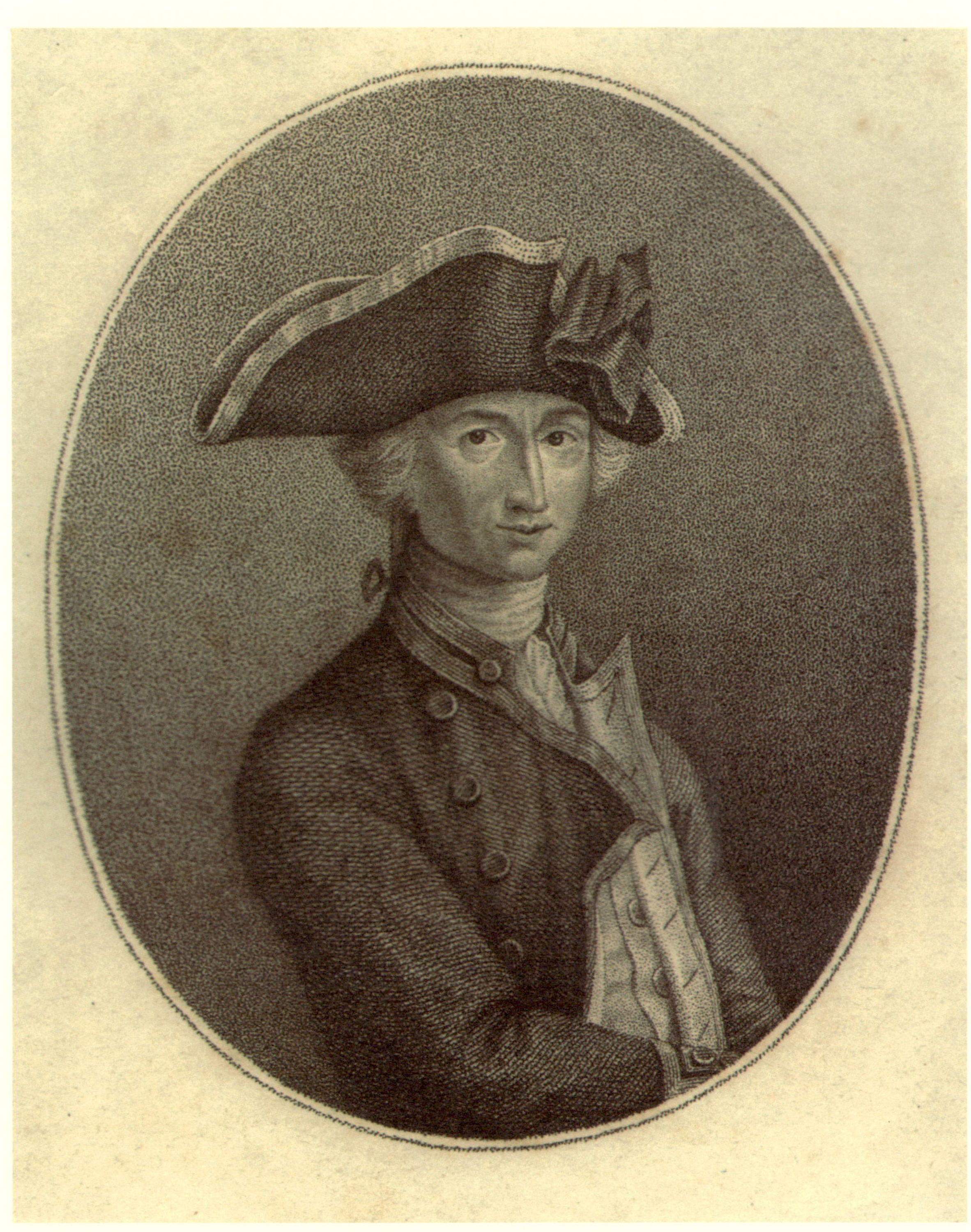

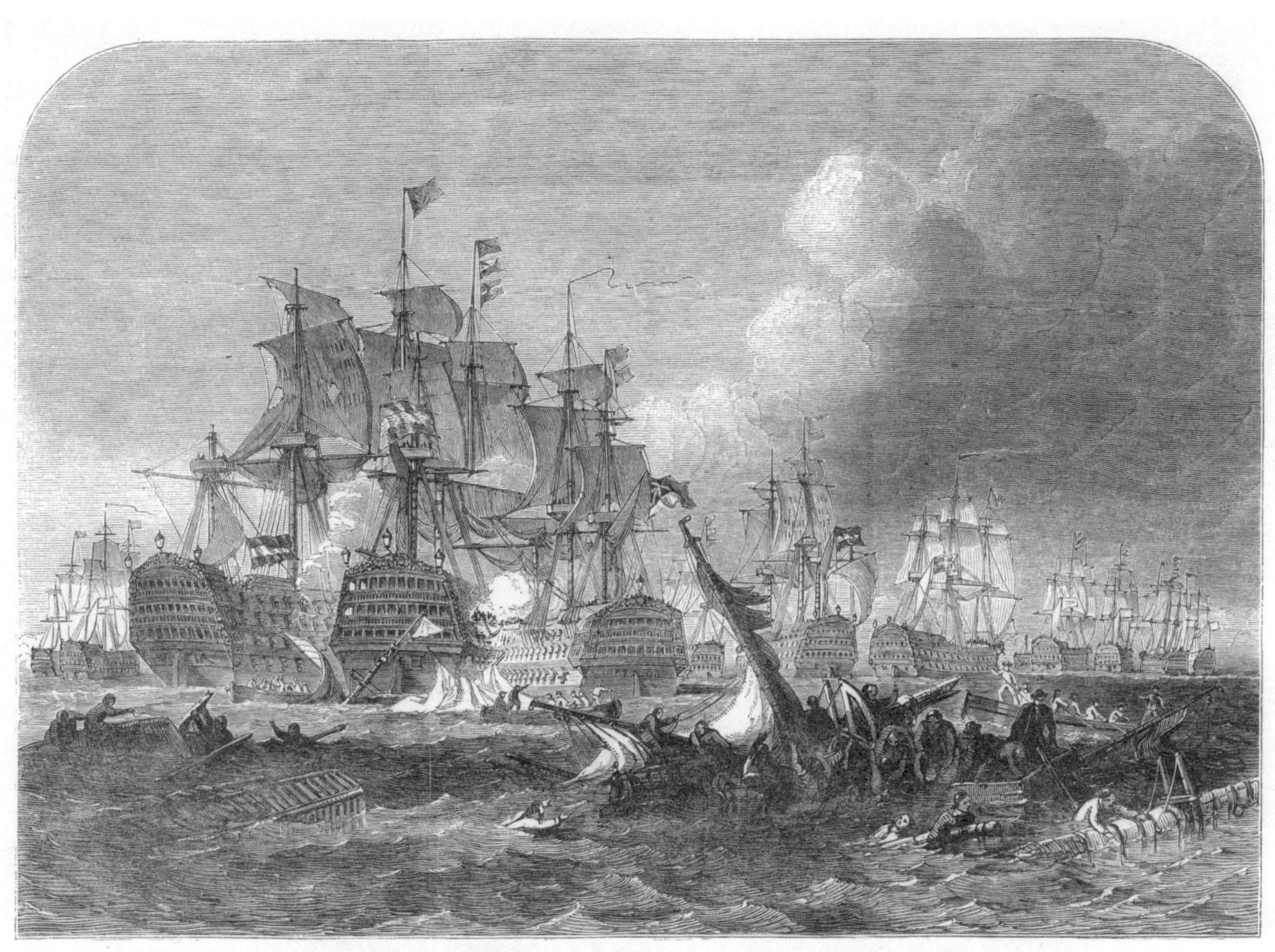



THE BATTLE OF CAPE ST. VINCENT. After an original painting by J. W. Carmichael, 1797. *The London News*, 1852. (2010.125.00.00001)

# IV



*As soon as I have fought the French fleet,*
*I shall do myself the honor of paying my respects to*
*your Ladyship at Naples*

NELSON fought the French in the Mediterranean and Atlantic—at Toulon, Corsica, Bastia, and Calvi, the last the engagement where he was blinded in his right eye.
In the Battle of Cape St. Vincent, Portugal (14 February 1797), a British fleet under John Jervis defeated a larger Spanish fleet under José de Córdoba y Ramos. While Nelson's forces were attempting to board the *San Nicolas*, the *San José* collided with the *San Nicolas* and their rigging became tangled. Nelson ordered his men to cross the first Spanish ship onto the second, and forced both ships to surrender. Later, this maneuver—using one enemy ship to cross to another—was wittily referred to as *"Nelson's patent bridge for boarding enemy vessels."* After the battle of Cape St. Vincent, in February 1797, he was promoted to the rank of Rear-Admiral of the Blue and was knighted.

Then, on 22 July 1797, he saw defeat. The Battle of Santa Cruz de Tenerife was an amphibious assault on the Spanish port city of Santa Cruz de Tenerife in the Canary Islands. Nelson's plan called for a night-time landing in order to surprise the Spanish batteries. The enemy was better prepared than Nelson expected and in the confusion several of the boats failed to land at the correct positions. Those that did were met with heavy gunfire and grapeshot. The operation ended in failure. Nelson was hit in the right arm by a musketball, which fractured his humerus bone. Most of the right arm had to be amputated, but within half an hour Nelson had returned to issuing orders to his captains.

Nelson returned to England and spent the last months of 1797 recuperating in London, eager to return to duty. In March 1798, he was assigned to the H.M.S. *Vanguard* and sailed back to the Mediterranean in search of the French fleet.

Meanwhile, Emma's influence in Naples was increasing; her behind-the-scenes political role had become significant. She carried letters and news from visiting diplomats to the court and reassured Queen Maria Carolina that the English could be trusted to protect Naples. At the same time, she was able to carry back to Sir William details of events at court and, in at least one instance, copies of letters supplied by the Queen concerning a potential alliance between Spain and

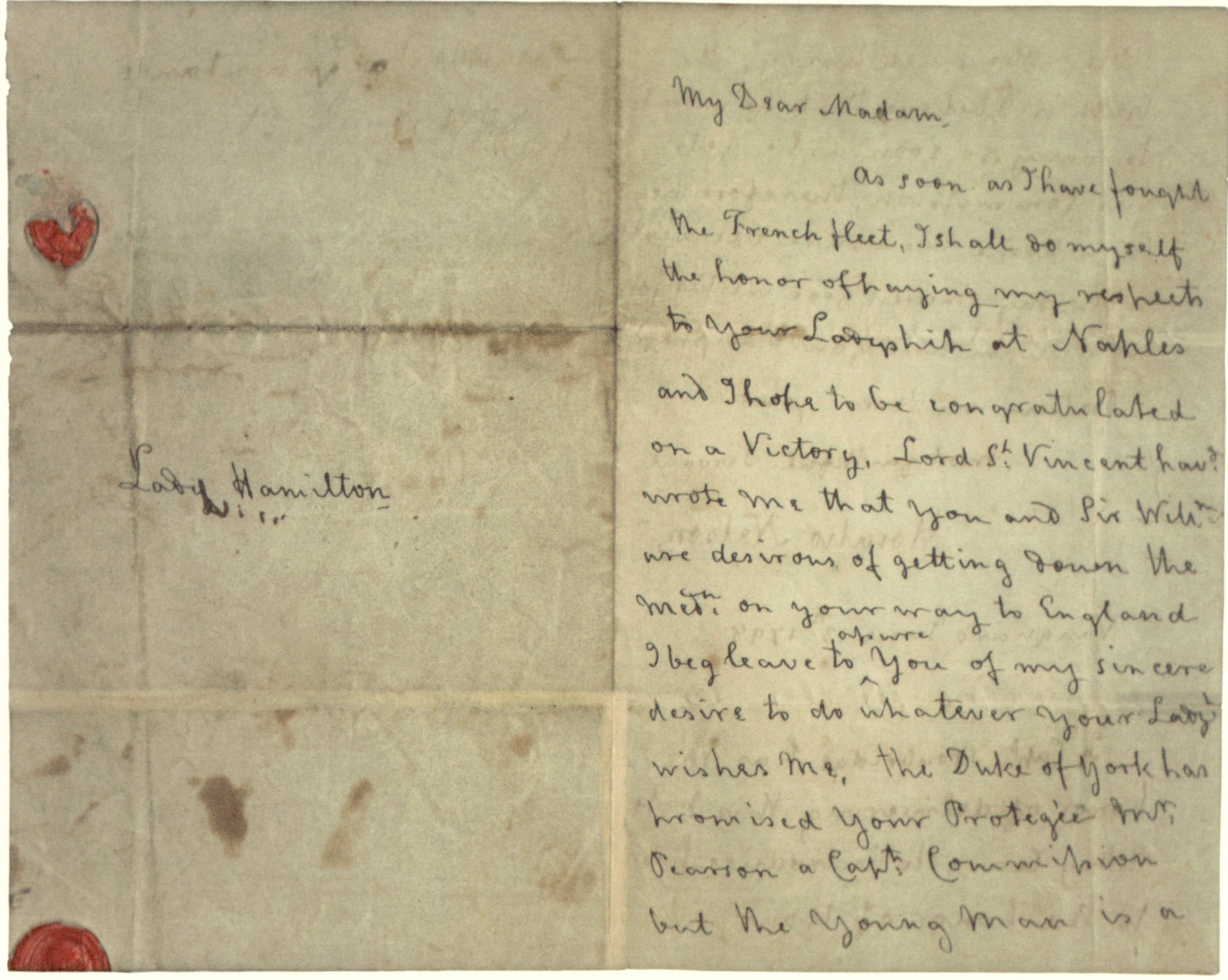





HORATIO NELSON. Autograph letter, signed: to Emma Hamilton. H.M.S. *Vanguard*, 13 June 1798. 3 pages, 8vo. (1993.002.00.0001)

France. Unfortunately for Emma, Sir William never acknowledged her role in his official reports.

*My Dear Madam, As soon as I have fought the French fleet, I shall do myself the honor of paying my respects to your Ladyship at Naples and I hope to be congratulated on a Victory ... Capt. Troubridge has the honor of delivering this note I beg leave to introduce him the honor of your Ladyships acquaintance.*

Although there had been official correspondence between Sir William, Emma, and Nelson, this is the earliest known letter from Nelson directly to Emma (*above*).

Lady Hamilton wrote back, via Captain Troubridge, saying *"God bless you and send you victorious ... I shall have a fever with anxiety ... Ever ever dear Sir, your obliged and grateful Emma Hamilton."*

After chasing the French fleet around the Mediterranean for three months, on 1 August 1798, Nelson caught them by surprise at Aboukir Bay, off Alexandria, Egypt. The ensuing two-day battle destroyed the French fleet. Nine ships were taken, two were sunk (including the flagship), and only two ships-of-the-line and two frigates escaped. An estimated 3,500 French sailors were lost. The Battle of the Nile, as it came to be called, dealt a major blow to Napoleon's ambitions in the east and left his army stranded in Egypt. The British sustained fewer than 1,000 casualties and did not lose a single ship. Nelson, however, sustained a severe head wound that caused him pain for the rest of his life. The victory made Nelson famous throughout Europe and a cult hero in England. He was awarded the title Baron Nelson of the Nile.

Perhaps Emma's single greatest diplomatic achievement was persuading Queen Maria Carolina to press Ferdinand to allow Nelson's ships to re-provision in Sicily, thus making it possible for him to sail for Egypt.

After his great victory, Nelson returned to Naples on 22 September. Sir William's barge was the first to come alongside the *Vanguard*. Emma was the first to board and collapsed into Nelson's arms. Sir William hailed him as the "Guardian Angel" of Naples. It was not long before they were describing themselves as *tria iuncta in uno* (three joined together as one).

Although not yet forty, Nelson was not the man who had left Naples five years earlier. The sea had aged him and war had left him exhausted, scarred, and maimed. Nelson and Josiah moved into the Palazzo Sessa where they were attended by Emma who took it upon herself to nurse Nelson back to health. He was eager for her attention.

They were instantly attracted to each other. Neither was in love with their spouse. Emma, at the height of her beauty, was married to a man approaching seventy. Fanny lacked Nelson's passion and drive for fame and glory. In less than two months, rumors of an affair circulated from Naples to London.

The political climate was also heating up. Although defeated at sea, the French army remained dominant in Europe. It was seen as an immediate danger to Naples when Napoleon's army occupied Rome in 1798, less than 200 kilometers away. Queen Maria Carolina convinced Ferdinand to take the initiative and launch a preëmptive attack. A hastily assembled Neapolitan army entered Rome on 29 November. Initially, the French fell back, then counterattacked. The ragtag Neapolitan army retreated—all the way back to Naples—with the French in hot pursuit.

As the French army approached, the royal family, the entire Neapolitan court, and assorted foreigners fled to Palermo, Sicily, on twenty of Nelson's ships, leaving the capital in a state of anarchy. "*We had a violent gale of wind, stronger, Lord Nelson says, than he ever had experienced in 30 years' service, & I fear a transport, with all the Corsican emigrants under British protection and pay, are gone to the bottom. Hatchets*

*were brought up to cut away the masts of the Vanguard if the gale had lasted..."* (Sir
William Hamilton to Charles Greville. Palermo, 6 January 1799. 5 pages, 4.^to.
[1990.035.05.0002] *see image opposite*).

*'Tis impossible my dear Miss Knight to come to you to day nor this even* FOR WE HAVE TO
GO OUT *things are as they were but keep yourselves in readiness do pray no embarkation for
the things the weather being bad so patience we shall see the Queen this eve. God bless you both*
    *your agitated & sincere*
    *Emma*
                          —Emma Hamilton to Miss [Cornelia] Knight, n.d.
                                    [December 1798]. (1991.345.00.0002)

In a five-page letter from Palermo, quoted above, Sir William Hamilton chron-
icles recent events to Charles Greville (Autograph letter, signed: from Sir
William Hamilton to Charles Greville. Palermo, 6 January 1799. 5 pages, 4.^to.
[1990.035.05.0002] *see image opposite*):

On the defeat of the Neapolitan army:

*My former dispatches to Lord Grenville will have prevented his Lordship from being too
much surprized at receiving one dated from Palermo ... I never could have imagined that a
fine army of near fifty thousand effective men ... [could] be reduced to less than 20 thousand
in 22 days without ever having had anything like what cou'd be called an action, and nothing
but treachery and stinking cowardice cou'd have caused such a cruel reverse, for the French
were never more than seven or eight thousand effective men.*

On their escape from Naples:

*[T]he King and Queen of Naples and all their Royal Family having been obliged to take
refuge on board the Vanguard, and by the contrivance and assistance of Lord Nelson and I
are safely lodged in their Palace here with a treasure in jewells and money of not less than
two and a half millions sterling. Emma has had a very principal part in this delicate business, as she is and has been for several years the real and only confidential friend of the Queen
of Naples ... The poor Queen of Naples is all despair, having also lost Prince Albert of
six years of age in our voyage, and who died in Emma's arms of repeated convulsions ... I
shall probably lose a great deal of valuable furniture in my houses of Naples and Caserta. I
have left my house at Naples, servants and all except two, to go on another month as if I was
there ...[Lord Nelson] lives always with us, and by his friendship I have at least secured
all my best pictures and collection of vases on board ... a good transport* [H.M.S. Colossus]
*and I hope to be with you early in the spring, but cannot think of leaving their Sicilijesties
in their present moment of distress.*

On his own failing health, a complaint often repeated to his nephew:

*I feel age creeping upon me, but I will bear up as long & as well as I can, & not give up as
my father did twenty years before he died, calling himself a dying man, and so we all are.
Adieu, my dear Charles, Emma's kind love attends you.*

what can the Emperor be doing
to allow of Naples & Tuscany
being lost ?

Palermo Jan.ry 6.th 1799.

My Dear Charles

You have certainly the
means of getting every intelligence of the
singular Events that have rapidly taken
place in the Kingdom of Naples and from
my last dispatch to Lord Grenville you
will hear of the King and Queen of Naples
and all their Royal Family having been
obliged to take refuge on board the Van—
guard and by the contrivance and assistance
of Lord Nelson and, I am safely lodged in
their Palace here with a Treasure in Jewells
and money of not less than two Millions &
a half Sterling, Emma has had a very prin
-cipal part in this delicate business as She is,
& has been for several years, the real and
only confidential friend of the Queen of
Naples. It is impossible for me to enter into

Rt Honble
Chas. Greville

particulars

SIR WILLIAM HAMILTON. Autograph letter, signed: to Charles Greville. Palermo,
6 January 1799. 5 pages, 4.to. (1990.035.05.0002)

The *Colossus* was bound for England with wounded men from the Battle of the Nile—along with Sir William's second collection of Greek pottery—when the ship was caught in bad weather off the Scilly Isles. It attempted to ride out the storm but after three days of worsening weather an anchor cable broke and the ship ran aground and sank. The crew and passengers were rescued but the entire cargo was lost. In 1974 divers located the ship and salvaged a few of Sir William's vases, which are now in the British Museum.

Sir William tells this sad tale of his abandoned homes and his collections lost at sea to Greville (Autograph letter, signed: Sir W. Hamilton to Charles Greville. Palermo, 8 April 1799. 5 pages, 4^to [1990.035.06.0002]):

*From being driven from my comfortable house at Naples to a house here without chimneys & calculated only for summer, we have all suffer'd in our health, but as I wax old it has been hard upon me having had both bilious and rheumatic complaints. I am still most desirous of profiting of the King's leave and of returning home by the first ship that Lord Nelson sends down to Gibraltar, as I am worn out and want repose … I realy now see a very good prospect of Ld Nelson's carrying back their Sicilian Majesties to Naples in the Vanguard & placing them again on that throne … Cardinal Ruffo's army in Calabria is increased to 15 thousand men, & is getting on to join the King's friends at Salerno … As to my 8 cases, all of the best vases in my collection that were on board the Colossus, I fear none will be recovered, & it is a pity, for never in this world will such a collection be made again … the French have taken most of my furniture at Naples, Caserta, & Pausilippo, which I had not time to carry off, having left Naples in such a hurry. Emma makes a great figure in our political line, for she carries on the business with the Queen, whose abilities you know are very great … I love Ld Nelson more & more—his activity is wonderfull, and he loves us sincerely.*

Nelson, meanwhile, apprises Sir William of the situation at sea (Autograph letter, signed: Horatio Nelson to Sir William Hamilton. Aboard the *Vanguard*, off Trapani, 27 May [1799]. 3 pages 4^to [2007.031.00.0002]):

*We are compleatly in the dark, to say the truth had I known or could have guessed at Ad[miral] Duckworth's intention not to have come to my help, I had no great business at sea, but being out I know had I returned the next day all Palermo would have fancy'd that I wanted to find shelter, & that the F[rench] F[leet] were at my heels … I would have you, the court, and all Palermo be assured that, whilst I have a ship left, their Majestys and the city shall be defended, therefore weither they hear of me this day or hour, they may rest assured I do not for a moment forget they are in my charge … I readily conceive your anxiety by my own, and that, if we do not hear from our friends, we fancy 10,000 things …*

*1 o'clock, morning of the 28^th*

*I thank you for your kind wishes about my health. I can say with truth that I have not been free from headache, sickness, and with want of rest, for I know not what sleep is since I left*

*Palermo. I am seriously unwell, and have given notice to my squadron that if I am ordered to blockade Toulon, that my health will not allow it, and I shall give up.*

At the time of this letter, the French fleet had escaped from Brest, France, and was sailing towards the Mediterranean. Nelson left Palermo on 12 May 1799 to begin an exhausting two weeks of sleepless patrols. He asks Hamilton to assure the anxious royal family that he is vigilant. This letter shows Nelson's reliance on Sir William, eight months into his affair with Emma, and testifies to his neglect of his own comfort and safety in the face of danger. He returned to Palermo on 29 May, where he recuperated for two weeks before moving on to Naples.

The French occupied Naples in January 1799, in spite of fierce resistance of the *lazzaroni*—there were 8,000 Neapolitan casualties—and established the Parthenopean Republic. The republic lasted only a few months, from January to June 1799. When French troops were recalled to northern Italy, the Neapolitan army under the command of Cardinal Ruffo "re-conquered" Naples and Ferdinand was returned to the throne. The aftermath was brutal and bloody. Queen Maria Carolina, enraged over the murder of her sister, Marie Antoinette, and the death of Prince Albert during their escape, carried out her vengeance. Ferdinand ordered wholesale arrests and executions of supposed liberals. No mercy was shown to the rebels.

Sir William informs Greville of the Neapolitan change of fortune (Autograph letter, signed: Sir W. Hamilton to Charles Greville. Dated on board the *Foudroyant*. Bay of Naples, 14 July 1799. 4 pages, folio. ([1990.035.07.0002] *see image overleaf*):

*By our present compleat success I am more than repaid for having, as you know, sacrificed both my health and private interests for the good of the common cause ... The arrival of the King's fleet in time has saved this capital from the utmost anarchy and confusion. Lord Nelson has secured all the chiefs of the Jacobine nobility & their party, who wou'd otherwise have escaped the hand of justice by the rascality or imbecility of the King's Vicar Gen[eral] [Cardinal Ruffo] ... we flatter ourselves that in a few days there will not be a Frenchman left in the kingdom of Naples ... In short, the King's fleet & a little good management & temper has placed their Sicn Majesties once more on their throne of Naples.*

Stress and persistent ill health had taken their toll on Sir William and he was eager to return to England to regain his strength.

*It will be a heart breaking to the Queen of N[aples]. When we go, she has realy no female friend but her, & Emma has been of infinite use in our late very critical business. Ld Nelson & I cou'd not have done without her, all of which shall be explain'd when we meet.*

For their efforts, Nelson and Emma were individually rewarded. Nelson was made the Duke of Bronte and granted an estate on the western slope of Mt. Etna in Sicily. Emma was granted her own title, Dame of the Order of Malta,

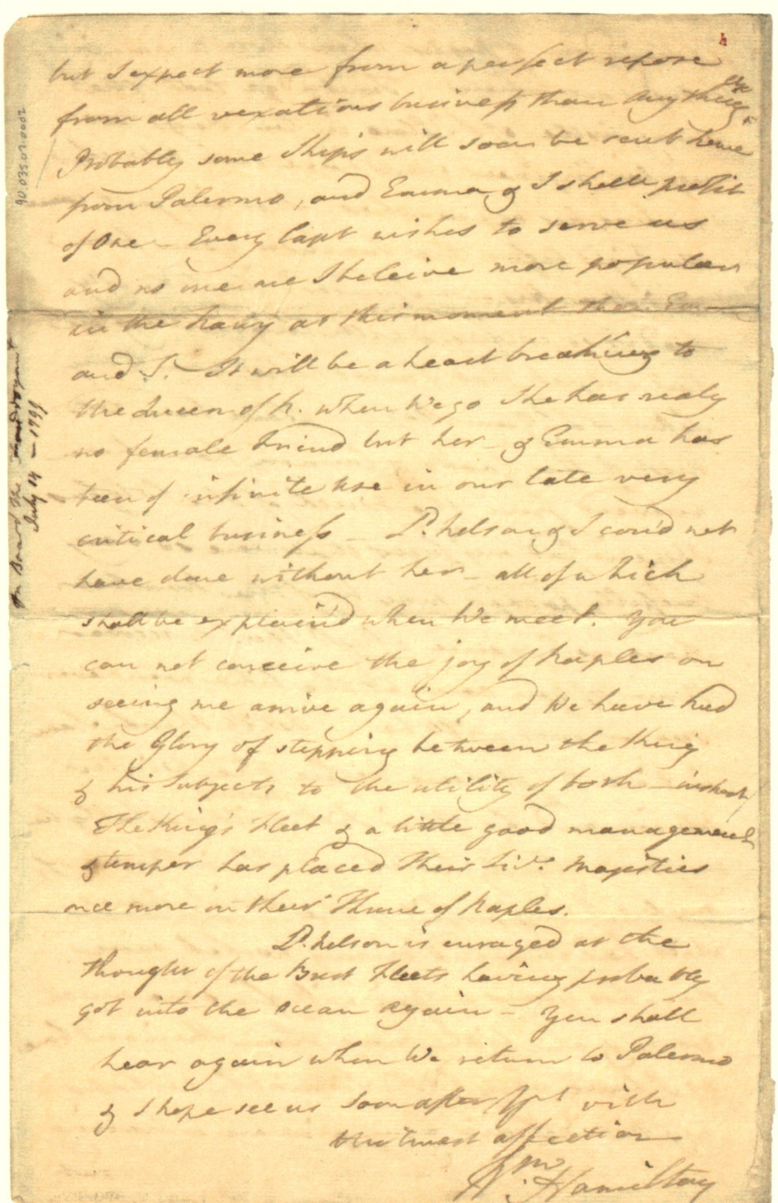



SIR WILLIAM HAMILTON. Autograph letter, signed: to Charles Greville. Dated on board the *Foudroyant*. Bay of Naples, 14 July 1799. 4 pages, folio. (1990.035.07.0002)

and received the Cross of Malta, which Queen Maria Carolina had mounted with diamonds.

After the Neapolitan debacle and the turmoil of its aftermath, Sir William was unceremoniously relieved of his post in January 1800. His expectation of grateful recognition and a pension for his thirty-seven years of service were gravely in doubt. As he prepared to depart for England, he made plans to return, expecting to live in retirement on the Bronte estate in Sicily. This was not to be.

Nelson also was in trouble. In February, displeased with his actions in Naples and rumors of the affair with Emma, the Admiralty called Nelson to Leghorn, Italy, to give an account of his command. Subsequently, Nelson was recalled to England. On his journey from Leghorn back to Palermo, Nelson writes to Emma (Autograph letter, signed: Horatio Nelson to Lady Hamilton. [Onboard the *Foudroyant*] 13 February 1800. 2 pages, 4$^{to}$ [1988.013.00.0003] *see image below*):

HORATIO NELSON.
Autograph letter, signed:
to Emma Hamilton. [Onboard the *Foudroyant*], 13 February 1800. 2 pages, 4$^{to}$. (1988.013.00.0003)

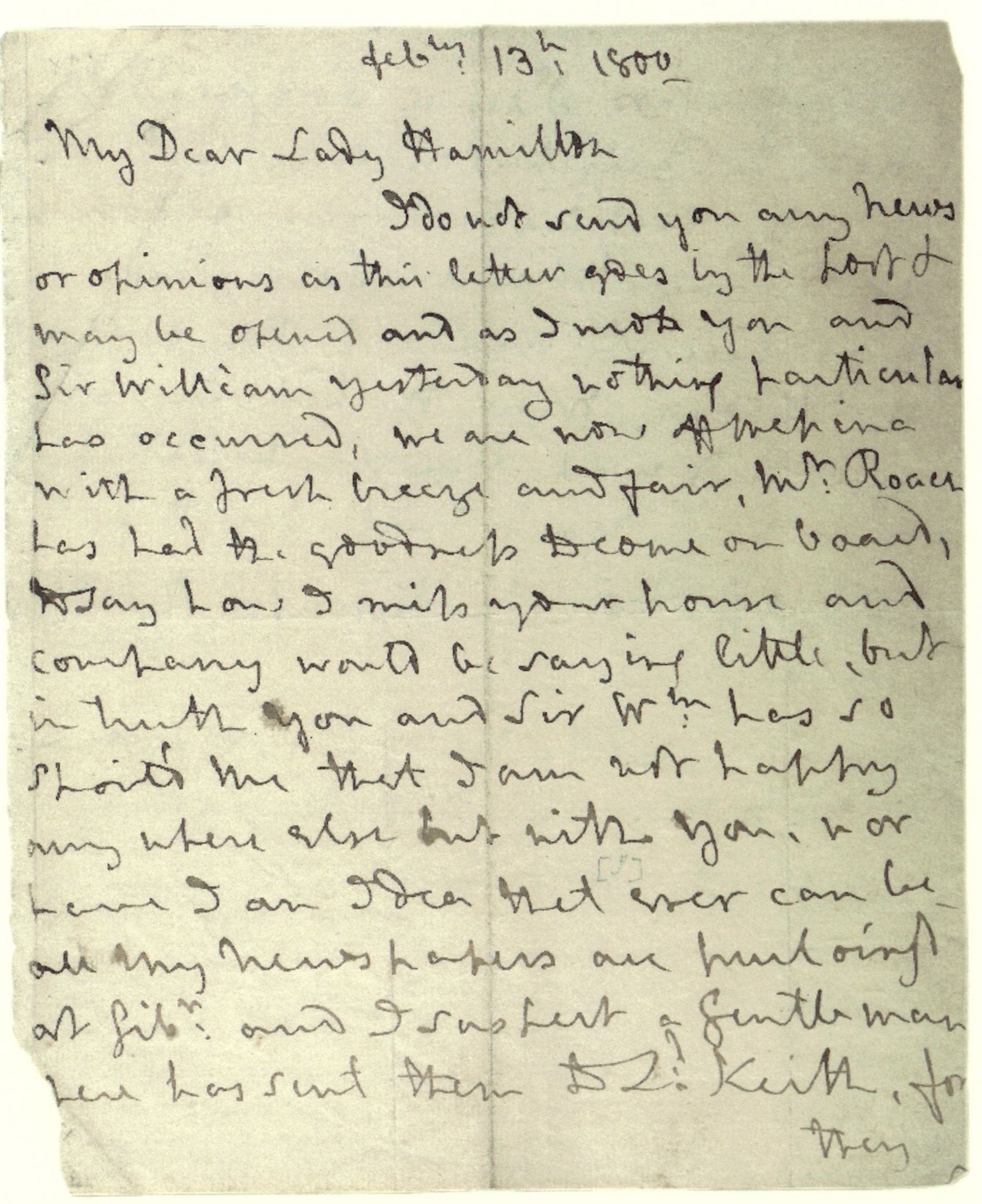

*We are now off Messina with a fresh breeze and fair ... To say how I miss your house and company would be saying little; but in truth you and Sir William have so spoiled me that I am not happy anywhere else but with you, nor have I an idea that I ever can be.*

On 10 June, together with the Hamiltons, he set out for the return journey to England. By this time, Emma was pregnant with Nelson's child. The *tria iuncta in uno* would never return.

They departed with their servants, secretaries, a group of English friends, Queen Maria Carolina, seven of her children, and a party of eighty bound for Vienna, all aboard the *Foudroyant*. In Leghorn they learned that the ship was needed for the war and the Admiralty refused Nelson's request to sail her to England. While the travellers were detained in Leghorn trying to organize transportation, an insurrection broke out caused by fears of an invasion by the French. Queen Maria Carolina and her entourage, Nelson, the Hamiltons, and the others travelled 150 miles east to the Adriatic where, after a three-week delay, they found Russian ships to take them to Trieste. Finally, on 10 August their fourteen carriages and three baggage wagons set off on a 700-mile journey across Europe bound for London—with frequent stopovers to enjoy their celebrity. Their greeting in Vienna was tumultuous. They were hailed as heroes, received by the emperor, and gala celebrations were held in their honor. During their month-long stay, Emma's voice impressed the great composer Joseph Haydn who composed an aria for her and a Mass in honor of Nelson.

Their eight-day visit to Dresden was recorded in the diary of Melesina Trench, an English traveller (Melesina Chenevix St. George Trench, *Journal Kept During a Visit to Germany in 1799, 1800*, edited by the Dean of Westminster [the author's son, Richard Chenevix Trench], [London: "not published," Parker, Son, and Bourn, Printers, 1861]; privately printed for her family and friends; presentation copy from the editor to the Earl of Hardwicke [2010.080.00.0001]):

3 OCTOBER: *It is plain that Lord Nelson thinks of nothing but Lady Hamilton, who is totally occupied by the same object. She is bold, forward, coarse, assuming, and vain. Her figure is colossal, but, excepting her feet, which are hideous, well shaped. Her bones are large, and she is exceedingly* embonpoint *... Lord Nelson is a little man, without any dignity ... Lady Hamilton takes possession of him, and he is a willing captive, the most submissive and devoted I have seen. Sir William is old, infirm, all admiration of his wife ... After dinner we had several songs in honour of Lord Nelson, written by Miss Knight, and sung by Lady Hamilton. She puffs the incense full in his face; but he receives it with pleasure, and snuffs it up very cordially.*

7 OCTOBER: *[H]er usual dress is tasteless, vulgar, loaded, and unbecoming ... Her waist is absolutely between her shoulders ... I think her bold, daring, vain even to folly, and stamped with the manners of her first situation much more strongly than one would suppose, after having represented Majesty, and lived in good company fifteen years. Her ruling*

*passions seem to me vanity, avarice, and love for the pleasures of the table. She shows a great avidity for presents, and has actually obtained some at Dresden by the common artifice of admiring and longing.*

8 OCTOBER: *The Electress will not receive Lady Hamilton, on account of her former dissolute life ... and I understand there will be no Court while she stays.*

Extensive excerpts from the *Journal*, including Trench's uncharitable description of Emma Hamilton and an account of a drunken Admiral Lord Nelson using foul language, were published on 9 October 1861 in the London *Times*.

They travelled—and partied—by riverboat on the Elbe for another eleven days to Hamburg where they boarded a mail ship bound for Yarmouth, arriving in London on 6 November 1800. Their first stop was Nelson's home, Roundhill. Due to poor communication, Fanny and Nelson's father, Edmund, had travelled to London to greet them. Nelson was appalled by the lack of welcome, and the incident set off a series of encounters that pitted the aging wife against Emma, the celebrity and soon-to-be mother of his child. A losing battle if ever there was one.

The *tria* moved into a house in London owned by Lord William Thomas Beckwith. Beckwith's mother was a cousin of Sir William. Beckwith inherited a fortune based on Jamaican sugar plantations estimated at £1 million, with an annual income estimated at £50,000, and the Fonthill estate of 6,000 acres of land. Newspapers of the period described him as "the richest commoner in England." Beckwith collected art on a massive scale and used his vast wealth to construct an enormous Gothic Revival mansion named Fonthill Abbey.

They spent Christmas at Fonthill. Emma, now eight months pregnant, performed the story of Agrippina in mime. The *Gentleman's Magazine* records that they arrived in the evening by coach and "*after having entered the great wall which incloses the abbey-woods the procession passed a noble Gothic arch.*" As they travelled through the wood, the way was brightly illuminated by innumerable lamps hung in the trees and by flambeaux moving with the carriages, and a militia volunteer band played. Once there, they sat down in the groined Gothic hall to a superb dinner on silver dishes. *Gentleman's Magazine* continues:

*Lady Hamilton appeared in the character of Agrippina bearing the ashes of Germanicus in a golden urn and as presenting herself before the Roman people with the design of exciting them to revenge the death of her husband ... Lady Hamilton displayed with truth and energy every gesture, attitude and expression of countenance ... The company left at 11 pm to sup at the Mansion House ... On leaving this strange nocturnal scene of vast buildings and extensive forest, now rendered dimly and partially visible by the declining light of lamps and torches, and the twinkling of a few scattered stars in a clouded sky, the company seemed, as soon as they had passed the sacred boundary of the great wall, as if waking from a dream ...*

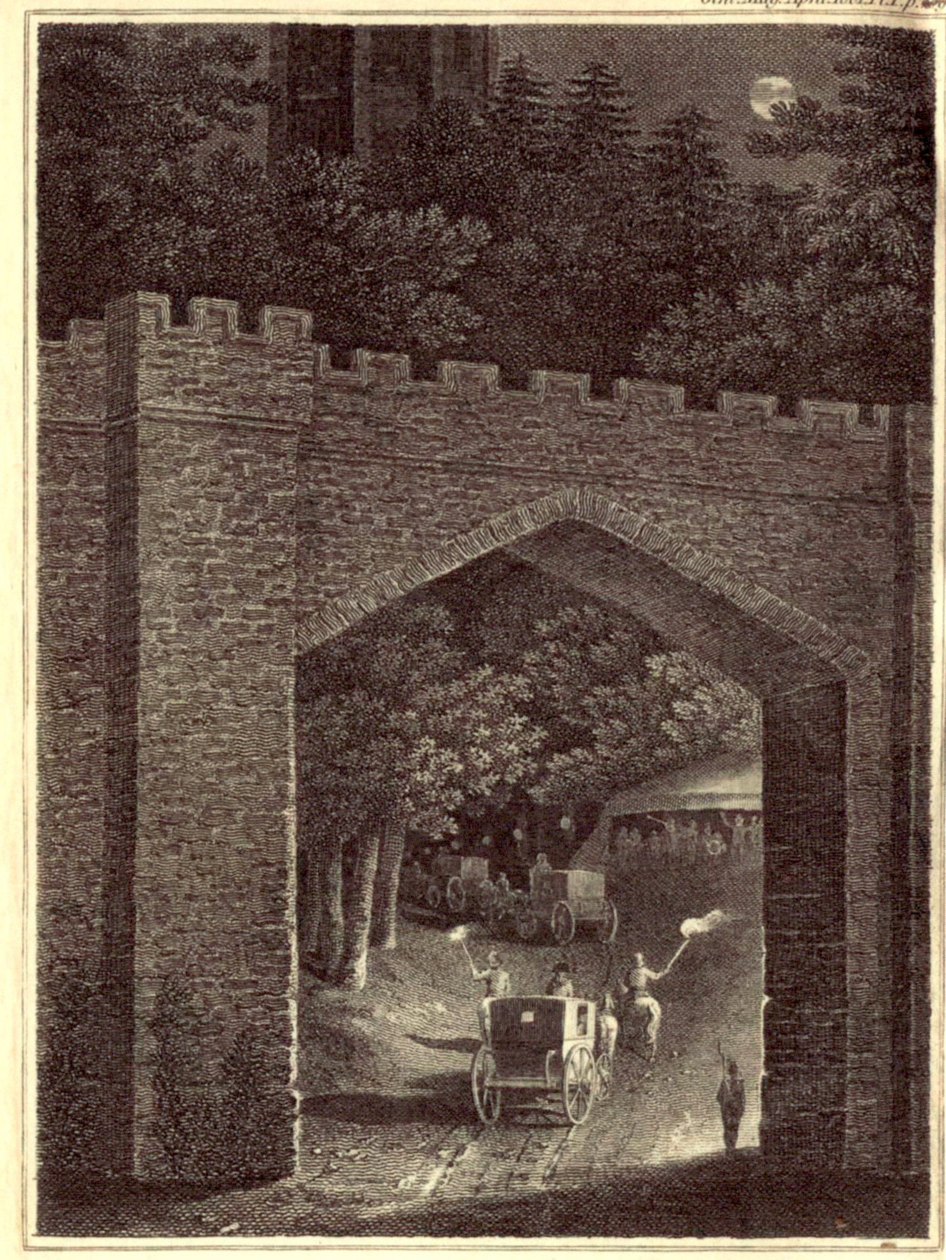



LORD NELSON'S RECEPTION AT FONTHILL. *Gentleman's Maga-zine*, Volume 71, April 1801, pl. 1, p. 28. London: J. Nichols & Son. (2010.117.00.0001)

*I can scarcely help doubting whether the whole of the last evening's enter-tainment were a reality, or only the visionary coinage of fancy.*

On his return to London on 1 January, Nelson learned of his appointment as Vice-Admiral of the Blue and second-in-command of the Channel Fleet. He hoisted his flag on the *San Josef* on 17 January, but not before a final confrontation with Fanny. It ended bitterly and they would never meet again.

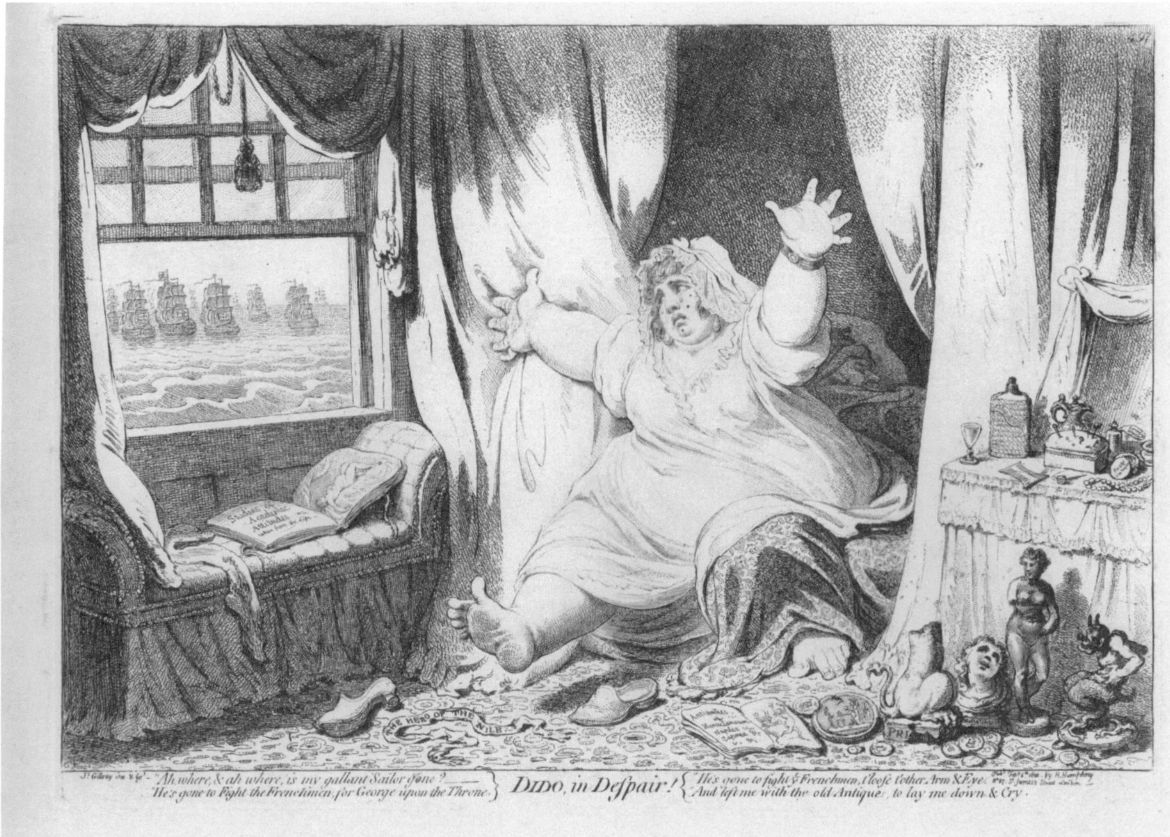



A contemporary print (*above*) satirizes the scandalous relationship between Nelson and Emma, casting them in the roles of Dido and Aeneas, the central love interest of Virgil's *Aeneid*. Spurred on by the gods and his sense of public duty, Aeneas abandons Dido in Carthage in order to found Rome. The print, therefore, refers to this parting, with Emma, excessively fat, in an "attitude" of despair, voicing the sentiments contained in the verse caption: *"Ah, where, & ah where, is my gallant Sailor gone?—He's gone to Fight the Frenchmen, for George upon the Throne, He's gone to Fight ye Frenchmen, t'loose t'other Arm & Eye, And left me with the old Antiques, to lay me down, & cry."*

DIDO IN DESPAIR. James Gillray and H. Humphrey. Published 6 February 1801. Etching, 25 × 35.3 cm. *The Works of James Gilray from the Original Plates.* London: Henry G. Bohn, 1847. (2010.112.01.0001)

73

The last line refers to Emma's aged husband asleep in the bed beside her. Meanwhile, a range of grotesque and suggestively ribald objects on the table, floor, and settee refer to the sexual improprieties of her and Nelson's relationship and undercut the pretensions of the classical allusions (*see* National Maritime Museum, Greenwich, www.nmm.ac.uk).

A companion image published in the same month (*opposite page*) is a complex and extremely pointed satire. It represents Hamilton as the great classicist and antiquary scrutinizing his motley and bizarre collection of objects, while blind to their real significance: he even contemplates them through his glasses the wrong way round. Everywhere they disclose Nelson and Emma's cuckoldry of Hamilton. The objects ranged around the room allude in various ways to the same subject. The headless statue of a Bacchante to the left assumes the pose of one of Emma's "Attitudes." On the far right, below the picture of Claudius, is a full-length statue of Midas, but with ass's ears: clearly a symbol for Hamilton himself, signifying that his ability to turn objects into gold will not stop him being a fool (*see* National Maritime Museum, Greenwich, www.nmm.ac.uk).

Already deep in debt, Sir William rented and furnished a grand house he could ill afford and prepared for the birth of Nelson's child. Horatia came into the world on 28 January and was put in the care of a nurse to allow Emma to return to "normal life"—dinners, gambling parties, theatre, and the opera.

Nelson was at sea when Horatia was born. The ensuing exchange of letters with Emma employed the subterfuge of addressing her as "Mrs. Thompson," care of Lady Hamilton. He wrote as if on behalf of Thomson, one of his crew, so that all remarks and enquiries about the child would be attributable to her fictitious parents. His difficulty in maintaining this disguise shows in frequent inconsistencies and slips of the pen. Later, after a pretended "adoption," Horatia was referred to as "Horatia Thompson Nelson."

The following is the first mention of Lady Hamilton as "Mrs. Thomson" (Autograph letter, signed: Horatio Nelson to Emma Hamilton. 25 January 1801. 2 pages, with superscription and seal [1993.151.00.0004]):

*If you'll believe me, nothing can give me so much pleasure as your truly kind and friendly letters, and where friendship is of so strong a cast as ours, it is no easy matter to shake it— mine is as fixed as Mount Etna, and as warm in the inside as that mountain ... I delivered poor Mrs. Thomson's to note; her friend is truly thankful for her kindness and your goodness. Who does not admire your benevolent heart. Poor man! he is very anxious, and begs you will, if she is not able, write a line just to comfort him. He appears to me to feel very much her situation; he is so agitated, and will be so for 2 or 3 days, that he says he cannot write, and that I must send his kind love and affectionate regards.*

Although estranged, Fanny had not given up her pursuit and determination to win Nelson back. She continued to write entreating him to return. In a scathing

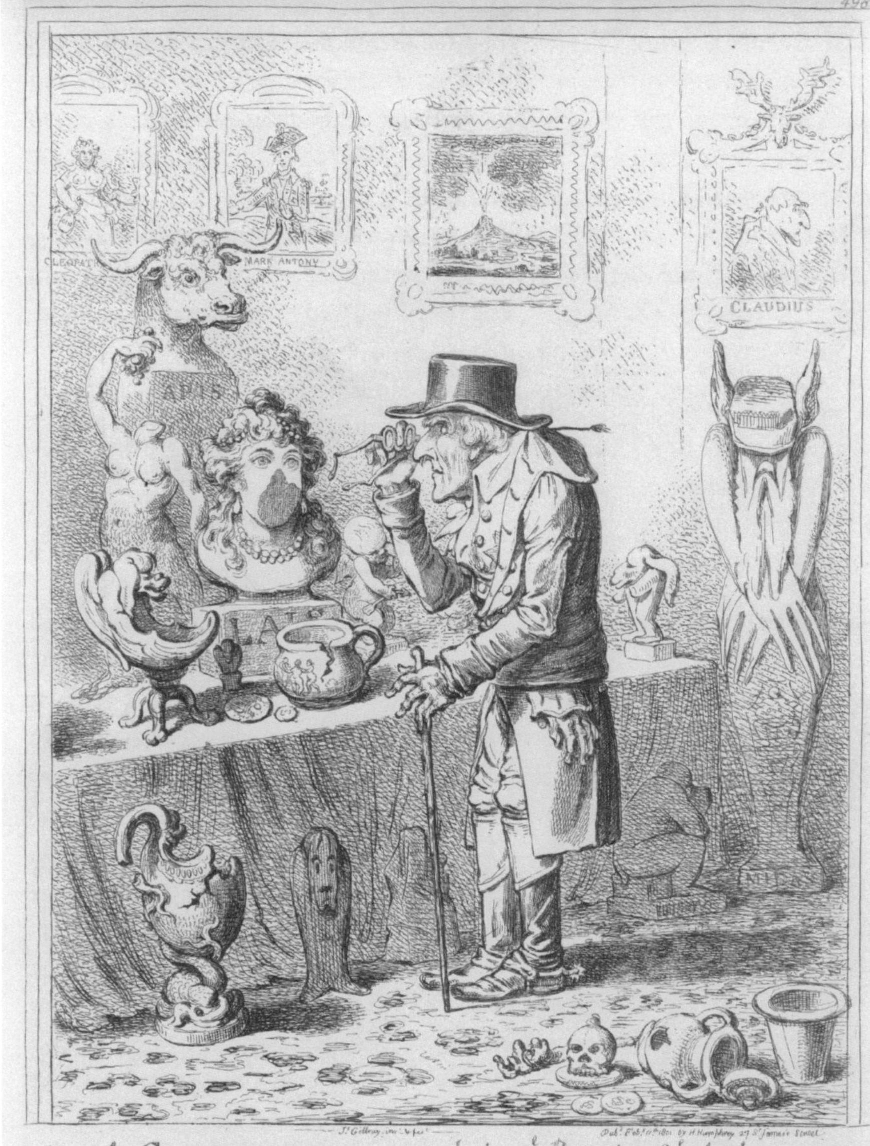


A COGNOCENTI CONTEMPLATING YE BEAUTIES OF YE ANTIQUE. James Gillray and H. Humphrey: Published 11 Februrary 1801. Etching, 26.3 × 37 cm. *The Works of James Gilray from the original plates.* London: Henry G. Bohn, 1850. (2010.112.01.0001)

aside in this letter, Nelson remarked, "*Let her go to Briton or where she pleases, I care not; she is a great fool, and, thank God! you are not the least bit like her.*"

Writing on "Thompson's" behalf, Nelson conveys his shipmate's joy (Autograph letter, signed: Horatio Nelson to Emma Hamilton. 1 February 1801. 8ᵛᵒ [1989.037.00.0001]):

*I believe poor dear Mrs. Thomson's friend will go mad with joy. He cries, prays, and performs all tricks, yet dare not show all or any of his feelings, but he has only me to consult with. He swears he will drink your health this day in a bumper, and damn me if I don't join him in spite of all the doctors in Europe, for none regard you with truer affection than myself. You are a dear, good creature, and your kindness and attention to poor Mrs T. stamps you higher than ever in my mind. I cannot write, I am so agitated by this young man at my elbow. I believe he is foolish; he does nothing but rave about you & her. I own I participate of his joy and cannot write anything … I trust I shall soon be at Portsmouth, and every endeavour of mine shall be used to come to town for three days … May the heavens bless you and yours, is the fervent prayer of your unalterable and faithful, &c.*

Nelson had learned of Horatia's birth two days before when he wrote that "*Mrs Thomson's friend will go mad with joy*" and continues the intrigue whereby Emma and Nelson pretended that they had adopted a child of one of Nelson's crew (Autograph letter, signed: Horatio Nelson ["Nelson & Bronte"] to "My Dear Mrs Thomson" [Lady Hamilton], n.p. [*San Josef*, Torbay], n.d. [3 February 1801], 2¼ pages, 8ᵛᵒ [2004.006.00.0003]):

*Your good and dear friend, does not think it proper at present to write with his own hand but he hopes the time may not be far distant when he may be united for ever to the object of his wishes, his only, only love. He swears before heaven that he will marry you as soon as it is possible, which he fervently prays may be soon. He charges me to say how dear you are to him, and that you must, every opportunity, kiss and bless for him his dear little girl, which he wishes to be called Emma, out of gratitude to our dear, good Lady Hamilton.*

Horatia was not to be christened for two years, but Nelson writes (Autograph letter, signed: Horatio Nelson to Emma Hamilton. No date [5 February 1801]. 1¾ pages 8ᵛᵒ, "Mrs. Thompson" [1989.037.00.0002]):

*Your dear and excellent friend has desired me to say that it is not usual to christen children till they are a month or six weeks old; and as Lord Nelson will probably be in town, as well as myself, before we go to the Baltic, he proposes then, if you approve, to christen the child, and that myself and Lady Hamilton should be two of the sponsors. Its name will be Horatia, daughter of Johem and Morata Etnorb. If you read the surname backwards, and take the letters of the other names, it will make, very extraordinary, the names of your real and affectionate friends, Lady Hamilton and myself.*

Nelson vows to "*steal a white bread sooner than my godchild should want*" (Autograph letter, signed: Horatio Nelson to Emma Hamilton. "Monday night, 9 o'clock" (17 February 1801). 3½ pages, 4ᵗᵒ [1990.035.00.0001] *see image opposite*):

*My dearest friend, I have read all your letters over and over … I would take an oath never to sleep out of the ship, unless absolutely forced by the impossibility of getting on board … I never would be far from you in case my presence should be necessary … But at the worst my dear friend can find a very good excuse to come and see me, altho' it would not be half so* *satisfactory as my going to see you in London … Ah! my dear friend, I did remember well the 12<sup>th</sup> February, and also the two months afterwards [the period they spent together during which Horatia was conceived]. I shall never forget them, and never be sorry for the consequences … I would steal a white bread sooner than my godchild should want.*

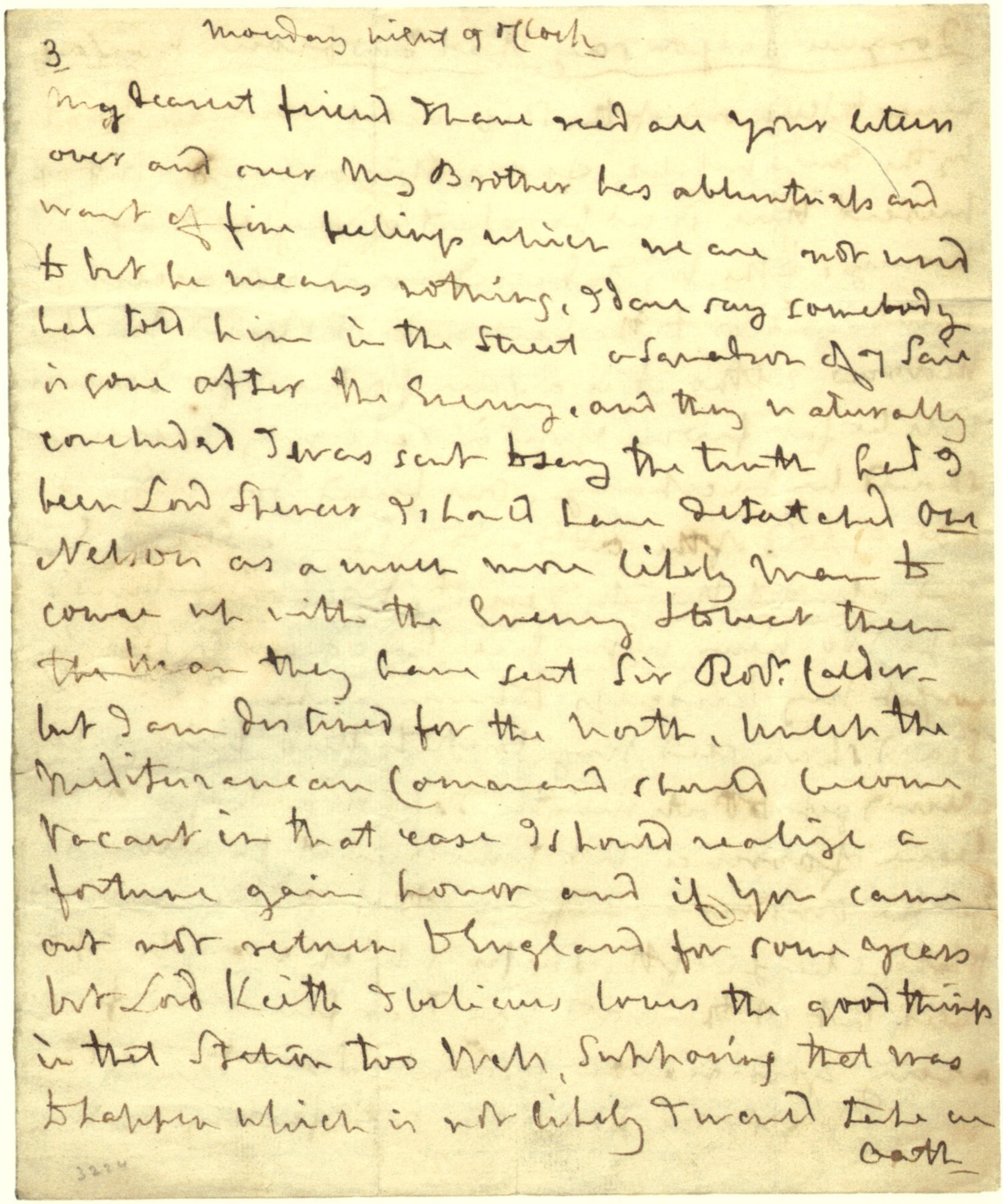

HORATIO NELSON. Autograph letter, signed: to Emma Hamilton. "Monday night, 9 o'clock" (17 February 1801). 4 pages, 4<sup>to</sup>. (1990.035.00.0001)

The philandering Prince of Wales had designs on Emma, and by mid-February an intensely jealous Nelson, suffering severe pain from his lost eye, expressed his rage and self-pity in a torrent of words (Autograph letter, signed: (Nelson & Bronte) [no place 18 February 1801] to Emma Hamilton. Dated Wednesday night. 3 pages, 4^{to} [1993.151.00.0005] *see image opposite*):

*'Tis not that I believe you will do anything that injures me that I cannot help saying a few words on that fellow's* [Edward, Prince of Wales] *dining with you, for you do not believe it is out of love for Sir William. No, you know the contrary, that his design is upon you. No! that I will never believe, but you have been taken in. You that are such a woman of good sence, put so often on your guard by myself ... I knew that he would visit you, and you could not help coming downstairs when the P[rince] was there, and notwithstanding all your declarations never to meet him, to receive him, and by his own invitation, en famille. But his words are so charming that, I am told, no person can withstand them. If I had been worth 10 millions I would have betted every farthing that you would not have gone into the house knowing he was there, and if you did, which I would not have believed, that you would have sent him a proper message by Sir William and sent him to hell. And, knowing your determined courage when you had got down, I would have laid my head upon the block with the axe uplifted and said strike, if Emma does not say to Sir William before the fellow, "My character cannot, shall not suffer by permitting him to visit." Oh! I wish I had been so placed then and there, then my head, my distracted head must have been off. Hush, hush, my poor heart, keep in my breast, be calm. Emma is true! But no one, not even Emma, could resist the serpent's flattering tongue, & knowing that Emma suits him, that even a stranger would not invite her to meet the fellow, what will they all SAY and think, that Emma is like other women, when I would have killed anybody who had said so, must now hang down my head and admit it ... I have eat nothing but a little rice and drank water; but forgive me, I know my Emma, and don't forget that you had once a Nelson, a friend, a dear friend, but, alas! he has his misfortunes. He has lost the best, his only friend, his only love. Don't forget him, poor fellow! he is honest. Oh! I could thunder and strike dead with my lightning. I dreamt it last night, my Emma. I am calmer; reason, I hope, will resume her place, please God. Tears have relieved me; you never will again receive the villain to rob me. But I will be calm & trust to Providence; but what will all the world say? Do modest women receive him? You nor I think so. May the heavens bless you! I am better. Only tell me you forgive me; don't scold me, indeed, I am not worth it, and am to my last breath yours, and, if not yours, no one's in this world. Ever yours.*

Finally, on 23 February, Nelson was granted leave and sped to London through the night. The lovers were re-united and Nelson had a first opportunity to meet their child. The visit was short; he was soon ordered to sail for the Baltic with the Channel Fleet.

At the end of March, Sir William sold most of his collections at auction to satisfy creditors, including his treasured portraits of Emma. To save her dignity, Nelson purchased the Vigeé Le Brun *Bacchante*, his favorite (see p. 46), for the princely sum of £300 (at that time about ten years' wages for a craftsman).

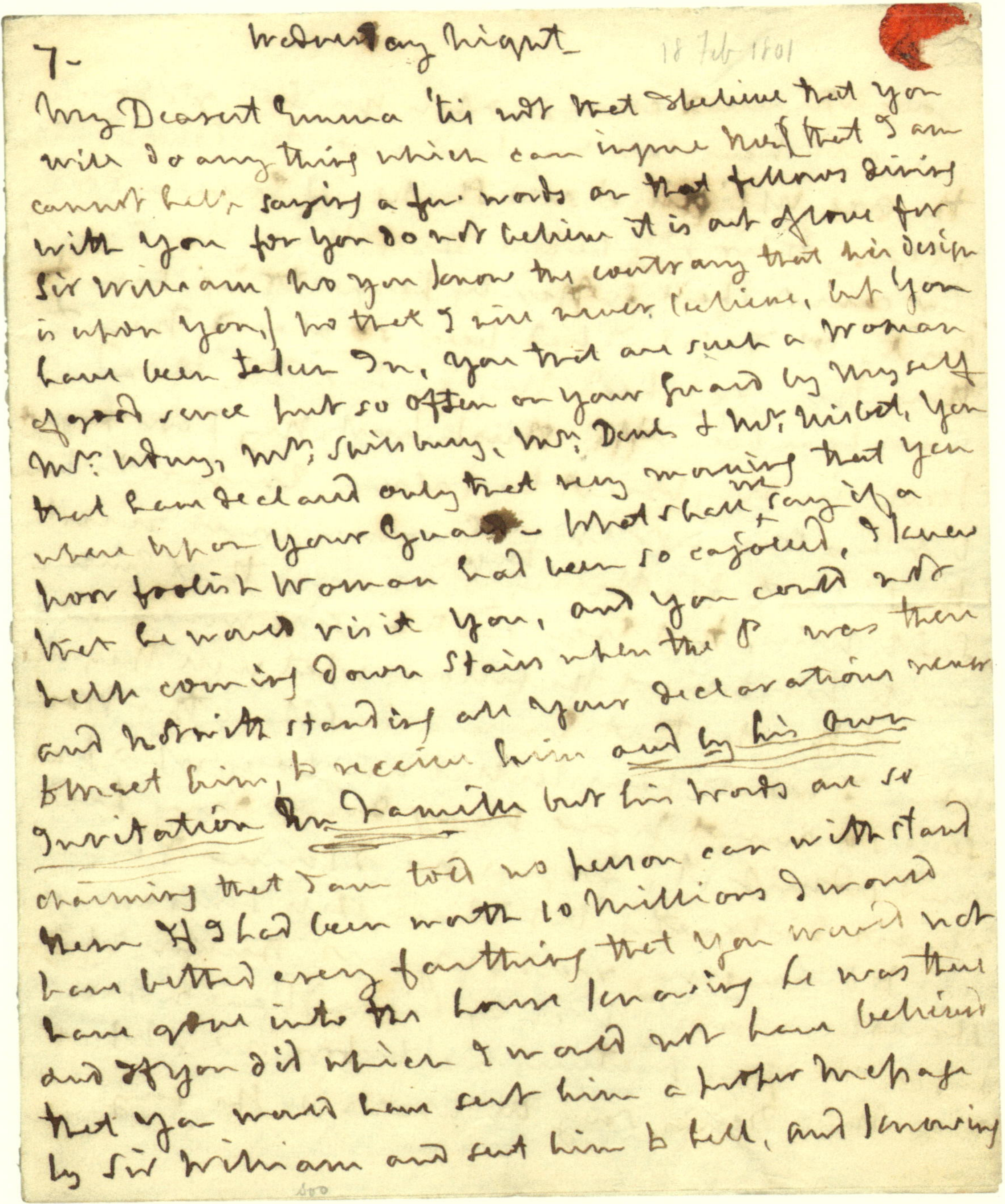

Once a British ally, the Russian Tsar Paul arranged a League of Armed Neutrality with Denmark, Sweden, and Prussia, in order to enforce free trade with France. The British viewed the league to be to French advantage and, thus, a serious threat. With the goal of breaking up the league, the British assembled a fleet under

NELSON & BRONTE. Autograph letter, signed: to Emma Hamilton. Dated Wednesday night [no place, 18 February 1801]. 3 pages, 4⁰. (1993.151.00.0005)

Admiral Sir Hyde Parker, with Nelson second-in-command. They defeated the Danish fleet anchored off Copenhagen on 2 April 1801. Nelson led the main attack and, when ordered to discontinue the engagement, famously disobeyed Parker's order to withdraw, replying *"Now damn me if I do!"* Parker's order is often misunderstood. It was in fact a highly unselfish and generous act. By providing an order to withdraw, Nelson could have done so with his honor and career intact. Although to withdraw was not in Nelson's character, Parker's conduct does equal credit to him.

Apparently Nelson had sent a letter with news of his victory to Emma even before the first report of the Battle of Copenhagen reached the British Admiralty on 15 April 1801 (Autograph letter, signed: Emma Hamilton to Lady Malmesbury. [Brighton] marked 15 April 1801. 1 page, 4.^{to} [1987.007.00.0001] *see image opposite*):

*My Dear Lady Malmsbery*

*All might be well but the post is wonting our great nelson covered with glory & himself safe 18 sail Large Small & all taken burnt & destroy'd & all by him god bless you & believe me your ever ob[edie]nt s[er]v[a]nt*
*E Hamilton*

*Lord h[amilton] writes that his friends will be in good health he has been on shore with the prince of Denmark he writes me that in the palace of the King the stairs were crowded & calling Long Live Nelson I will send more particulars tomorrow.*

My dear Lady Malmesbury

all right all well but the post is waiting our great Nelson covered with glory & himself safe 18 sail large small be all taken burnt & destroyed & all by him god bless you & believe me ever your oblidged

E Hamilton

Lord H writes that all his friends well & in good health he has been on shore with the prince of Denmark he writes me that in the pallace of the king the stairs were crowded & calling Long live Nelson I will send you more particulars tomorow

EMMA HAMILTON. Autograph letter, signed: to Lady Malmesbury. [Brighton] marked 15 April 1801. 1 page, 4to. (1987.007.00.0001)

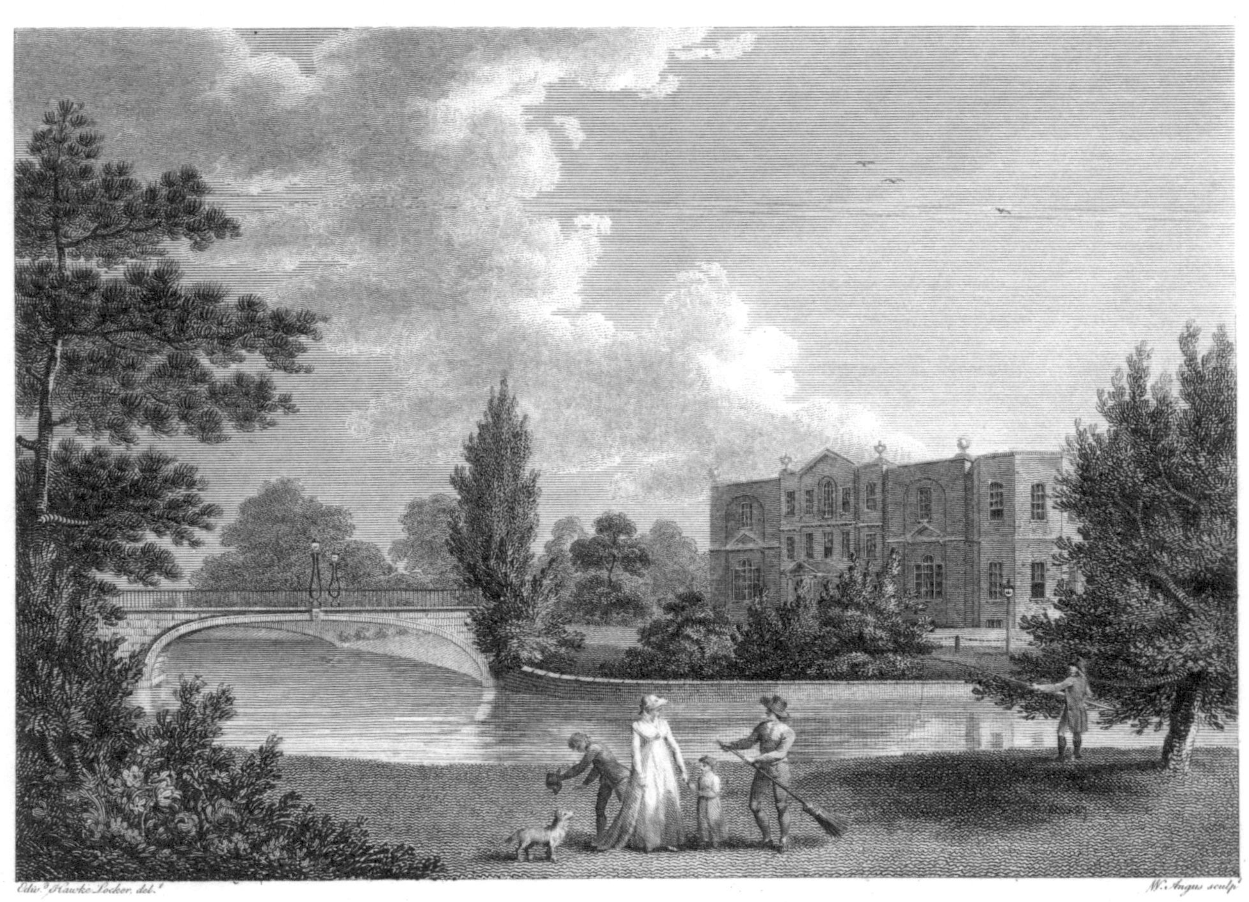



**MERTON PLACE** in Surrey, the Seat of Admiral Lord Nelson. After a drawing by Edward Hawke Locker. Islington [i.e., London]: W. Angus, 1804. Illustration size approx. 13 × 19 cm. Together with a separate page of descriptive text. (2010.073.00.000)

# V

## Paradise Merton

NELSON returned to England in July 1801, and the *tria iuncta in uno* celebrated on a two-week sojourn in the English countryside with friends. They discussed future plans and Nelson asked Emma to find a "little farm" outside London where they could live.

News of a threatened French invasion ended their vacation and Nelson was sent to protect the Channel. On 15 August 1801, Nelson's force mounted a surprise attack on the French flotilla at Boulogne. The attack was a dismal failure. Britain lost 12 boats and 45 men, with 128 more wounded. The French did not lose a single ship and suffered few casualties. Nelson wrote to Emma in despair: *"I am in silent distraction. My dearest wife, how can I bear our separation? Good God! What a change, I am so low that I cannot hold up my head."*

In September Emma found a house in the county of Surrey, southwest of London, in the village of Merton, near Wimbledon. The fifty-two-acre property was described as "elegant and commodious," but was condemned by Nelson's surveyor: *"I am astonished anyone can think of it as nearly compleat for any family ... circumscribed by a dirty black looking canal ... which keeps the whole place damp."* Even though the house was in disrepair, the couple pressed forward, anxious to be settled. In mid-September 1801, Nelson bought Merton for £9,000. Emma took on the mission to transform the property into a residence befitting a hero, a home in which he could entertain friends and family and receive dignitaries.

Improvements were quickly made—at extravagant expense—mature landscaping plants were put in, streams were stocked with fish and ponds with wildfowl, and sheep were brought to the meadows. The house was elegantly furnished and decorated as a celebration of Nelson. Emma, Sir William, and their servants moved in. Sir William Hamilton wrote to Nelson that *"the house is so comfortable ... you have nothing but to come and enjoy immediately."*

Peace negotiations led to the signing of an armistice, the Treaty of Amiens, on 27 March 1802, signaling a respite in the war with France. Freed from active duty, Nelson returned to England in late October. Emma, Sir William, Horatia, and Paradise Merton were waiting to welcome him.

For Emma and Nelson, the next nineteen months were the happiest of their lives, marred only by the deaths of Nelson's father on 26 April 1802 and Sir William on 6 April 1803.

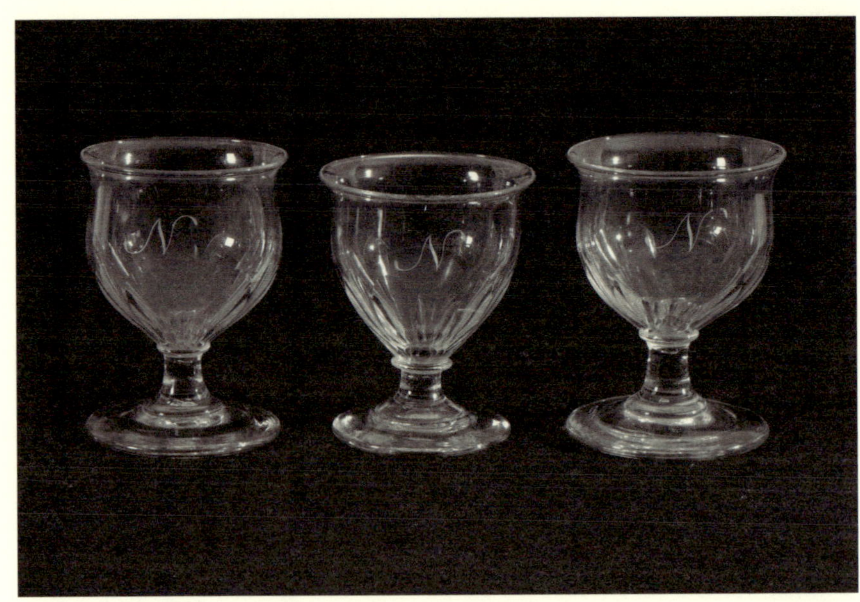



SET OF SEVEN ENGRAVED RUMMERS. Each tulip-shaped bowl cut with a band of flutes and inscribed with the initial N, set on a collar above stem and solid conical foot. 13 cm. (2006.017.00.0001)

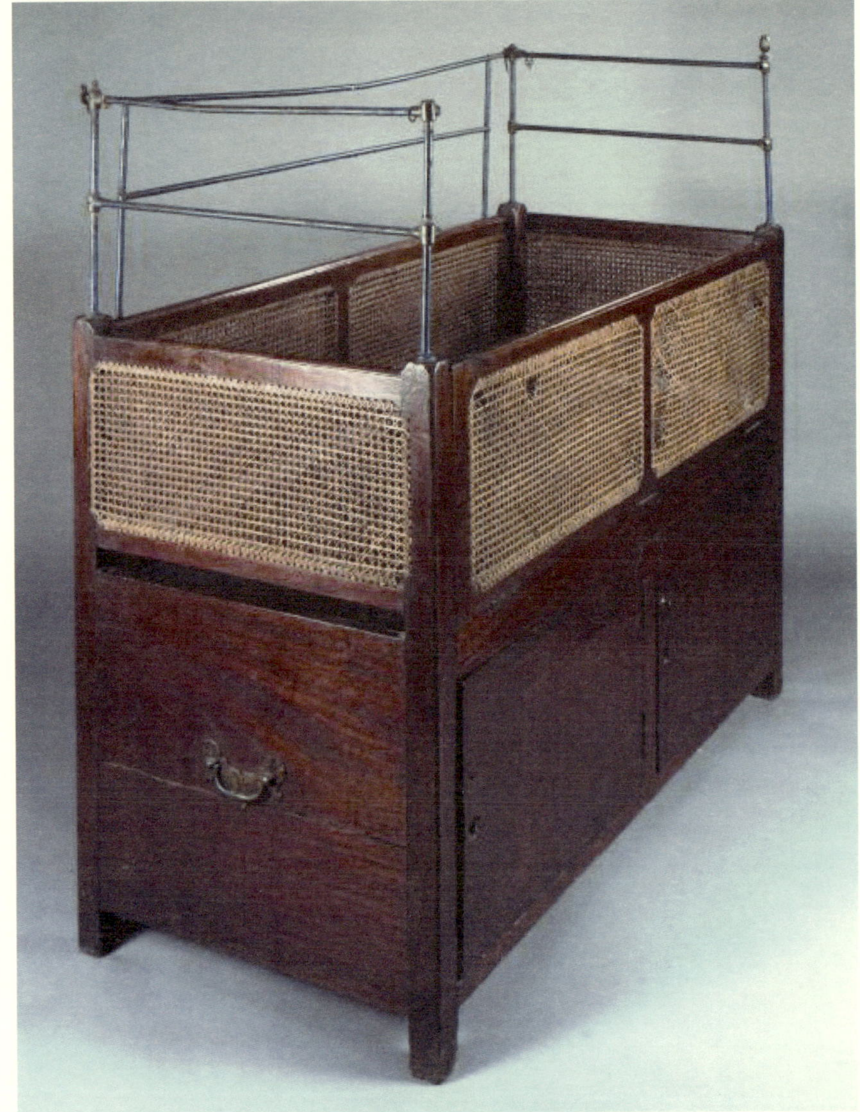

HORATIA'S BED. George III Mahogany and Caned Cot, with a hinged fall-front above a pair of paneled doors on stile feet. (2006.017.00.0002)

Alexander Davison owned various interests from textile factories to shipping and acted as a supply agent for the British government, procuring coal and other supplies for the military. In 1798, after the Battle of the Nile and the Battle of Copenhagen, Nelson designated him prize agent to the Admiralty responsible for negotiating the sale of enemy ships captured during the actions and distributing the proceeds among Nelson and his men. Acting as Nelson's financial overseer, Davison was also responsible for keeping track of expenditures at Merton, which brought him into conflict with Emma when he tried to restrain what he considered to be her extravagant spending.

In the following letters, he responds to accusations of meddling with her *"exclusive prerogative in schemes"* at Merton. He defends his actions, referring to *"the trust imposed in me by our mutual & dearest friend Lord Nelson"* and explains that her plans would cost £4,000 when Nelson intended to spend no more than three or four hundred (Autograph letters, signed: Alexander Davison to Lady Hamilton. 19 and 28 June 1804. Retained drafts. Pages, folio, and 4^to, King's Bench Terrace, 19–28 June 1804):

*[I]f you will not be offended by my offering an opinion ... the sooner the pleasure grounds & Gardens are finished the better, as the season by & bye will not be so favorable for such work ... I am well aware that you are as desirous as myself to be correct in the expenditure of his money and that every shilling should be laid out to the best possible advantage ... I am sure on more mature reflection, you will acknowledge me to be right ...*

The second letter conveys *"all the Plans of Merton"* and assures her that he is acting in Nelson's best interest (*"... I ever shall discharge the Trust to the best of my Power for His Interest to the best of my Judgement"*).

By 1801 Sir William was feeling the financial strain of maintaining two households as well as Emma (Autograph letter, signed: Sir William Hamilton to Charles Greville. Merton Place, 5 December 1801. 3 pages, 4^to [1990.035.08.0002]):

*When was Davis to remit the rents due at Michaelmas to Messrs. Coutts? Nothing has yet arrived ... and I find nothing is to be got out of the Treasury, that I may not be distressed in looking out for money to pay the current expenses of our house ... for really at my time of life ... it is cruel to find myself in the situation I am at present.*

In April 1802 Nelson's father, Reverend Edmund, became seriously ill. Nelson failed to visit him before he died on the 27th and, curiously, did not attend the funeral. Complaining of a stomach ailment, he stayed at Merton and celebrated Emma's thirty-seventh birthday.

Sir William wrote to Greville in the early days of 1789, presciently observing: *"foreseeing that the difference of 57 & 22* [referring to Emma] *may produce events"* (see p. 41 above). The "events" he was foreseeing probably did not extend to his own demise. Now, at seventy-two, Sir William was simply worn out. Illness, financial strain, and, perhaps, his attempts to keep up with Emma had all taken their toll. On 6 April Sir William died in the arms of Emma with Nelson at their side. The *tria* was no more.

Considering her lifestyle, the terms of Sir William's will were not generous to Emma. He left almost the entirety of his estate to

WILL OF SIR WILLIAM HAMILTON, K.B. of Colby in Pembrokshire. 28 May 1801, with his codicil of 31 March 1803. 2 pages, folio, integral blank and endorsement. (2002.151.01.0001)

Greville. To Emma, he bequeathed £300 immediately and £800 *per annum*, and to Nelson, *"The copy of Madame Le Brun's picture of Emma, in enamel, by Bone, I give to my dearest friend, Lord Nelson, Duke of Bronte—very small token of the great regard I have for his Lordship, the most virtuous, loyal, and truly brave character I ever met with. God bless him, and shame fall on all those who do not say Amen!"*

Emma left the London residence at 21 Piccadilly and moved to a smaller house on Clarges Street. She hoped Greville would help settle her debts, but to no avail. Nelson's letter to Greville bespeaks his warm feeling toward Sir William (Autograph letter, signed: Horatio Nelson to Charles Greville. 13 May 1803 [1995.023.00.0002] *see image overleaf*):

*My Dear Sir,*

*I can have no demand on Sir William anything which I might have laid out for our mutual comfort He was most heartedly and sincerely welcome to. Dear Sir Williams room at Merton has not been looked into since he left it. Probably His Telescope, some Books &c are there I will write to Mrs. Cadogan & send them to Town.*

*I do not know anything about the sociable I feel most sensibly your good wishes for me and 'till I see you in person which certainly will be before I go off, and believe me Dear Mr. Greville you're much obliged &*

*faithful friend*

*Nelson & Bronte*

The letter, on black-bordered mourning paper, was written to Greville on 13 May 1803, the same day that Horatia was christened at Marylebone Church.

«═════»

Meanwhile, a tempest was brewing. Under the terms of the Treaty of Amiens, England was to give up most of its islands in the West Indies, Egypt, and Ceylon. France was required to surrender the Papal States and the Kingdom of the Two Sicilies and retain control of the northern Italian lands of Piedmont and the French side of the Rhine River. Napoleon had used the time of peace to consolidate power and reorganize his domestic administration and now refused to implement concessions. England, in turn, refused to restore Malta to the Knights Hospitalers. Tensions heightened. On 16 May 1803, Britain declared war and the Royal Navy imposed a blockade on France. On the 22nd Napoleon responded, ordering the imprisonment of all British males between the ages of 18 and 60 in France. The war resumed; peace had lasted barely a year.

Nelson was appointed Commander-in-Chief of the Mediterranean Fleet and sailed on the *Victory "to give M. Villeneuve* [admiral of the French fleet] *a drubbing."* His pursuit of the French fleet would end with its annihilation at Trafalgar ... and with Nelson's death.

HORATIO NELSON.
Autograph letter, signed:
to Charles Greville. 13
May 1803. 1 page, 4<sup>to</sup>.
(1995.023.00.0002)

When he left, Emma was pregnant. Between Christmas and New Year's Day, she gave birth to Nelson's second child, named Emma. The baby did not survive; the circumstances of the birth and short life are unknown.

Distraught and in grief, Emma drifted between Merton and her house on Clarges Street, passing the time with friends and Nelson's extended family. Nelson remained at sea for two years. Although he provided £100 per month for expenses at Merton, Emma sank ever deeper into debt.

Realizing her precarious financial situation, Emma began appealing to the government for support in recognition of her services to the nation while in Naples. In the following letter she writes to her cousin in despair over her ongoing struggle and begs the Duke of Hamilton to exercise his influence, *"you know what I did to serve*

Government," and also refers to Queen Maria Carolina's pledge, "*as soon as we have peace [to] get the King to provide for me as He owes all he has to me & my Exertions.*"

*My Dear Lord*

*Will you Excuse me in thus Troubling you on my own Private affairs and very very Private they are owing to the King's illness and now Mr A* [Henry Addington, Prime Minister from 1801 to 1804] *being out. I am again Thrown in to Despair for the moment altho I think I may perhaps move this administration more than I did the other if you My Dear Lord have any influence with any of the party you would make me very happy by writing a line for me & thus commending my Case to them for I really do not know what to do nor what I shall do if they do not assist me …*

*Grateful Emma Hamilton*

Unfortunately for Emma, Sir William never acknowledged her contributions to his diplomatic efforts in his official dispatches. While Emma's role was common knowledge among friends, and even to travellers who visited Naples, the lack of corroboration in official documents made it possible for the government to ignore Emma's pleas for compensation.

In his biography of Emma, published in 1905, Walter Sichel argued that Lady Hamilton had indeed contributed to Nelson's great victory at the Battle of the Nile, but critics pointed out that no state documents had survived to support this point of view. A few years later, however, Sichel found indisputable proof in the Dropmore Papers—a letter from Sir William Hamilton to Lord Grenville, Minister for Foreign Affairs, with another letter enclosing from the Queen of Naples, both attesting to Emma's political role. Lord Grenville never placed these documents among the official archives.

Sir William Hamilton to Lord Grenville:

*1798, June 18. Naples.—Having so good an opportunity, I cannot resist the pleasure of sending to your Lordship the enclosed copy of a most interesting letter, for the perusal of your Lordship and of your select friends. Enclosure.*

The Queen of Naples to Lady Hamilton (translation):

*1798, June 11. [I]t is solely due to the appearance of the courageous English squadron in the Mediterranean that we owe the departure of the Republican squadron without their having perpetrated violence upon our territory; but this same squadron could return ... I ask you therefore in the name of the friendship you have always shown to me and because of the confidence that draws me so sincerely to your great and respectable nation, to assure Lord St. Vincent* [John Jervis, 1st Earl of St Vincent, commander of the Mediterranean fleet] *of our respect, confidence and eternal gratitude for the promptness with which he rushed to our defense ... I ask you to tell the worthy and devoted knight your husband to make known to his court, nation and valiant admiral* [Nelson] *that if at this very moment we are unable to follow our heart, to open all doors to the entire squadron, to fulfill different requests—which would produce immediate and open war—it is out of necessity and prudence ... We are devoted to your brave nation ... I entrust this letter to your discretion and prudence; it could infinitely compromise me. It is the Country and the State that I fear leading into sorrow by avowing so strongly my hate and the loathing my heart feels for them; because for myself, personally, I would take pride in avowing these feelings loudly and in proving them on all occasions. I ask therefore that this remain between us ... do not let any occasion pass to assure your brave respectable nation and admiral that the king my husband, his sons, my future grandchildren will all nurture the same sentiments of friendship, trust, gratitude for you all and that these sentiments will last as long as I shall live.*

For four months—from April to July 1805—Nelson pursued Admiral Villeneuve and the French fleet across the Atlantic to the Caribbean and back.

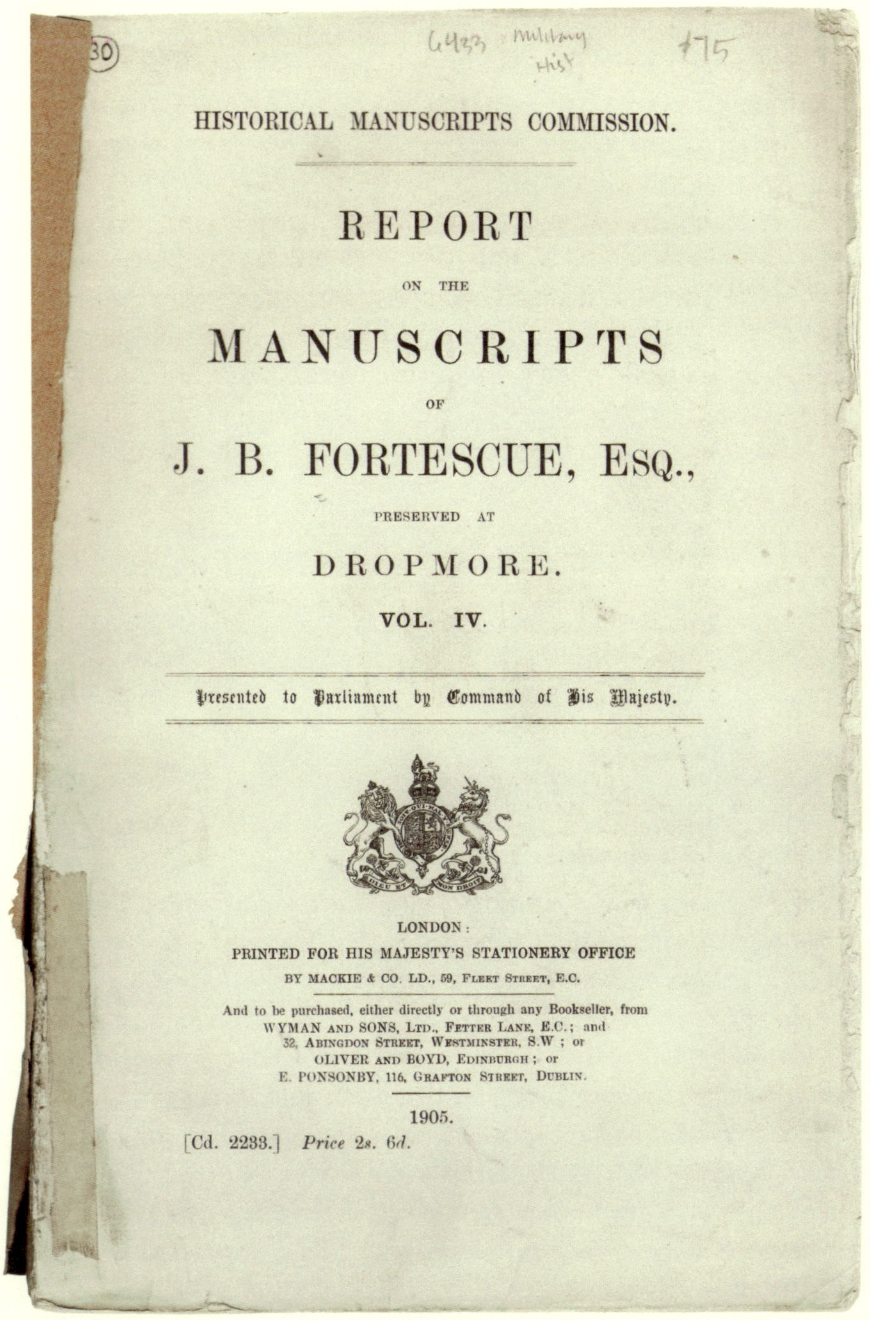

HISTORICAL MANUSCRIPTS COMMISSION.

# REPORT

ON THE

# MANUSCRIPTS

OF

# J. B. FORTESCUE, Esq.,

PRESERVED AT

# DROPMORE.

## VOL. IV.

Presented to Parliament by Command of His Majesty.

LONDON:
PRINTED FOR HIS MAJESTY'S STATIONERY OFFICE
BY MACKIE & CO. LD., 59, FLEET STREET, E.C.

And to be purchased, either directly or through any Bookseller, from
WYMAN AND SONS, LTD., FETTER LANE, E.C.; and
32, ABINGDON STREET, WESTMINSTER, S.W ; or
OLIVER AND BOYD, EDINBURGH ; or
E. PONSONBY, 116, GRAFTON STREET, DUBLIN.

1905.

[Cd. 2233.]   Price 2s. 6d.

*Report on the Manuscripts of J. B. Fortescue, Esq., Preserved at Dropmore.* London: His Majesty's Stationary Office, 1905. (2010.089.00.0001)

Since her birth, Horatia had been under the care of Mrs. Gibson in Marylebone. In the following letter, Nelson authorizes Emma to bring his five-year-old "adopted" daughter to live at Merton and offer Mrs. Gibson a substantial annuity of £20 per year on condition that she make no attempt to keep Horatia:

HORATIO NELSON. Autograph letter, signed: to Emma Hamilton. *Victory*, at Sea, 16 May 1805. 4 pages, 4⁰. (2004.006.00.0004)

*My Dearest Lady Hamilton*

*As it is my desire to take my adopted daughter Horatia Nelson Thompson from under the care of Mrs Gibson and to place her under your Guardianship in order that she may be properly educated and brought up I have therefore most earnestly to entreat that you will undertake this charge and as it is my intention to allow Mrs. Gibson as a free will offering from myself (She having no claim upon me having been regularly paid for her of the child) the sum of twenty pounds a year for term of her natural life, and I mean it should commence when the child is delivered to you, but should Mrs. Gibson endeavor upon any pretence & keep my adopted daughter any longer in her care then I do not hold myself bound to give her one farthing and I shall most probably take other measures ... I again and again My Dearest friend request your care of my adopted daughter whom I pray for God to help. I am Ever for Ever My Dear Lady Hamilton your most faithful & affectionate Nelson & Bronte*

On 18 August 1805, the *Victory* docked at Portsmouth. Nelson was granted leave, his first in two years, and he sped to Merton to be with Emma and Horatia. This was the only time they lived alone together in the same house (Autograph letter, signed: Horatio Nelson to Emma Hamilton. Victory, Northernbank [Portsmouth] 19 August 1805. 3 pages, 4.^to [2003.111.00.0001]):

*I am in quarantine for the first time in my ... I hope to be out of quarantine tomorrow fore-noon ... You may believe I shall not stay ten minutes in Portsmouth only to Bow to the Com-mander and in Chief & the Commissioner ... I cannot be at Merton before 9 o'clock and if not by that time ... don't expect your faithful loving Nelson after that hour ... I shall my Emma rejoice to have you in my arms. Men need not envy a thing I am all all Yours & I shall rejoice to see dear Horatia ... may Heaven sends us a speedy meeting a happy one I am sure it will be Ever for Ever my Emma*
*Your own faithful*

*Nelson & Bronte*

Over the next three weeks, there was constant activity, a stream of visitors and frequent trips to London for meetings with ministers and the Admiralty to discuss the escalating French threat.

On 2 September, Captain Henry Blackwood arrived with news; the French fleet under the command of the Admiral Pierre Villeneuve had reached Cadiz and joined the Spanish fleet to form a massive combined force. On the evening of 13 September 1805, Nelson left Merton for the last time. Unable to tear himself away, he returned to Horatia's room several times, knelt to pray at her bedside, then bade farewell to Emma. As he drove away, he wrote in his diary:

*Friday night, at half-past ten, drove from dear, dear Merton, where I left all which I hold dear in this world, to go to serve my king and country; and if it is His good pleasure that I should return, my thanks will never cease being offered up to the throne of His mercy. If it is His good Providence to cut short my days upon earth, I bow with the greatest submission, relying that He will protect those so dear to me, that I may leave behind. His will be done. Amen Amen Amen.*
—*Nelson's Last Diary, September 13 October 21, 1805.*
London: Elkin Mathews, Cork Street, 1917

On the 15th Nelson sailed on the *Victory* with orders to blockade or destroy the combined French and Spanish fleet. On 21 October, off the southwest coast of Spain at Cape Trafalgar, twenty-seven British ships led by Nelson destroyed the Franco-Spanish fleet. Twenty-one of thirty-three French and Spanish ships were captured or sunk. Not a single British vessel was lost.

The battle commenced with Nelson's famous words signaled to his fleet: "England expects that every man will do his duty." Nelson's plan called for his ships to attack in two parallel lines, break into the enemy's formation, and open fire at close quarters.

The *Victory*, under the command of Thomas Hardy, was in the heart of the battle, which soon became a confusion of ships, smoke, and fire. The *Victory* be-came entangled with the French ship *Redoubtable* and, as each ship continued to

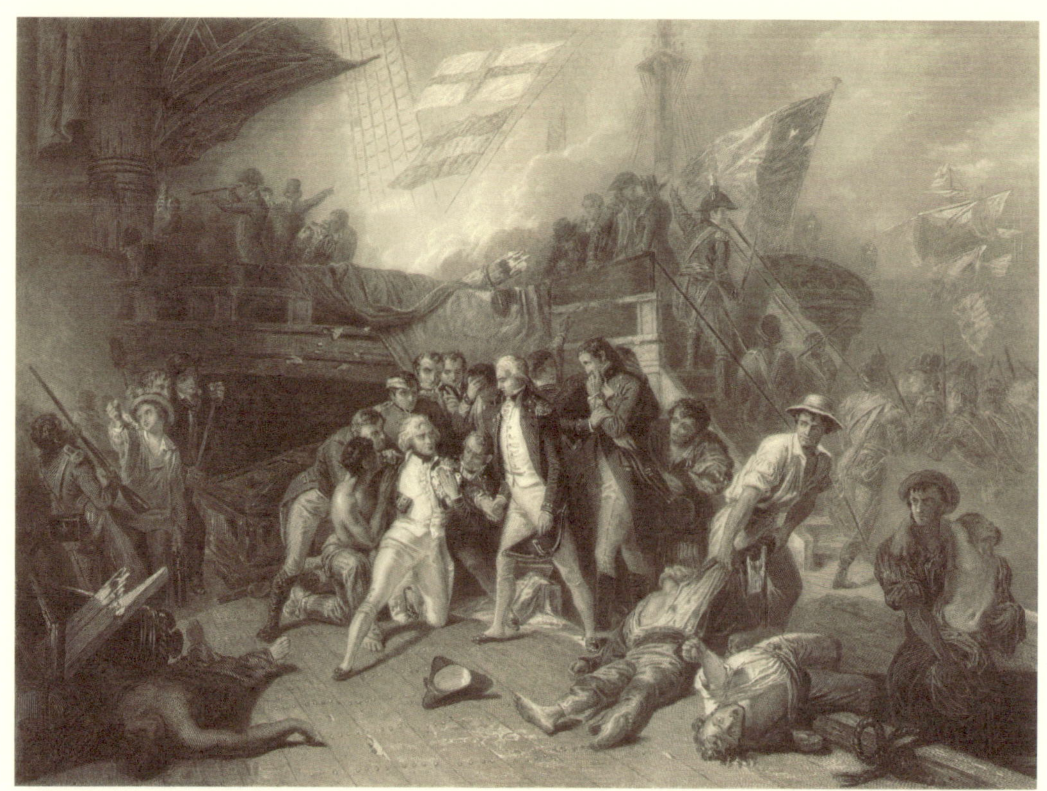

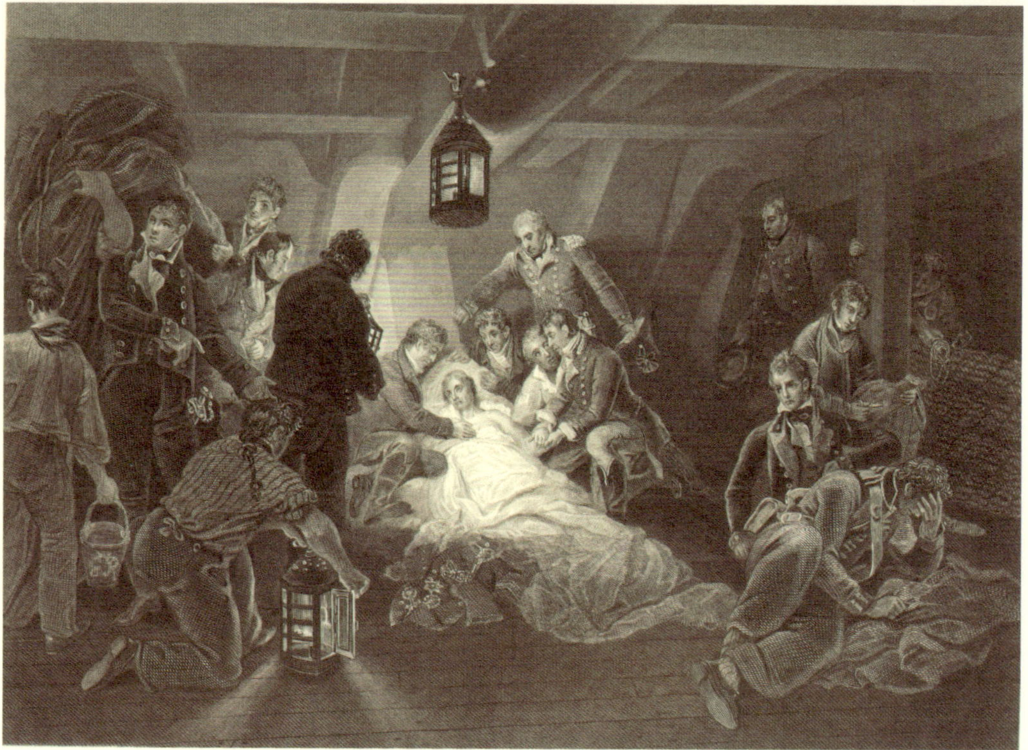

THE DEATH OF NELSON. W. Greatbach after Ernest Slingeneyer. London: G. Virtue, ca. 1854. Steel engraving. 24.9 × 32.7 cm. (2010.148.00.0001)

THE DEATH OF NELSON. W. Hulland after A. W. Davis from: Hume and Smollett, *The History of England*. London: George Virtue, ca. 1850. Steel engraving. 24 × 17 cm. (2010.132.00.0001)

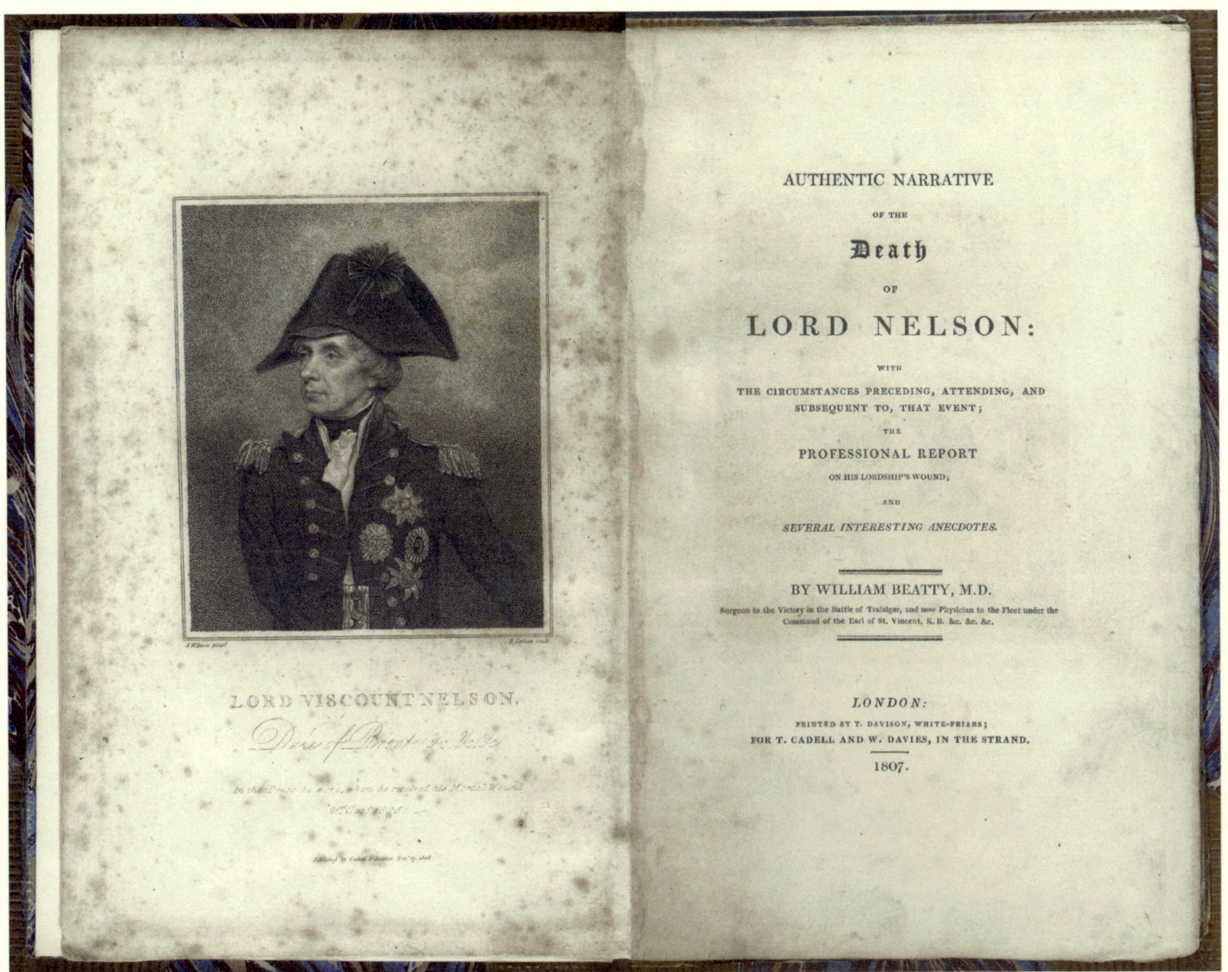

fire on the other, a French sharpshooter in the rigging of the *Redoubtable* fired a musket ball into Nelson's left shoulder. The shot passed through his chest and lodged in his lower back. It would prove fatal.

Nelson was carried below deck. "*I am a dead man, Hardy. I am going fast: it will be all over with me soon. Come nearer to me. Pray let my dear Lady Hamilton have my hair, and all other things belonging to me.*" (Dr. William Beatty, *Authentic Narrative of the Death of Lord Nelson*).

He lived long enough to learn of the *Redoubtable's* surrender and the final victory after four and one-half hours of combat. He is depicted in the engraving opposite in the final moments of his life.

Emma did not learn of Nelson's death until 6 November. At the news she was plunged into the depths of inconsolable despair.

William Beatty, the ship's surgeon aboard the *Victory*, attended Nelson until his demise. There was such great interest in the

WILLIAM BEATTY, *Authentic Narrative of the Death of Lord Nelson: With the Circumstances Preceding, Attending, and Subsequent to, that Event; the Professional Report on His Lordship's Wound; and Several Interesting Anecdotes*. London: Cadell and W. Davies, 1807. (1995.036.00.0001)

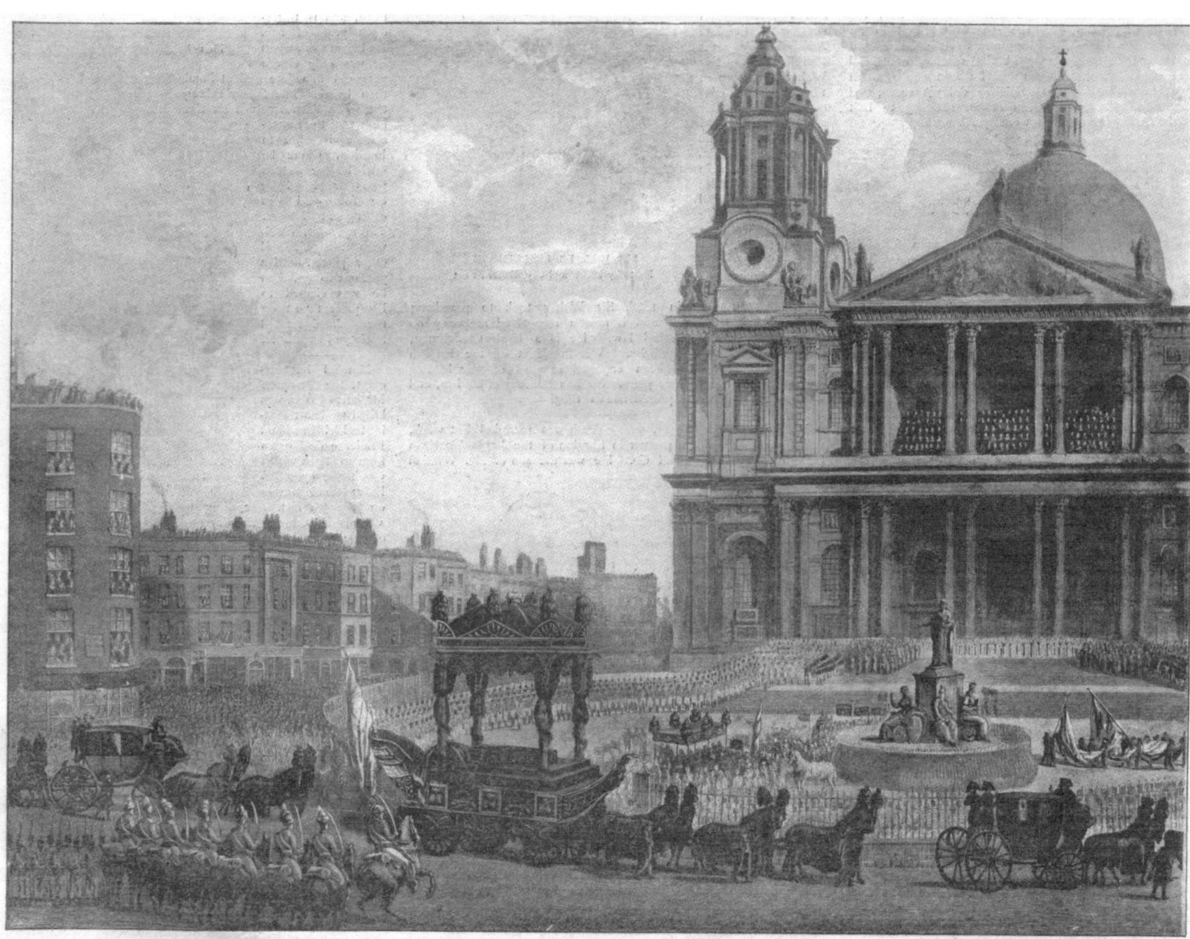



details of Nelson's death that Beatty's description was widely published in magazines and the "authentic narrative" was published in 1807.

Nelson's death at the moment of victory propelled his image to near-mythic proportion. The press and the state fashioned him into a symbol of the British will to survive and triumph over those who would destroy her. Nelson now belonged to the nation. His remains were brought back to England and he was accorded a hero's funeral.

Thirty thousand people filed past Nelson's coffin at Greenwich Hospital on the 5th and 6th of January. On the 8th his body was taken in a waterborne procession from Greenwich to the Admiralty building at Whitehall, and on the 9th a four-hour funeral procession brought his remains to St. Paul's Cathedral for interment. Excluded, Emma grieved at home.

Nelson's death spawned an industry of commemorative memorabilia.

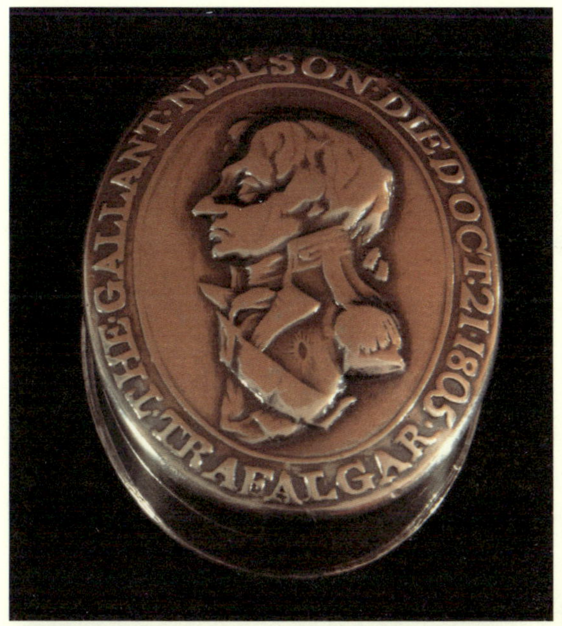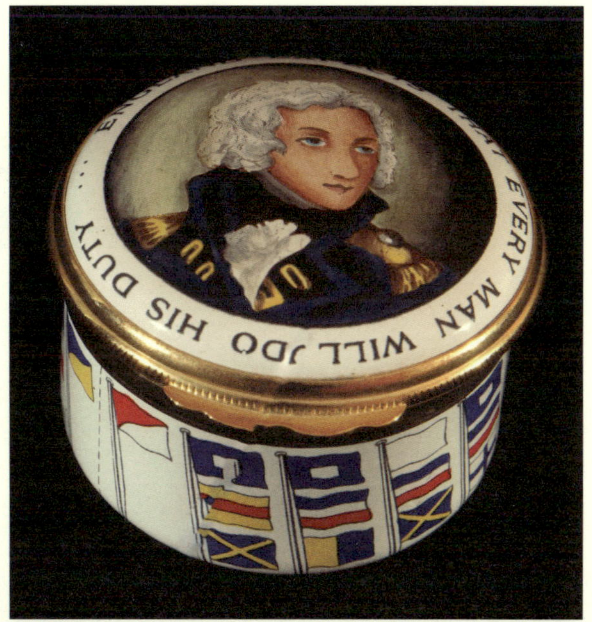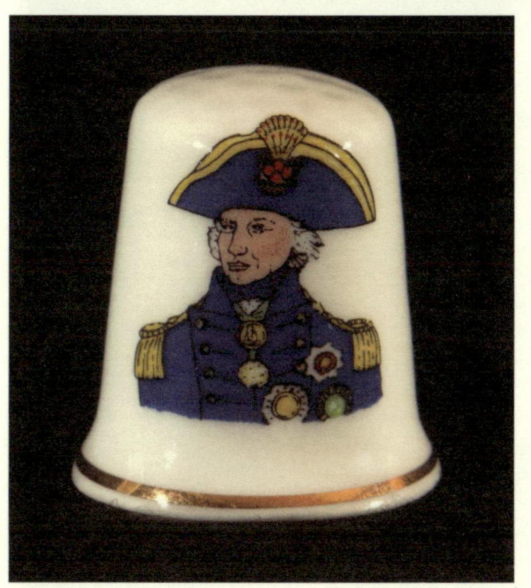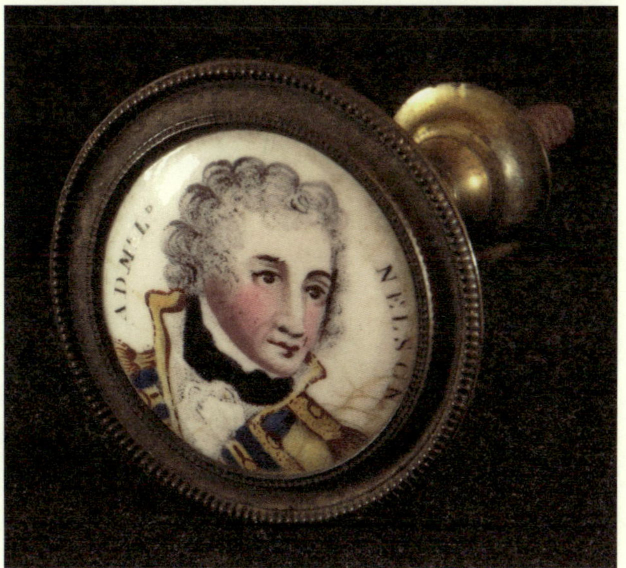

*Top left*: SILVER PILL BOX. Hallmarked for William Pugh, Birmingham, England, 1805, with Nelson portrait in cameo and the inscription "The Gallant Nelson, Died Oct. 26, 1805, Trafalgar." (1988.012.00.0001)

*Top right*: CERAMIC AND METAL PILL BOX, ca. 1810. (2010.145.00.0001)

*Bottom left*: CERAMIC THIMBLE, (n.d.). (2010.144.00.0001)

*Bottom right*: CERAMIC AND METAL DRAWER PULL, ca. 1810. (2010.146.00.0001)

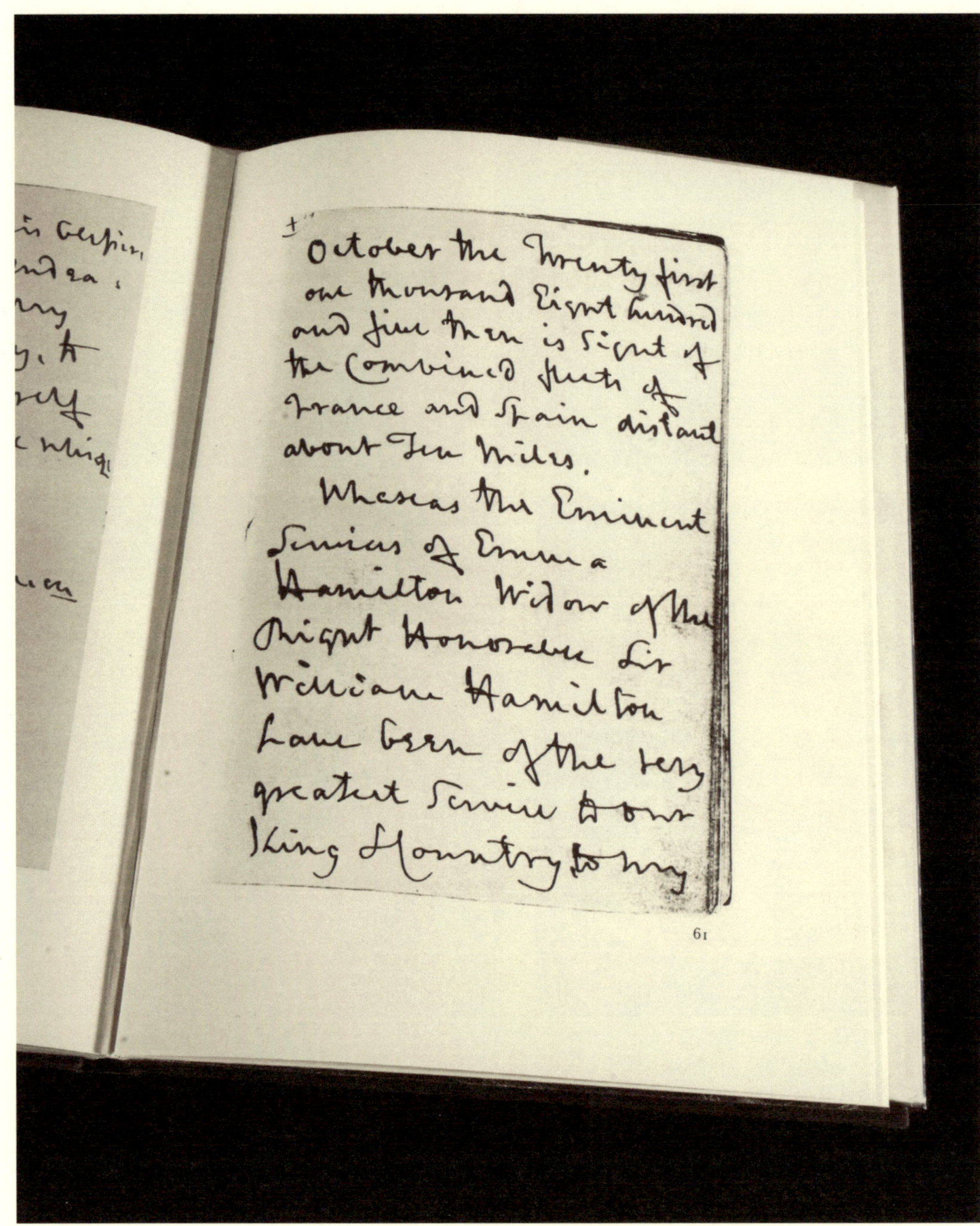





FINAL CODICIL TO NELSON'S WILL, Nelson's Diary, 21 October 1805.
Oliver Warner (editor), *Nelson's Last Diary and the Prayer Before Trafalgar.*
Kent, Ohio: Kent State University Press, 1971. (2010.124.00.0001)

# VI

*You will not see me an ambassadress*
*nor in splendor but you will ever find me firm &*
*my mind uncorrupted*

IN THE PENULTIMATE HOURS OF LIFE, Nelson not only expressed his love and loyalty for Emma and Horatia, but also, in a final act—a codicil to his will—attempted to further the recognition and redress the neglect of the government for Emma's services to Nelson and the nation:

*October the Twenty first, one thousand Eight hundred and five, then in sight of the Combined Fleets of France and Spain, distant about Ten Miles ...*

*Whereas the Eminent Services of Emma Hamilton, Widow of the Right Honourable Sir William Hamilton, have been of the very greatest service to our King and Country, to my knowledge, without her receiving any reward from either our King or Country, first, that she obtained the King of Spain's letter in 1796 to his brother the King of Naples acquainting him of his intention to declare war against England, from which letter the Ministry sent out orders to then Sir John Jervis to strike a stroke, if opportunity offered against either the Arsenals of Spain or her Fleets; that neither of these was done is not the fault of Lady Hamilton, the opportunity might have been offered. Secondly, the British Fleet under my command could never have returned the second time to Egypt had not Lady Hamilton's influence with the Queen of Naples caused Letters to be wrote to the Governor of Syracuse, that he was to encourage the Fleet being supplied with everything should they put into any Port in Sicily. We put into Syracuse and received every supply, went to Egypt, and destroy'd the French Fleet. Could I have rewarded these services I would not now call upon my Country, but as that has not been in my power, I leave Emma Lady Hamilton therefore a Legacy to my King and Country, that they will give her ample provision to maintain her Rank in Life. I also leave to the beneficence of my Country my adopted daughter Horatia Nelson Thompson and I desire she will use in future the name of Nelson only. These are the only favours I ask of my King and Country at this moment, when I am going to fight their Battle. May God bless my King and Country, and all those who I hold dear. My Relations it is needless to mention; they will of course be amply provided for.*

*Nelson & Bronte*

*(Witness)*
*Henry Blackwood*
*T. M. Hardy*

The following letter, now in the British Library, was found open on Lord Nelson's desk:

*Victory, October 19th, 1805, Noon, Cadiz, E.S.E., 16 Leagues.*
*My dearest beloved Emma, the dear friend of my bosom. The signal has been made that the Enemy's Combined Fleet are coming out of Port. We have very little wind, so that I have no hopes of seeing them before to-morrow. May the God of Battles crown my endeavours with success; at all events, I will take care that my name shall ever be most dear to you and Horatia, both of whom I love as much as my own life. And as my last writing before the Battle will be to you, so I hope in God that I shall live to finish my letter after the Battle. May Heaven bless you prays your*
*Nelson & Bronte*

At the end of the letter, Emma has written, "*This letter was found open on HIS desk, & brought to Lady Hamilton by Captain Hardy. Oh, miserable, wretched Emma! Oh, glorious & happy Nelson!*"

On the same day Nelson also wrote to Horatia:

*My dearest Angel, I was made happy by the pleasure of receiving your letter of September 19th, and I rejoice to hear that you are so very good a girl, and love my dear Lady Hamilton, who most dearly loves you. Give her a kiss for me. The Combined Fleets of the Enemy are now reported to be coming out of Cadiz; and therefore I answer your letter, my dearest Horatia, to mark to you that you are ever uppermost in my thoughts. I shall be sure of your prayers for my safety, conquest, and speedy return to dear Merton, and our dearest good Lady Hamilton. Be a good girl, mind what Miss Connor says to you. Receive, my dearest Horatia, the affectionate parental blessing of your Father.*

Nelson's will left almost the entirety of his estate, including his lands in Sicily, to his brother William and provided £1,000 a year to his wife, Fanny. To Emma Nelson left £2,000, the Merton estate with all its furnishings, 70 acres of land, and £500 yearly income from the Bronte estate (to be paid by William). In a previous codicil to his will Nelson provided for Horatia:

*Codicil to Nelson's, 13 May 1803*

*... I give and bequeath to Miss Horatia Nelson Thompson (... who I acknowledge as my adopted daughter), the sum of £4,000 sterling money of Great Britain ... and I leave my dearest friend Emma, Lady Hamilton, sole guardian of the said Horatia Nelson Thompson, until she shall have arrived at the age of 18 years, and the interest of the said £4,000 to be paid to Lady Hamilton, for her education and maintenance. This request of guardianship I earnestly make of Lady Hamilton, knowing that she will educate my adopted child in the paths of religion and virtue, and give her those accomplishments which so much adorn herself ...*

Emma tried in vain to pursue the intention of Nelson's codicil, and was ignored. Others took up her cause, including Davison, who made direct appeals to the Prince of Wales; all to no avail.

The government awarded Fanny an annuity of £2,000 per year. Nelson's sisters each received £10,000, and his brother, the new Earl Nelson, was granted a £5,000 annuity and £99,000 with which to purchase an estate. There was nothing for Emma—not even Sir William's pension—and nothing for Horatia. Emma briefly cooled towards Davison, perhaps suspicious that Davison was more interested in the Nelson clan than in her.

Still a favorite party guest, Emma continued to pretend—and spend—as if she were a lady of wealth. As William Nelson's family distanced themselves, Nelson's sisters made increasing demands

JAMES HARRISON, *The Life of the Right Honourable Horatio, Lord Viscount Nelson: Baron Nelson of the Nile, and of Burnham-Thorpe and Hilborough in the County of Norfolk … London: Printed at the Ranelagh Press, by Stanhope and Tilling, 1806. 2 volumes. (2004.015.00.0001)* Harrison's biography of Nelson was written under Emma's guidance. This copy of Harrison's *Life of Nelson* was once owned by George Elphinstone, Viscount Keith (1746–1823), Nelson's superior officer.

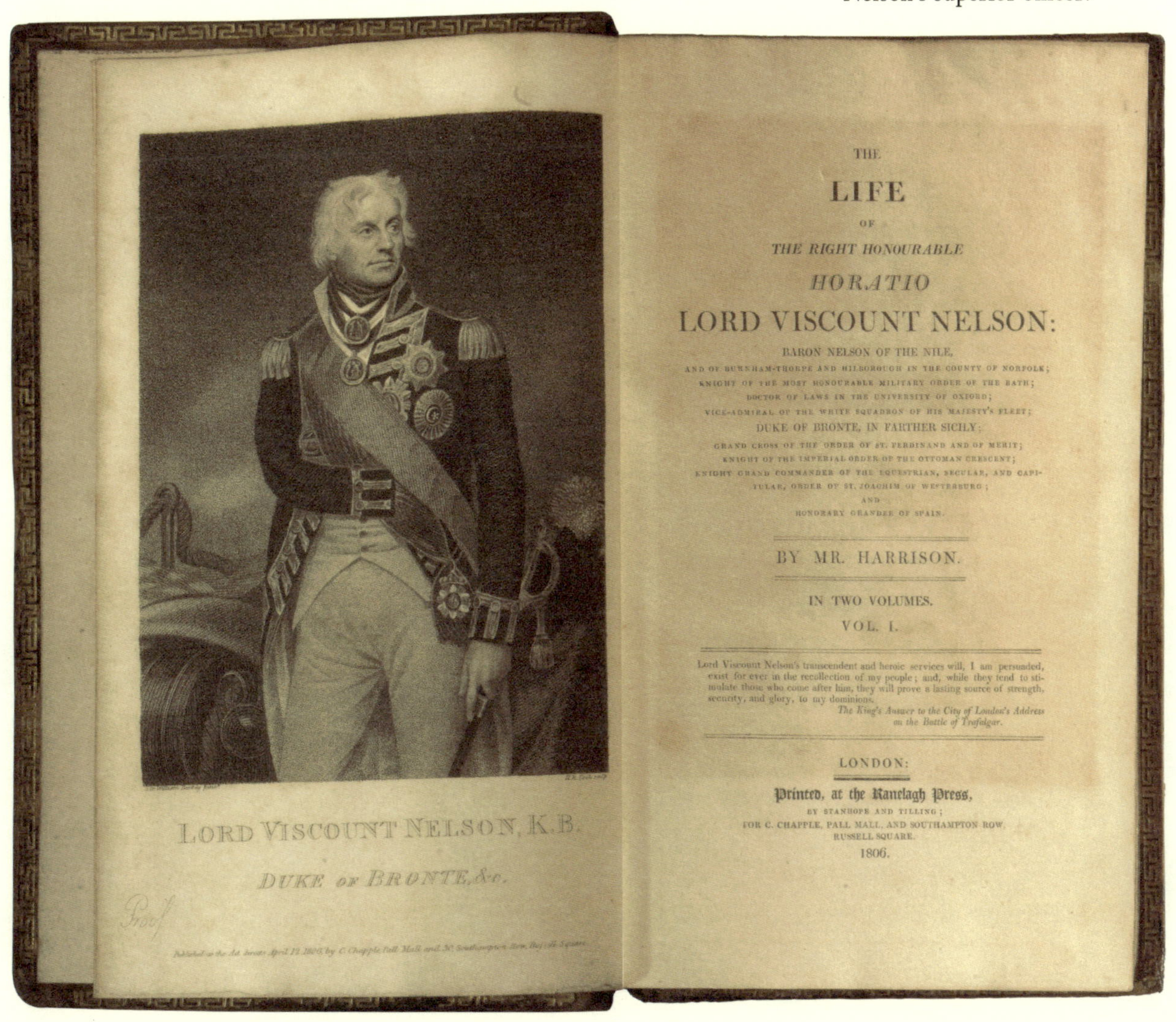

on Emma to groom and educate their daughters. Her mother's relatives—the Kidds and the Connors—also had expectations. She could not bear the thought of giving up the financially draining Merton, and over the next two years her financial affairs spiralled out of control.

Alexander Davison had responsibilities that did not end with Nelson's funeral. As much a friend and adviser to Emma as he was to Lord Nelson, Davison continued to manage the Merton estate and Emma's affairs.

By 1808 Emma's situation had deteriorated to such an extent that Davison and seven other financiers appointed themselves her trustees and sought to tackle her mountain of debts.

Emma called upon John Willock in the spring of 1808 to value the house, furniture, and other property at Merton with a view to selling everything but a few pictures. The property was offered at auction on 10 June, but failed to make the reserve and was bought in. Various attempts followed to sell the house to private buyers. Finally, on 25 November 1808, Alexander Davison and Emma's friends advanced her several thousand pounds and agreed to assume responsibility for disposing of Merton Place as advantageously as possible. The following April, financier Asher Goldsmid, a brother of one of the trustees, agreed to pay £13,000 for the house and timber, and to take the furniture and effects at a valuation of £1,801. 10s. Willock's account for a year and a half's work came to more than £5,000, half of which was paid from Goldsmid's deposit, and the rest mostly from the auction sale of Nelson's wine for £2,351. 10s. 11d.

Charles Greville died in April 1809, and Mrs. Cadogan passed away in January 1810. To save money, Emma moved to a hotel and then to even less expensive quarters at 150 Bond Street—alone and adrift, assailed by creditors, pressured by family, and abandoned by former friends.

ALEXANDER DAVISON. Retained autograph draft of a letter: to Lady Hamilton. 2 pages, 4to, St. James's Square, 31 August 1812. (2002.151.05.0001)

In the letter above, Davison responds to Emma's letters about her *"embarrassment in pecuniary matters,"* which has unfortunately occurred at a time of *"universal distress"* when bankers are down to their *"last shilling."* Nevertheless, considering her circumstances and *"in the absence of the Admiral,"* he agrees to a temporary loan of £450 *"till the Harvest has been got in."* Davison's reference to income from "the harvest" probably refers to the £500 *per annum* pledged by Nelson to be paid from the Bronte estate.

Emma's financial problems were caused as much by her extravagance and generosity as the failure of the government to provide the support requested in the codicil to Nelson's will. She borrowed heavily at exorbitant interest rates, hoping that one of her wealthy friends or the Prince of Wales would come to her rescue. They did not.

To avoid her creditors, she committed herself to the King's Bench Prison in December 1812. Debtors could buy the right to live within a three-quarter-mile radius, "within the Rules" of the prison where they could not be hounded by creditors or arrested for other crimes. An alderman, Joshua Smith, gave her money to rent a residence at 12 Temple Place, where she moved with some of the furnishings from Merton. By March 1813, Smith and other friends were able to stave off her creditors and she was able to return to her Bond Street home. She renewed her pleas—and demands—for recognition and compensation.

In a lengthy petition (*shown opposite*), Emma recounts her activities in great detail, beginning with her friendship with the Queen of Naples in 1791, to her role in influencing Nelson to accept command of the fleet which culminated in his victory at Trafalgar in 1805.

She explains her many services: "*...for the fourteen Years that I was Ambassador's Wife at this court ... my sole view was to maintain the Dignity of our Royal and beloved Master, to advance His Interests, and Wishes; and to sooth and alleviate the toils of His brave loyal Seamen in a distant Clime. In a place of hoarding at such times, and occasions, it was my sole pride, my glory, my ambition, thus to have expended what private friendship had bestow'd for my own immediate Comforts and use...*"

Emma's concluding paragraph embodies the poignancy of her continuing appeals:

*I ... now find myself in embarrassments that imperiously press on me to look for remuneration for those Services, Expenditures and Losses that I have recited; and not alone for immediate but as well for payment of that support for the time past ... I may ... without fear of exaggeration, affirm that my private Funds in Monies expended, and losses sustaine'd, have suffer'd a diminuation of full £20,000. Had I hoarded these Sums that 'I must be permitted to' say I generously expended for the honor and advantage of the 'Country,' I might at this Hour, have a competence independent of any remuneration for the Services I have quoted, and which I have no doubt the Country would wish me to enjoy.*

In September 1791 I went with my
Husband thro' France to Naples. At Paris I waited
on the Queen, then at the Thuilleries, who entrusted
me with the last Letter she wrote to her Sister
the Queen of Naples; this led to an ascendency
in Her Majesty's Esteem, that I never after fail'd to
exert in favor of every British Interest.

In the Year 1793 when Lord Hood
had taken possession of Toulon and Sir John Jervis
was employ'd upon the reduction of Corsica; the
latter kept writing to me for every thing he wanted,
which I procur'd to be promptly provided him, and
as his Letters to me prove had considerably facilitated
the reduction of that Island: I had by this time
the King induced thro' my influence with the Queen,
to become so Zealous in the good Cause that both
would often say "I had de Bourbonitz'd them,
"and made them all English"!

By unceasing Cultivation of this influence,
and no less watchfulness to turn it to my Country's
good

EMMA HAMILTON. Autograph letter, signed: to the Prince Regent (from 1820, King George IV), (n.p. [12 Temple Place]), 28 February 1813. 4 pages, 4⁰. (2004.006.00.0005)

The letter above was preceded by a lengthy memorial, perhaps the one described above, addressed to the Prince Regent, listing her services to the country, and her grievances:

*Most humbly do I beseech forgiveness for my again intruding on your Royal Highness but my necessity is such and so peculiar is my immediate situation that no other mode of seeking Relief appears to me left … for indeed I am sinking in misery & am most unhappy …*

The petitions and entreaties Emma and her friends, counselors, and advisors fired off for years never succeeded. In this petition, writing for herself and desperate, Emma tried to speak directly to the Prince Regent (acting for the King during the madness of his father, George III), using Horatia's needs as one of the justifica-

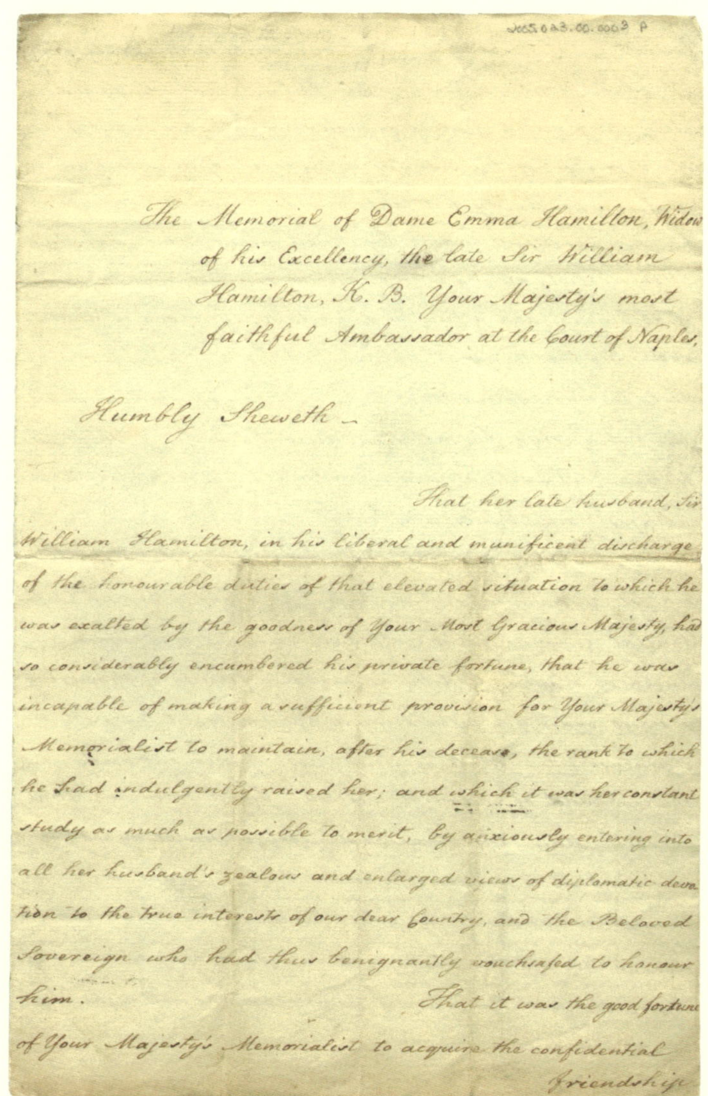

EMMA HAMILTON. Manuscript document, signed (not her hand): "Memorial of Dame Emma Hamilton." No date (ca. March 1813). 4 pages, folio. (2005.023.00.0003)

tions for her demands, and declaring in the present letter that the *"slender provision left by Lord Nelson for the bringing up of his daughter Horatia comes short of which I deem necessary for the Education of one of her descent the only Living Blood of that glorious man."*

Drafted by a Mr. Russell, the letter above may be Emma's final appeal to receive Nelson's legacy. As was the convention with royal petitions, it is neither in the hand of the petitioner, nor signed, although Emma clearly played a large role in it. This petition having failed, Emma was imprisoned for debt.

A series of mostly undated notes and letters during 1813 to Sir Richard Puleston, an admirer, attest to her deteriorating health and increasing anxiety.

Autograph letter, signed: Emma Hamilton to Sir Richard Puleston, n.p., n.d., 1
page integral address leaf, seal (2004.006.02.0006):

*ten ten thousand Thanks to you my dear Sir for your goodness I never can ? nor express my
gratitude enough but let me see or Hear from you tomorrow as I wish to Consult with you*

> *EH*

Autograph letter, signed: Emma Hamilton to Colonel Puleston, Warrens Hotel,
Charles, St. St. James Sq. From 15 Bond St., n.d., 1 page integral address leaf, seal
(2004.006.03.0006):

*Dear Sir*

*I hope you will call on me today before two o'clock that Horatia & I may thank you for your
kind attentions your ever grateful*

> *E Hamilton*

Autograph letter, signed: Emma Hamilton to Colonel Puleston. n.d [1813], n.p.,
Friday noon, 1 page, 8ᵛᵒ (2004.006.05.0006):

*We cannot go this evening to Vauxhall but will arrange for another day & soon Excuse this
script but I am in the midst of business but ever your most obliged & faithful*

> *Emma Hamilton*

Autograph letter, signed: Emma Hamilton to Sir Richard Puleston. 11 Temple
place. n.d., 1 page, 8ᵛᵒ (2004.006.06.0006):

*I did not foresee the difficulty you mention or wou'd not have asked it but feel the same obliged
to you*

*If Lord Early will not do any thing then I am Lost Life Liberty & all gone god bless you
ever & for ever your affectionate & gratefull*

> *EH*

In June 1813, under threat of arrest by her creditors, Emma auctioned many of
the remaining things of value—jewelry, furniture, books, and items associated
with Nelson. It was not enough. On 28 June she was arrested and sentenced to
prison until she could pay the £400 debt. She moved again to 10 Temple Place.
Although desperate (or perhaps out of desperation) she continued to entertain
lavishly and borrow heavily.

In July, Emma writes to Puleston:

*If you are in Town & will take a drive to see one who will ever Love & respect you (you
will make me happy) you will not see me an ambassadress nor in splendor but you will ever
find me firm & my mind uncorrupted Shame on those who will let me and Nelsons daughter
pass the first of August* [anniversary of the Battle of the Nile] *in anguish*

> *EH*

And in November, Emma writes to Puleston (*see overleaf*):

*I have been confined to bed my dear Sir Richard for some time with the remains off of the jaundice but I am getting better although I was at deaths door and I feel stronger and better than I have been for thee 3 years … I shall have gained one Experience that of knowing my true friends from those who feigned to be my friends …*

EMMA HAMILTON. Autograph letter, signed: to Colonel Puleston, Ivy Rock, Woodside, Chester. No 12 Temple place, opposite the Drury Lane Theatre. 24 July 1813. 1 page, 8vo. (2004.006.04.0006)

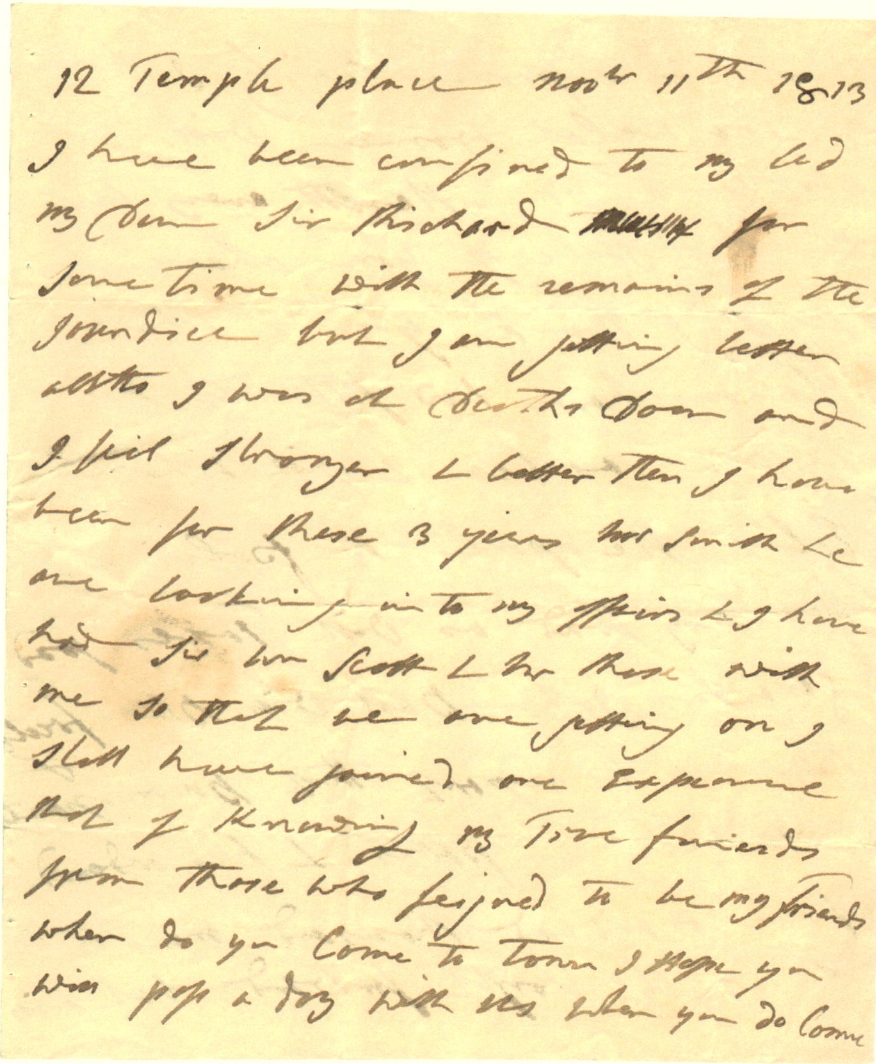

Emma had been living "within the Rules" at Temple Place for nine months when, in April 1814, Nelson's letters were published. The ensuing scandal tarnished Nelson's image and exposed Emma to public ridicule. The details of their relationship, including Nelson's candid remarks about the government, alienated her supporters and doomed any further appeals to the Prince of Wales, who was disparaged by Nelson.

James Harrison, who lived at Merton while writing his biography of Nelson, is often cited as the editor, but it is also possible that Nelson's secretary, Francis Oliver, could have been responsible. Thomas Lovewell, the publisher, went bankrupt in 1817 and sold the letters to John Wilson Croker, acting for the Admiralty that purchased them to avoid further embarrassment.

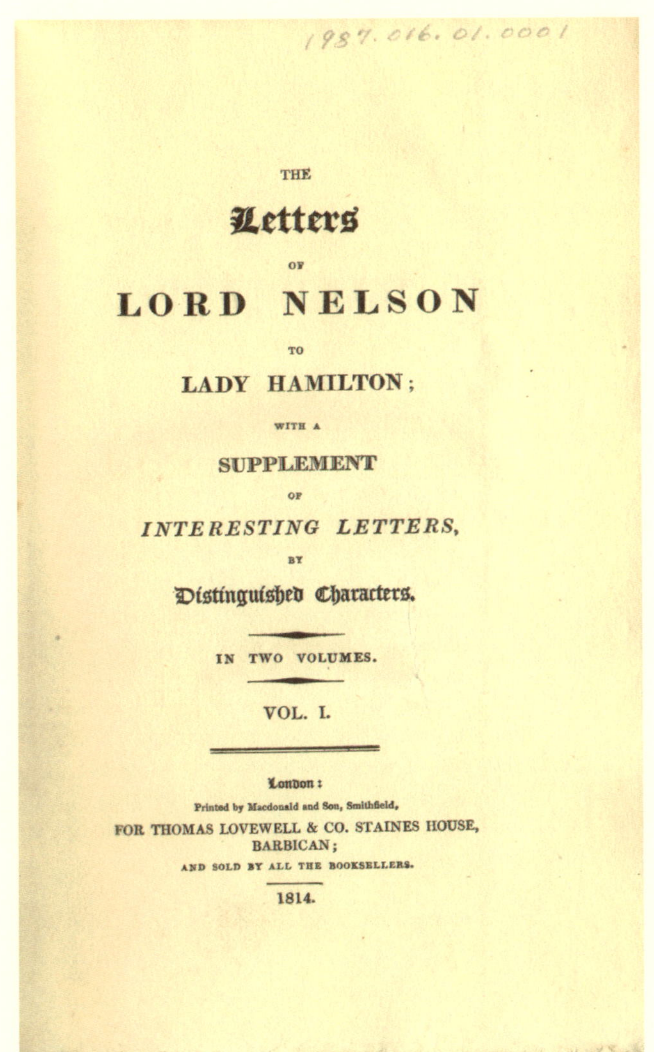

[HORATIO NELSON]. *The Letters of Lord Nelson to Lady Hamilton.* London: Printed by Macdonald and Son for Thomas Lovewell & Co., 1814. 2 vols. (1987.016.00.0001)

Emma's health deteriorated rapidly—anxiety and fear aggravated the intestinal problems that had plagued her and Sir William since their time in Naples. She was brought to the brink of despair. Seeing no possibility of release from her creditors, Emma made plans to flee to France.

The progressive disintegration of her hand during the course of the following letter suggests that despair is complete:

*I know not what to do my mind is so distrest for I find next week there will be more detainers ... I will sell as I many things as I can get fifty pounds for then I shall have only have fifty if you can procure me That I will give a receipt for it to be received of mssrs Davisons & Co paid next for the 21st of October when he receives two hundred & twenty pounds for me good as the bank pray do it if you Love me ... God Sake if it is possible let me have*

I know not what to do my mind
is so distrest for I find next
week there will be more
detainers do not leave the
letter if you can see him do if
not I will sell as many things
as I can get fifty pounds for
them I shall have only have fifty
if you could procure me that I
will give a receipt for it to be
received of messrs Davisons & Co
paid in full for the 21st of October
when He Receives Two Hundred &
Twenty pounds for me good as
the Bank pray do if you

*the fifty ... if one detainer comes I am lost for ever May Heaven bless you your affectionate*

*Emma H*

With the help of Alderman Smith, she sold her few remaining things and obtained enough money to make bail on 22 June. With only £50, Emma Hamilton and Horatia made their escape to Calais in the first week of July 1814.

Emma never lost her ability to charm and impress and was even able to borrow again, this time in French francs. She set up residence in the fashionable Dessein's Hotel, where she hosted dinner parties and continued to live, as we might say, "in denial."

Her luck was not to hold. Eventually she ran out of credit and in September she moved to a farmhouse outside of town. By November her condition worsened. She needed constant medical attention and moved back to Calais. She spent her final weeks of life unable to leave her bed, taking laudanum and spirits to dull the pain.

Emma Lady Hamilton died on 15 January 1815. Her wish to be interred beside her mother in the Paddington church was ignored, and she was buried in the churchyard of St. Pierre's in Calais. Many naval officers followed her hearse to the cemetery, which was converted into a timber yard in 1816. In 1833 a guide to Calais mentioned a Latin inscription on her headstone which was only partially decipherable:

QUAE

... CALESIAE

VIÂ IN GALLICÂ VOCATÂ

ET IN DOMO C.VI. OBIIT

DIE XV. MENSIS JANUARII. A.D. MDCCCXV.

ÆTATIS SUAE LI.

*[Who ... at Calais in the rue Francais died in No. 106 on the 15<sup>th</sup> day of January A.D. in the 51<sup>st</sup> year of her age]*

By the end of the 19th century, the headstone had disappeared and her grave could no longer be found.

*The maison Damy, now Grandin, in a room of which poor Lady Hamilton breathed her last, is situated in the Rue Française, the street running parallel with the southern rampart and fossé, and is at present numbered 111. From its aspect being due north, the house in question is as cheerless and dreary as can be well imagined; not a ray of sunshine ever gladdens*

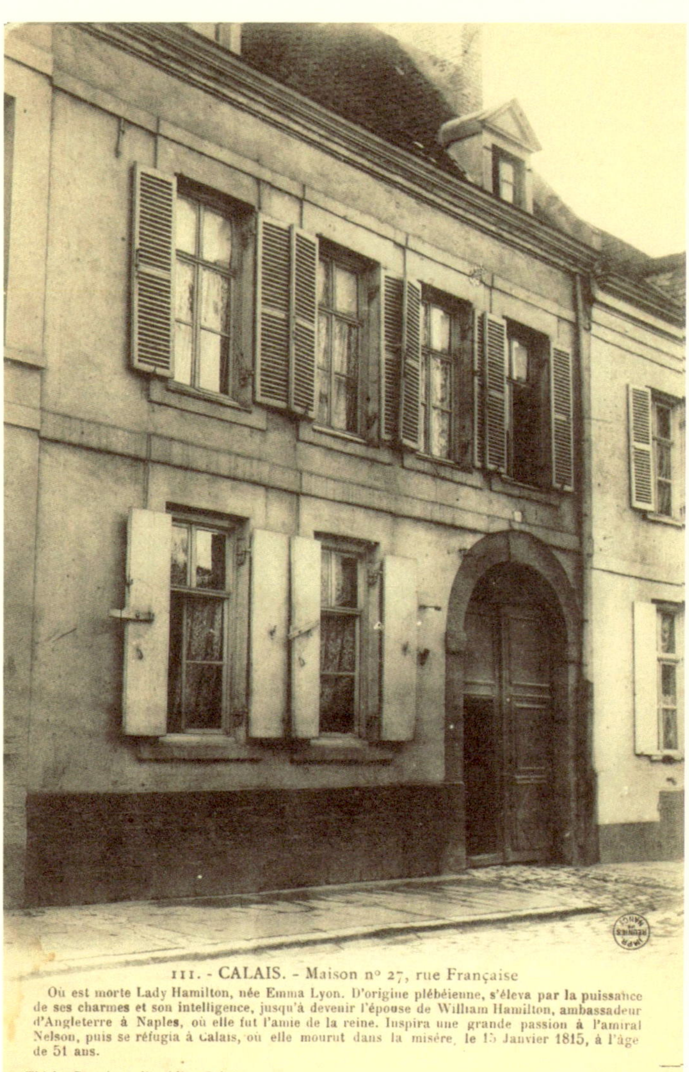

111. - CALAIS. - Maison nº 27, rue Française
Où est morte Lady Hamilton, née Emma Lyon. D'origine plébéienne, s'éleva par la puissance de ses charmes et son intelligence, jusqu'à devenir l'épouse de William Hamilton, ambassadeur d'Angleterre à Naples, où elle fut l'amie de la reine. Inspira une grande passion à l'amiral Nelson, puis se réfugia à Calais, où elle mourut dans la misère, le 15 Janvier 1815, à l'âge de 51 ans.

Thiriat-Deguines, lib.-édit., Calais

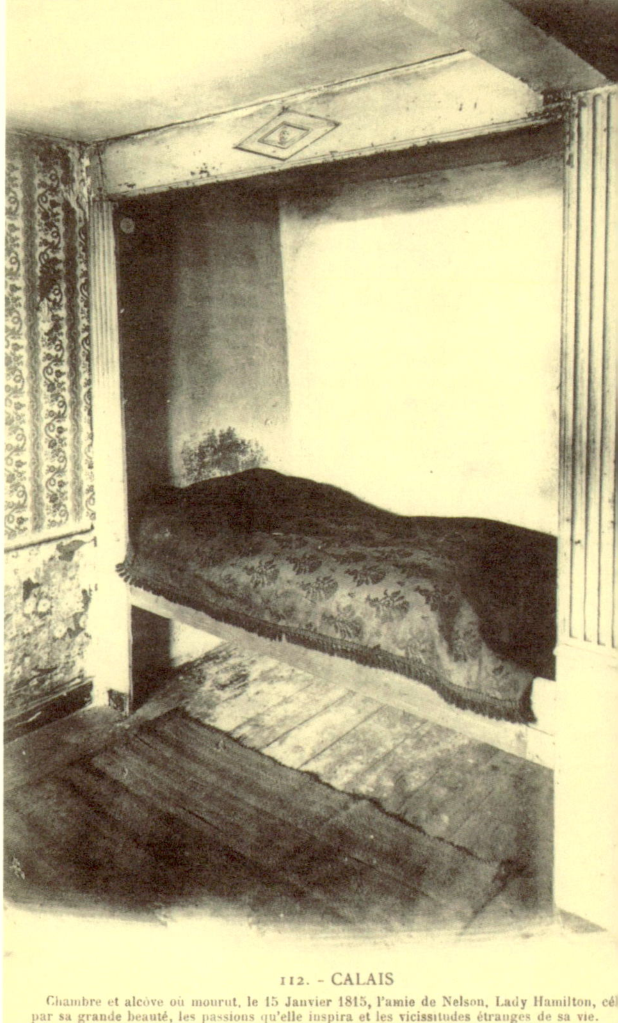

112. - CALAIS
Chambre et alcôve où mourut, le 15 Janvier 1815, l'amie de Nelson, Lady Hamilton, célèbre par sa grande beauté, les passions qu'elle inspira et les vicissitudes étranges de sa vie.

Thiriat-Deguines, lib.-édit., Calais

THE HOUSE AND ALCOVE WHERE EMMA DIED. Postal cards. Thiriat-Deguines. Nancy, France: Reunies, n.d. (2010.159.00.0001 and 2010.159.00.0002)

*the side of the street in which it is situated, or plays for an instant even in summer on the ever-shaded, cold-looking casements.*

— Robert Bell Calton, *Annals and Legends of Calais.*
London: John Russel Smith, 1852, pp. 182–3.

The British Consul made the funeral arrangements, paid Emma's outstanding debts, and gave Horatia enough money to return to England. Horatia was met by Nelson's sister, Catherine Matcham, and spent the next two years caring for the Matchams' children. After two years with the Matchams, Horatia went to live with her uncle, the widower Thomas Bolton, formerly married to

Nelson's other sister, Susanna, who died in 1813. She worked as his housekeeper.

Emma's best epitaph may be found in the touching lines by Nelson's doctor, William Beatty, who had himself known and liked her (from Walter Sichel, *Emma Lady Hamilton from New and Original Sources and Documents, Together with an Appendix of Notes and New Letters*. London: Archibald Constable, 1909, p. 475):

> *... All know thy shame, thy mental sufferings, none.*
> *All know thy frailties—all thou wast and art!*
> *But thine were faults of circumstance, not heart.*
> *Thy soul was formed to bless and to be bless'd*
> *With that immortal boon—a guiltless breast,*
> *And* BE *what others* SEEM*—had bounteous Heaven*
> *Less beauty lent, or stronger virtue given!*
>
>             *... Yet 'tis come*
> *To this! When all but slander's voice is dumb,*
> *And they who gazed upon thy living face,*
> *Can hardly find thy mortal resting-place.*

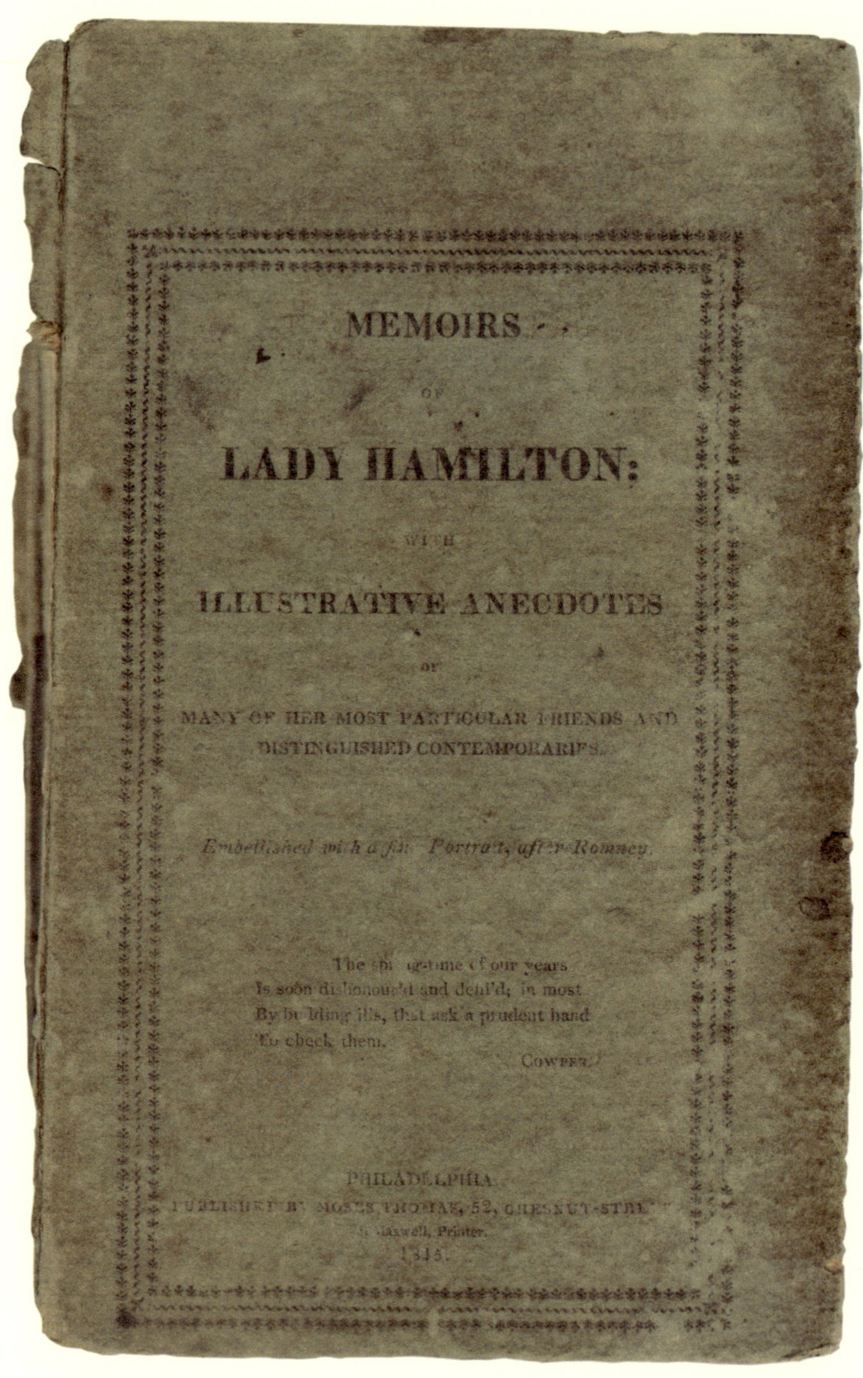

# VII

## An Inglorious Aftermath

**P**UBLISHED the year Emma died, the *Memoirs of Lady Hamilton* was not a book written by any of Emma's friends. It expresses a moralistic attitude towards Emma and portrays her as a grasping social climber. Four editions were printed in 1815, two in London, one in New York, and a fourth in Philadelphia. It was translated into French and published in Paris the following year.

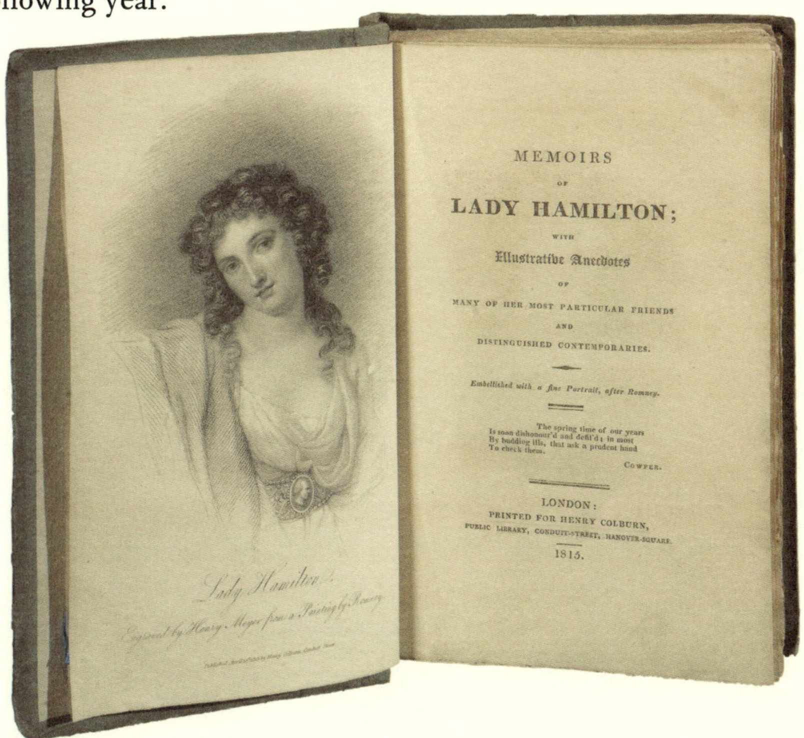

[ANONYMOUS], *Memoirs of Lady Hamilton; with Illustrative Anecdotes of Many of Her Most Particular Friends and Distinguished Contemporaries. Embellished with a fine Portrait, after Romney.* London: Printed for Henry Colburn, 1815. 8ᵛᵒ. 1st edition. (2010.139.00.0001)

*The maxim, that 'nothing should be said of the dead, but what is good,' though it has become proverbial by the frequency of repetition, and the benevolence which it seems to inculcate, is too often made an excuse for error, and an apology for depravity. But whatever may be the nature or the extent of the rule, it never could have been intended to operate as an act of indemnity, to cover in oblivion the deeds of those who have endeavoured to loosen the foundations of morality by their principles, or to render vice attractive by their example...*
      *Memoirs of Lady Hamilton* ... Chapter 1.

117

RICHARD B. H. RIDGWAY.
Autograph document, signed.
London, 14 March 1818. Memorandum detailing charges
for legal services rendered in
connection with Lady Ham-
ilton's debts. Annotated in
pencil by Alexander Davison.
(2004.151.15.0001)

As expressed by Elbert Hubbart in *Little Journeys to Homes of Great Lovers Lord Nelson and Lady Hamilton* (East Aurora, N.Y.: The Roycrofters, Vol. XIX, November, 1906): *"Lady Hamilton was unfortunate in having her history written only by her enemies—written with goosequills … Nelson in his innocence did not know English society; otherwise he would not have commended Lady Hamilton to the gratitude of the English. It was a little like commending her to a pack of wolves. The sum of ten thousand pounds was voted to each of Nelson's sisters, but not a penny to Lady Hamilton, 'my wife before the eyes of God,' as he himself expressed it …"*

The sheer magnitude of Emma Hamilton's extravagance and consequent debts is reflected in documents that show that the repercussions for her creditors were still being felt three years or more after her death, as in the memorandum above, which, in a pencil annotation by Alexander Davison, states "1st April 1818, drew at sight in favor of Mess Coutts & Co P £242. 16[s.] 10[d.] the balance."

Detailed in the next and final document (*opposite*) (J. Dawson. Retained autograph draft: to Alexander Davison. Swarland Hall, 1 April 1818 [2002.151.10.0001]) concerns the receipt of £457. 1s. 9d. the *"fourth part of the Annuity to Lady Hamilton and Interest."*

Thus ends the paper trail in this archive.

118

Swarland Hall 1.ᵗ April 1818

Dear Sir

I have had the pleasure to receive Your letter of the 18 Ult.
informing me of your having received £457. 1. 9 one fourth part of the
Annuity to Lady Hamilton and Interest; and enclosing your account of 1812
1813. 1814 & 1818, Amounting to £65. 12. 5 and the Legacy Duty of £148. 12. 6
making together £214. 4. 11, which sum You deduct from the money received, leaving
a balance of £242. 16. 10 which You say You will pay as I direct —
I have in consequence, drawn upon You at sight for
the balance in favor of Mess.ʳ Tho.ˢ Coutts & Co. and
am glad to hear the Residue of the Annuity will very shortly
be paid — I sincerely thank You for the exertion You have made in the
business, tho' it has been attended with an extraordinary Expense —

I shall be in Town in all this month, and shall soon after my
arrival have the pleasure to call upon You — But for letting some Farms
which are out of Lease, I would now been in London

Yours very faithfully.

J. Dawson Esq.
Savile Place
New Burlington Street —

J. DAWSON. Retained autograph draft: to Alexander Davison. Swarland Hall, 1 April 1818. 1 page, 8ᵛᵒ. (2002.151.10.0001)

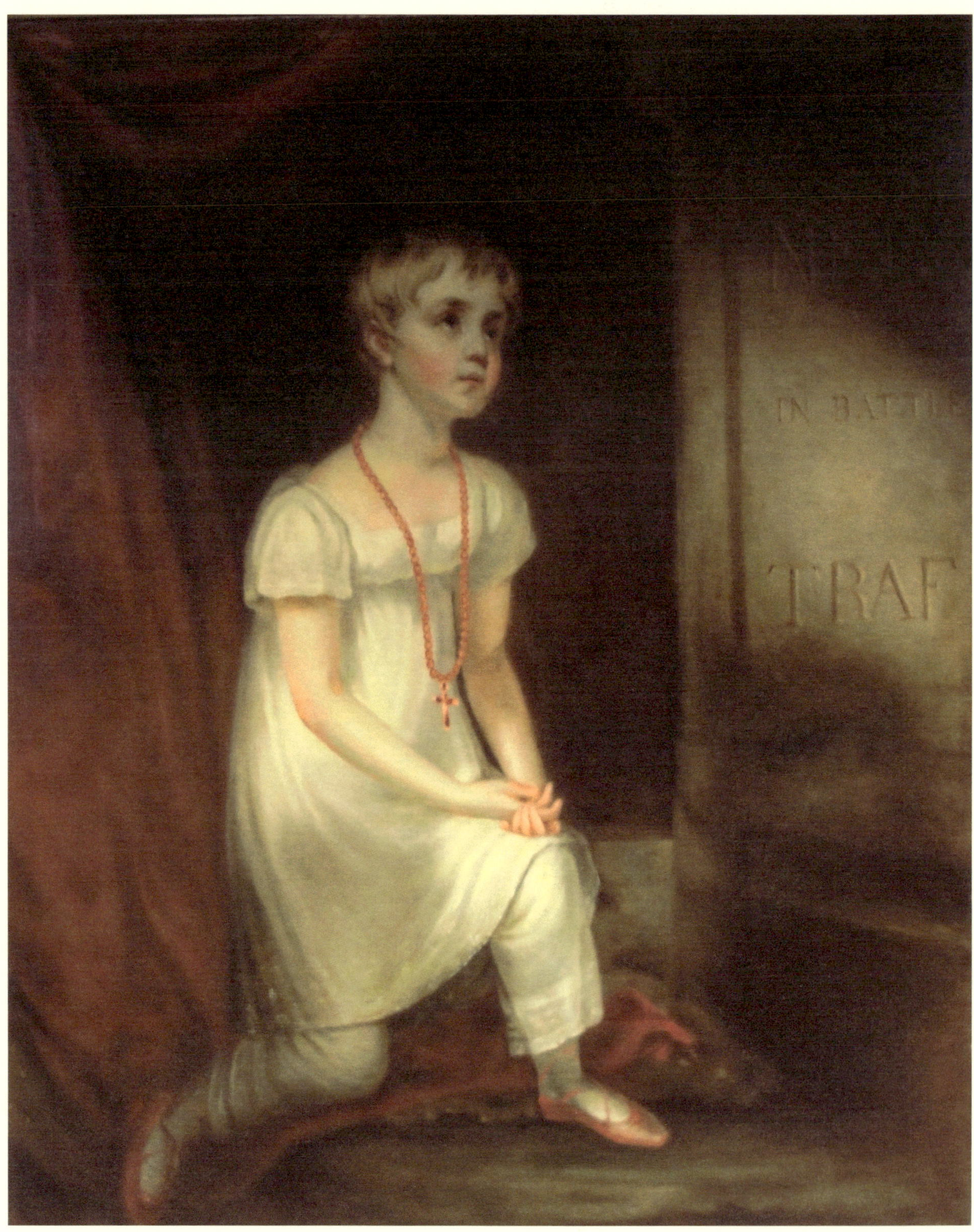
IN BATTLE
TRAF

## Mother & Daughters

Horatia's relationship with her mother was fraught with the tribulations of Emma's latter days, including her time with Horatia in debtors' prison, so much so that Horatia never acknowledged her filial connection to Emma. She did, however, from early youth, revel in and benefit from the reflected glory of her father.

The young Horatia is portrayed by William Owen (*shown opposite*), full length on bended right knee at the imaginary tomb of her father, on which is visible the inscription "NELS...," "IN BATTLE...," "TRAF...." Owen came to London in 1780 and entered the Royal Academy Schools in 1791. He was appointed Portrait Painter to the Prince of Wales in 1810 and Principal Painter to the Prince Regent in 1813. He eschewed sparkle and flash, preferring a considered sober approach which especially suited his depictions of children and elderly sitters. Another version of this picture by Owens, in inferior condition, exists in the National Maritime Museum at Greenwich.

Horatia Nelson's future husband, the Reverend Philip Ward, first met her in 1819 at Burnham, Norfolk, where he later took up the position of Curate. It seems Horatia had been rather fond of the Reverend Blake, his predecessor, but Philip won her heart. They were married in Burnham Westgate Church on 19 February 1822. The ceremony was conducted by Horatia's uncle, Reverend William Bolton.

Over the years, she raised a family of nine children. Horatia died on 6 March 1881, in her 81st year. Not once in her life did she acknowledge Emma Hamilton as her mother. It is said that Horatia wrote a life of Emma (some extracts were published in the London *Athenaeum* in 1877), but a publisher was never found and the manuscript was lost or destroyed.

Inscribed to eight-year-old Horatia on the front end paper of *Moral Maxims from the Wisdom of Jesus*, her mother records the following sentiment: "*Richmond. August 26ᵗʰ 1809 Given to Horatia Nelson May*

---

*Opposite*: HORATIA NELSON kneeling before her father's tomb, after 1807, by William Owens (1769–1825). Oil on canvas. 127 × 101.5 cm. Picture credit: Gunnar Bengtsson's private collection at the Victory Hotel in Stockholm, Sweden.

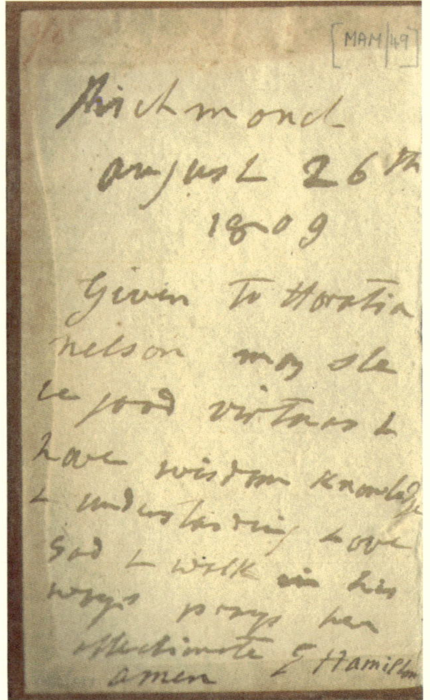

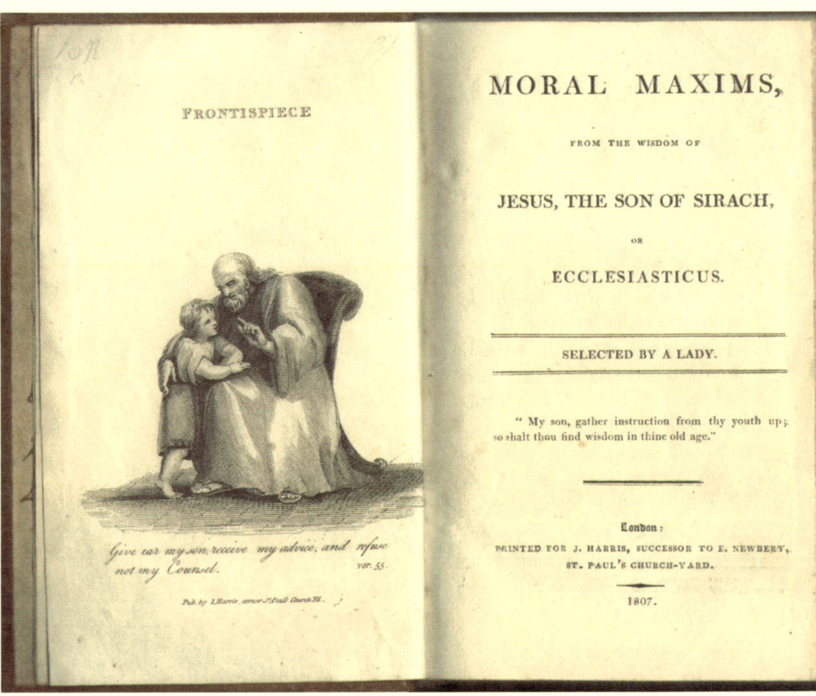

[ELIZABETH SEMPLE], *Moral Maxims from the Wisdom of Jesus, the Son of Sirach, or Ecclesiasticus Selected by a Lady.* London: J. Harris, 1807.

Horatia Nelson's copy with presentation from Emma Hamilton. (2006.017.00.0003)

she be good virtuous & have wisdom knowledge & understanding love God & walk in his ways Prays her affectionate E Hamilton Amen."

Later in life, Horatia's mature reflections upon "Lady Hamilton" are recorded in *Tait's Edinburgh Magazine* (Vol. 12, No. 11, November 1845, p. 788): "*Miss Horatia Nelson lived with Lady Hamilton until her decease, and she bears this satisfactory testimony to Lady Hamilton's conduct towards her: 'With all Lady Hamilton's faults—and she had many—she had many fine qualities, which, had she been placed early in better hands, and in different circumstances, would have made her a very superior woman. It is but justice on my part to say that through all her difficulties, she invariably till the last few months, expended on my education, &c, the whole of the interest of the sum left me by Lord Nelson, and which was left entirely at her control.'*"

In all likelihood, neither Horatia nor Nelson ever knew of the existence of Emma's elder daughter, born in 1782 from her mother's relationship with Sir Harry Featherstonhaugh. Known as Emma Carew, this lonely child lived with a series of relatives, her mother never secure enough to send for her during the years spent in Naples or, later, at Merton. Near the end of Lady Hamilton's life, Miss Carew wrote to her for help, but by then Emma had nothing to give. The rest of Emma Carew's life is unknown.

## The Legacy of Emma Hamilton

BY KATE WILLIAMS

EMMA HAMILTON is one of the most iconic women of the eighteenth century. Famed for her beauty, glamour, and intense passion for life, she was also intelligent and creative. Her work with George Romney had a vital impact on portraiture, and in her Attitudes she created a new art form. A gifted singer, she charmed Joseph Haydn. Her energy and talents lit up England and Europe, and she has been continually represented and refigured since her death in 1815.

Emma had her faults, as satirists have pointed out, and she has been reviled for her adultery. And yet her artistic talents and drive have often been overlooked. Nelson's love made her famous, but her life would have been fascinating even if she had never met him. She was born into poverty in an age when land and power were the possession of a few prominent families. At the time the average life expectancy was seventeen, and for impoverished female children much lower. Very little could be expected of the little girl born Amy Lyon on 26 April 1765.

Emma's energy and intelligence served her well. She became the wife of one of the greatest collectors of his day, a confidant of the Queen of Naples, and a friend of the future George IV and William IV. Many were delighted by her beauty, but she secured friendships with her quick mind and zeal for experience. Nelson was charmed by her flamboyant play for his heart, but he also admired her fluent French and Italian and intimacy with the Neapolitan Royal Family.

Emma was widely celebrated for her artistic innovation. In her Attitudes, conceived soon after she arrived in Naples aged twenty-one, she created what Elisabeth Vigée Le Brun called "un nouveau genre." Dressed in white, Emma used shawls and her dramatic abilities to mimic poses from classical myth—from Medea to Niobe. One of the earliest spectators, Johann Wolfgang von Goethe, wrote in his *Italian Journey* (1816) how she "gives so much variety to her poses, gestures, expressions that the spectator can

KATE WILLIAMS studied her B.A. and D.Phil. at Oxford and her M.A. at the University of London. Her biography of Emma, *England's Mistress*, was Book of the Year in the *Times* and *Independent*, and the film and stage musical are in production. She has since written *Becoming Queen* about Princess Charlotte and Queen Victoria. Her first novel is due out next year and her next biography in 2012.

hardly believe his eyes." She revealed, he thought, "what thousands of artists would have liked to express."

As muse to George Romney, Emma had already exercised an influence over portraiture. Romney's determination to show her as vulnerable to the viewer, unlike the popular mannered style of portraits of ladies, fed into the Romantic desire to show the self without props. The freedom and seemingly improvised nature of the Attitudes proved equally striking and they were widely described and painted, perhaps most delicately by Friedrich Rehberg in his 1794 collection of drawings.

When success as an actor meant ensuring that a large and noisy theatre audience could hear your words, Emma's revelation of emotion using shawls and the expressions of her face was revolutionary. We can see her work as encouraging a movement to a naturalistic style of acting and dance. Eighteenth-century ballet was often stiff and dancers paused between poses. Emma's agility made her a precursor of Isadora Duncan, who transformed modern dance with her emphasis on graceful movement.

Emma was repeatedly figured by artists, playwrights, musicians, and writers. We can see characters who resemble her in many eighteenth-century novels, including Mary Charlton's *The Wife and the Mistress* (1802) and Eliza Parson's *The Convict; or The Navy Lieutenant* (1807). Madame de Staël's *Corinne* (1807) is surely one of the greatest works she inspired.

The beautiful poetess, Corinne, an Englishwoman living in Rome, enchants Lord Nelvil, a visiting aristocrat with a name rather similar to Britain's greatest naval hero. Corinne has an appearance like Emma's: long dark hair, white, draped gowns, and a figure that is "tall and rather full, after the manner of the Grecian statues." She excels at the Tarantella dance, at which Emma was skilled. She even strikes characteristic poses. She is "so well acquainted with all the attitudes which the ancient painters and sculptors have represented" that with her movements and "incredible dexterity, she recalled to mind the dancers of Herculaneam, and gave birth successively to a crowd of new ideas for painting and design."

Corinne is a woman of ardour and imagination, who follows her heart and refuses to be kept to stultifying social norms. Emma was at her best when so figured, an expansive woman who would kiss Nelson's sword at dinner in front of the company and inspire him to heights of passion in his letters. It was fitting that she was

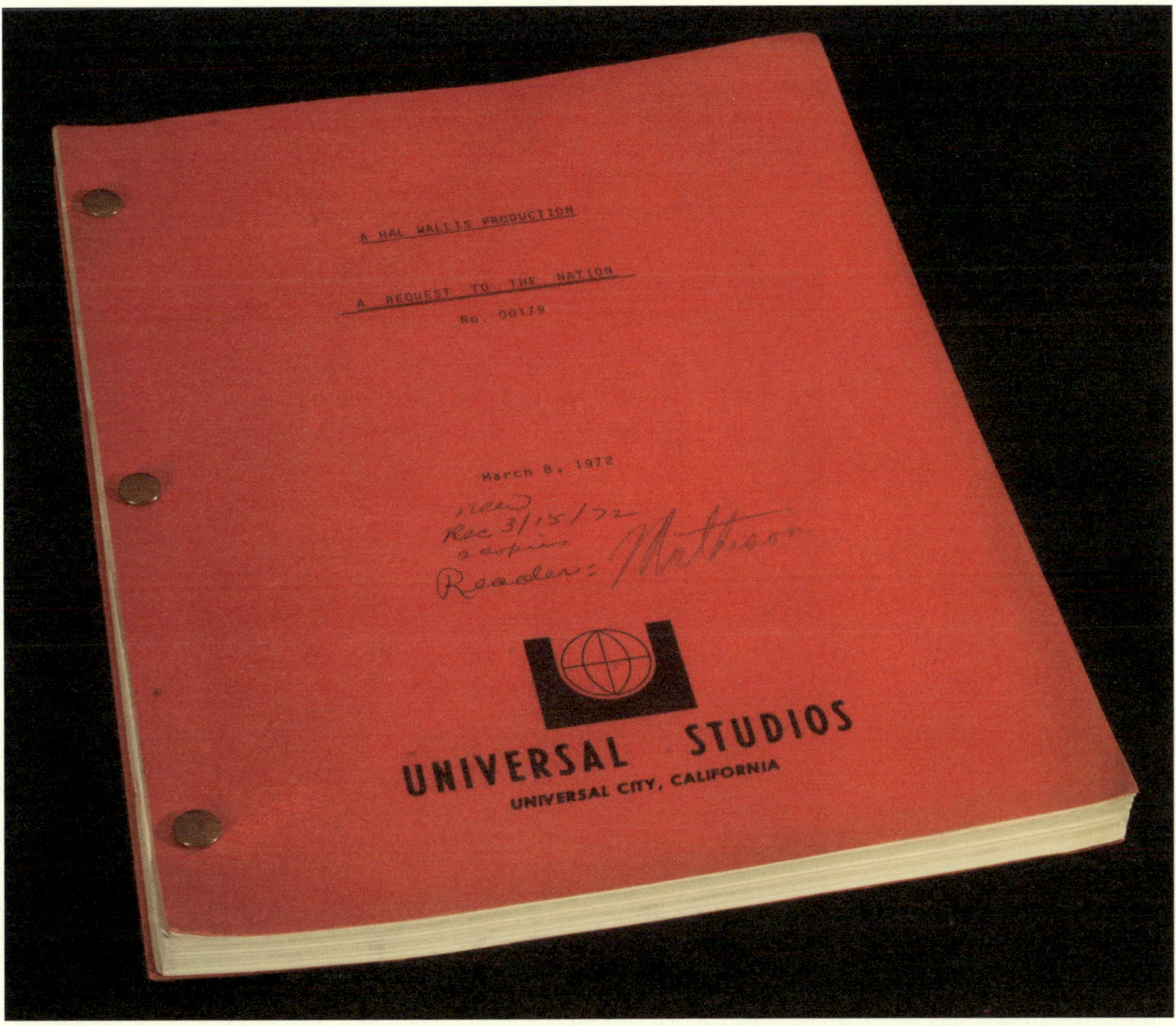



such an accomplished singer, for she lived her life on an operatic scale.

Emma has been much represented in film, with one of the most recent favourites Glenda Jackson in *Bequest to the Nation* in 1972. A particularly appealing film is the 1929 *The Divine Lady*, in which Corinne Griffiths played Emma without words. With music and sound effects but no spoken dialogue, the film won an Oscar for best direction and Griffiths was nominated for Best Actress. The expressiveness of her eyes proves intense emotion can be communicated without talk—as in the case of the Attitudes.

The most lavish biopic was Alexander Korda's 1941 *That Hamilton Woman!* With Vivien Leigh as a skittish Emma and Laurence Olivier as a painfully restrained Nelson, the film, released in the

TERENCE RATTIGAN.
A Bequest to the Nation.
Original script of first-draft
screenplay, 8 March 1972.
(2010.082.00.0001)

E. BARRINGTON, *The Divine Lady* (*with Illustrations from the Photoplay*). This "romance of Nelson and Emma Hamil-ton" is illustrated with scenes from the photoplay starring Corinne Griffith. New York: Grosset & Dunlap, 1924. (2010.138.00.0001)

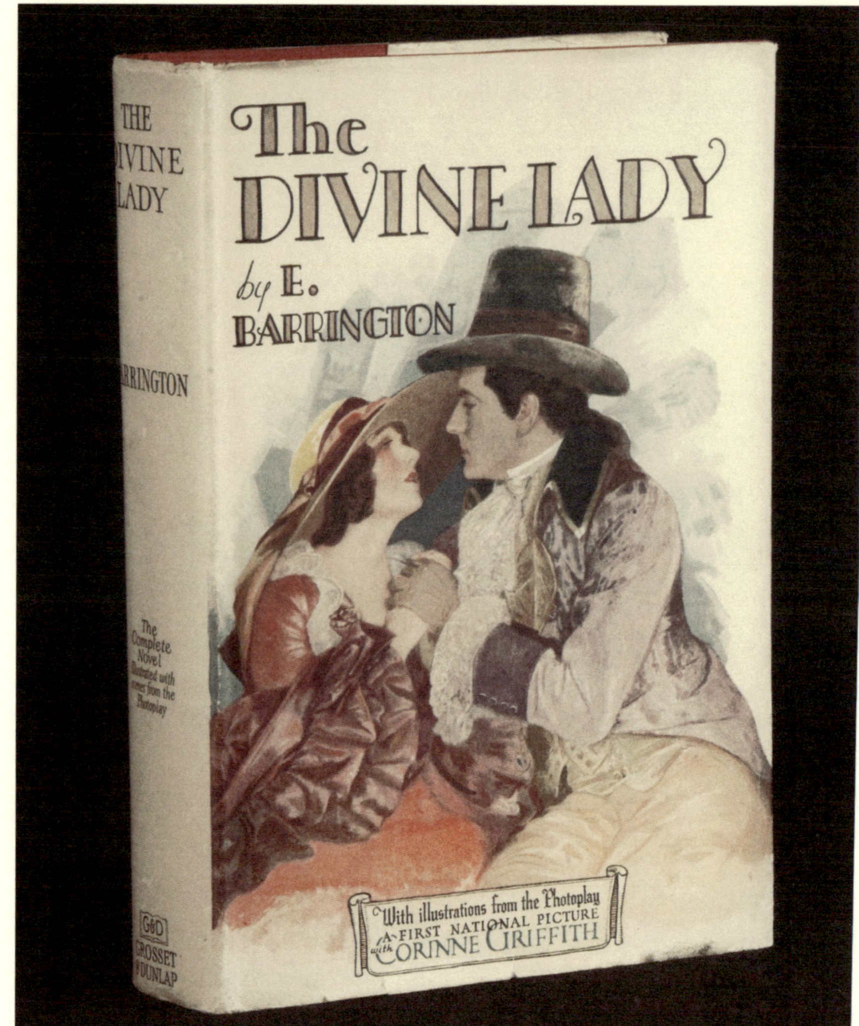


United Kingdom as *Lady Hamilton*, was intended to raise spirits in wartime—with magnificent sets, opulent (if historically in-accurate) costumes, and intensely romantic scenes. The British Prime Minister Winston Churchill was a devoted admirer. Scenes in which Olivier announces his desire to resist those who dictate mirrored Churchill's determination to fight on against the Third Reich.

In the film, Emma meets Nelson privately and falls in love with him because he is wounded. "They told us of your victories, but not of the price you had paid," she tells him, while staring at his damaged eye and arm. In actuality, Emma wrote to Nelson in 1798, begging him to come to Naples and offer them protection. She was attracted by both his heroism and his celebrity and she threw herself into his arms on his ship, in front of the entire receiving party. Nelson's wounds had been widely publicised. Korda confers erotic force on Nelson because he has suffered while fighting for his country. It was crucial in 1941 for women and men to believe that those disabled by battle could be more romantically attractive than they had been when whole in body.

The Victorians found Emma's excess and blatant adultery disagreeable. Now, perhaps, in an age of greater equality between the sexes we feel more sympathy for the position of women at the time. With little chance of making their own money, most relied on men—whether as wives or mistresses. Legally, a woman had a status little different to a child. When she married her assets, possessions, and any income became the property of her husband. He would usually bequeath his (and indeed her) property to his male heir. As Jane Austen showed so deftly in the opening of *Sense and Sensibility* (1811), women without sons often struggled to make the heir ensure their comfort in widowhood.

Nelson left Emma Merton Place, but the property was already indebted and Emma's resolve to retain his bequest condemned her finances. Her flamboyance and rebellion against social norms made her vulnerable after Nelson's death, as many of her friends turned their backs on her. Aristocratic women could flaunt society and fall back on the money of their families—Emma had nothing.

Most of Emma's belongings were lost, Merton Place was sold and later demolished and she lived in increasingly cheap rental properties. She died in poverty in Calais, just short of fifty, in the same year that the Napoleonic Wars were finally ended by the victory of the allies at the Battle of Waterloo. Poor orphaned Horatia was sent back to England to live with Nelson's sisters in turn, before marrying a young curate, Philip Ward, at the age of twenty-one. She had ten children, but only one line still remains, a family who are a credit to Nelson. In them the spirit of Emma remains.

George Romney missed his muse after she left for Naples. Drafting a letter in the August after her departure, he wrote of *The Spinstress* that, compared to "the great number of ladys of fashion sitting to me since you left England … it is the sun of my Hemispheer and they are but twinkling stars."

Emma, Lady Hamilton, the "sun" of so many hemispheres died sadly but she lives on in her luminous portraits, and in her legacy to art and culture, so much of which can be seen in this marvellous exhibition. When we regard a dance of great fluidity, look at a portrait in which the very soul of the model seems exposed, or even watch an actress weep on stage, we are appreciating part of the spirited woman whose beauty, creativity, and intense emotions at once dazzled and confounded her eighteenth-century contemporaries.

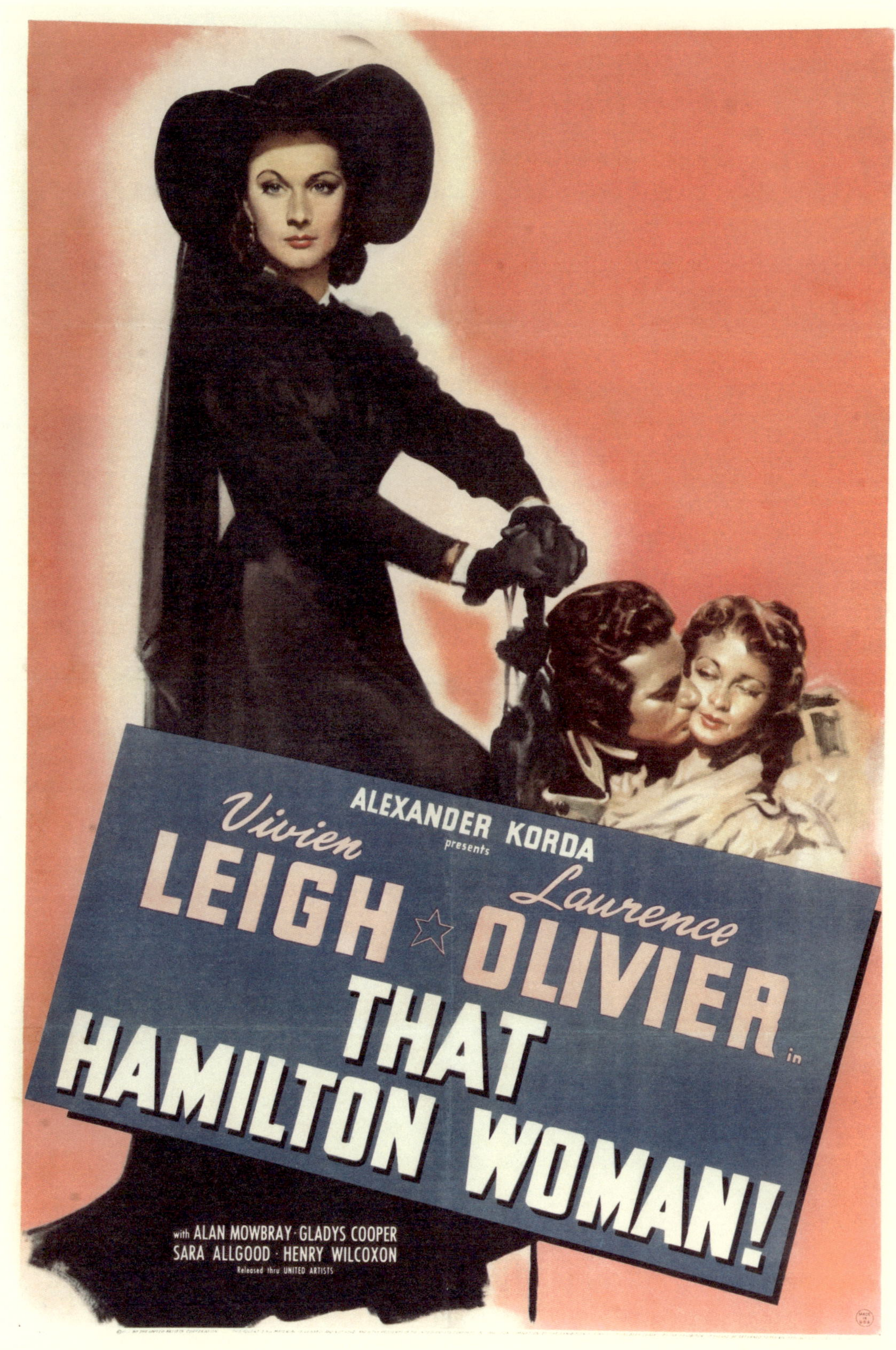



[FILM POSTER]. *That Hamilton Woman!* (1941). An historical film drama produced and directed by Alexander Korda for Alexander Korda Films. (2010.104.00.0001)

# The Jean Kislak Collection of
## Works About or Inspired by the Life of Emma, Lady Hamilton


1852     CALTON, Robert Bell. *Annals and Legends of Calais.* London: John Russell Smith, 1852. (2010.083.00.0001)

1874     PAGET, John. *Paradoxes and Puzzles, Historical, Judicial, and Literary.* Edinburgh: William Blackwood & Sons, 1874. (2010.095.00.0001)

1889     JEAFFRESON, John Cordy. *The Queen of Naples and Lord Nelson: An Historical Biography …* London: Hurst & Blackett, Ltd., 1889. (2000.096.01-02.0002)

1891     GAMLIN, Hilda. *Emma Lady Hamilton: An Old Story Re-told.* Liverpool & London: Simpkin, Marshall, Hamilton, Kent & Co., 1891. (2010.081.00.0001)

1892     ——— *Memoirs of Emma, Lady Hamilton, with Anecdotes of her Friends and Contemporaries.* W. H. Long (ed. & annotated). London: William W. Gibbings, 1892. Second Revised and Enlarged Edition. (2000.054.00.0001)

1893     MORRISON, Alfred. *The Collection of Autograph Letters and Historical Documents: The Hamilton & Nelson Papers, 1798–1815.* 2 vols. [London]: Private Circulation, 1893–94. (1989.039.00.0002)

1894     GAMLIN, Hilda. *George Romney and His Art.* London: Swan Sonnenschein, 1894. (2010.088.00.0001)

1895     PORTER, Mrs. Robert P. "The Nymph of the Attitudes," *The Cosmopolitan, a Monthly Illustrated Magazine,* XVIII (November 1894–April 1895). (2010.136.00.0001)

1897     BERESFORD, Charles, and H. W. WILSON. *Nelson and His Times.* London: Harmsworth Brothers, [1897]. (2010.029.00.0001)

1897     MAHAN, Captain A. T. *The Life Of Nelson: The Embodiment of the Sea Power of Great Britain.* London: Sampson, Low, Marston & Co., 1897. (2000.076.01.0001)

1900     JEAFFRESON, John Cordy. *Beaux & Belles of England: Lady Hamilton and Lord Nelson.* London: The Grolier Society, 1900. Edition limited to 1,000 copies for England and America. (2000.053.01-02.0001)

1903     DUMAS, Alexandre. *The Lovely Lady Hamilton, or The Beauty and the Glory.* New York: Street & Smith, [1903]. (2010.076.00.0001)

1903     GIGLIOLI, Constance H. D. *Naples in 1799: An Account of the Revolution of 1799 and of the Rise and Fall of the Parthenonian Republic.* London: John Murray, 1903. (2010.037.00.0001)

1903     HOOPER, James. *Nelson's Homeland.* London: G. Nelson, Dale & Co., 1903. (2010.016.00.0001)

1904     ROBERTS, William. *Romney: A Biographical and Critical Essay with a Catalogue Raisonne of his Works.* London & New York: Thos. Agnew & Sons and Charles Scribner's Sons, 1904. (2000.096.00.0014)

1904    VIGÉE LE BRUN, Louise-Élisabeth. *The Memoirs of Madame Vigée Lebrun* (trans. by Lionel Strachey). London: Grant Richards, 1904. (2010.072.00.0001)

1905    BAILY, J. T. *The Life of Emma, Lady Hamilton: A Biographical Essay with a Catalogue of Her Published Portraits*. London: W. G. Menzies, 1905. First Edition. (2000.096.00.0015)

1905    SICHEL, Walter. *Emma Lady Hamilton: From New and Original Sources and Documents.* London: Archibald Constable, 1905. (1992.004.00.0004)

1906    GRAHAM, Winifred. *Emma Hamilton's Miniature.* London: George Bell & Sons, 1906. (2010.095.00.0002)

1906    MOORHOUSE, E. Hallam. *Nelson's Lady Hamilton.* London: Methuen, 1906. (1992.005.00.0003)

1906    HUBBARD, Elbert. *Little Journeys to Homes of Great Lovers: Lord Nelson and Lady Hamilton.* East Aurora, N.Y.: The Roycrofters, Volume XIX, November 1906. (2010.127.00.0001)

1907    SICHEL, Walter. *Emma Lady Hamilton from New and Original Sources and Documents, Together with an Appendix of Notes and New Letters.* London: Archibald Constable, 1907. (1989.039.00.0001)

1910    ——— *Memoirs of Emma, Lady Hamilton, the Friend of Lord Nelson and the Court of Naples.* New York: P. F. Collier & Son, 1910. (2000.057.00.0001 & 2000.059.00.0001)

1911    FRANKAU, Julia. *The Story of Emma, Lady Hamilton.* London: Macmillan & Co., Ltd., 1911. Limited to 250 copies signed by the author. Finely bound by The Chelsea Bindery in full navy blue morocco, with a portrait of Horatio Nelson in the center of the front board surrounded by a further 12 vignette portraits each depicting Lady Emma Hamilton in a different pose. (2000.096.01-2.0016)

1912    MOORHOUSE, E. Hallam. *The Story of Lady Hamilton.* London: T. Foulis, 1912. (2000.085.00.0001)

1912    SCHUMACHER, Henry. *The Fair Enchantress: A Romance of Lady Hamilton's Early Years.* London: Hutchinson, 1912. (2000.063.00.0001)

1914    TURQUAN, Joseph, and Jules D'AURIAC. *The Great Adventuress: Lady Hamilton and the Revolution in Naples (1753–1815).* London: Herbert Jenkins, 1914. (2010.011.00.0001)

1915    DANBY, Frank (pseudonym of Julia Frankau). *Nelson's Legacy: Lady Hamilton, Her Story & Tragedy.* New York: Charles Scribner's Sons [1915]. (1992.005.00.0001)

1922    HENDERSON, B. L. K. *Romney.* London & New York: Philip Allan & Co. and F. A. Stokes, 1922. (2000.087.00.0001)

1924    BARRINGTON, E. *The Divine Lady (with Illustrations from the Photoplay).* This "romance of Nelson and Emma Hamilton" is illustrated with scenes from the photoplay starring Corinne Griffith. New York: Grosset & Dunlap, 1924. (2010.138.00.0001)

1924    SICHEL, Walter. *The Sands of Time: Recollections and Reflections by Walter Sichel.* New York: George H. Doran, 1924. (2010.085.00.0002)

1927    SHERRARD, O. A. *A Life of Emma Hamilton.* London: Sidgwick & Jackson, 1927. (1992.005.00.0006)

# WORKS ABOUT EMMA HAMILTON

1929    [THEATRE PROGRAM]. THURSTON, Temple. *Emma Hamilton: Souvenir Theatre Program Performed at New Theatre, St. Martin's Lane.* [24 printed pages with photographs and scenes throughout. Starring D. A. Clare-Smith, Ion Swinley, Mary Cobb, Basil Beale, Renne de Vaux, Ellen Hare, Wilfred Babbage; produced by Leslie Banks.] London: [New Theatre], 1929. (2010.104.00.0001)

1932    ARETZ, Gertrude. *The Elegant Woman from the Rococo Period to Modern Times.* New York: Harcourt, Brace & Co., 1932. (2010.086.00.0001)

1935    BOWEN, Marjorie. *Patriotic Lady: Emma Lady Hamilton. A Study of Emma, Lady Hamilton, and the Neapolitan Revolution of 1799.* London: John Lane, 1935. (2000.056.00.0001)

1936    D'AUVERGNE, Edmund B. *The Dear Emma: The Story of Emma Lady Hamilton, Her Husband, and Her Lovers.* London: George G. Harrap & Co., Ltd., 1936. (2000.051.00.0001)

1939    KEATE, E. M. *Nelson's Wife: The First Biography of Frances Herbert, Viscountess Nelson.* London: Cassell and Company, Ltd., 1939. (2000.088.00.0001)

1941    [FILM POSTER]. *That Hamilton Woman!* (1941). An historical film drama produced and directed by Alexander Korda for Alexander Korda Films. 71 × 101 cm. (2010.084.00.001)

1942    FIELD, Bradda. *Miledi. Being the Strange Story of Emy Lyon, a Blacksmith's Daughter, Who Married His Britannic Majesty's Envoy Extraordinary and Minister Plenipotentiary at the Court of Naples and Became, Emma, Lady Hamilton, Companion of Royalty and the True Friend of Vice-Admiral Lord Nelson, K.B., Duke of Bronte.* London: Constable & Co., Ltd., 1942. (2000.052.00.0001)

1949    RAWSON, Geoffrey. *Nelson's Letters from the Leeward Islands, and Other Original Documents in the Public Record Office and the British Museum.* London: Staples Press, 1949. (2000.093.00.0001)

1950    OMAN, Carola. *Nelson.* London: The Reprint Society, 1950. (2000.078.00.0001)

1955    KENYON, F. W. *Emma, Lady Hamilton.* New York: Thomas Y. Crowell Co., 1955. (2010.025.00.0001)

1956    FENWICK, Kenneth. *Southey's Life of Nelson.* London: The Folio Society, 1956. First edition. (2000.083.00.0001)

1957    HAMILTON, Gerald. *Emma in Blue: A Romance of Friendship.* London: Allan Wingate, 1957. (2000.067.00.0001)

1960    WARNER, Oliver. *Emma Hamilton and Sir William.* London: Chatto & Windus, 1960. (2000.068.00.0001)

1962    [EXHIBITION CATALOGUE]. MILNE-HENDERSON, Patricia. *The Drawings of George Romney.* An exhibition held from May to September 1962 at the Smith College Museum of Art, Northampton, Mass.: Smith College Museum of Art, 1962. (2010.038.00.0001)

1963    TOURS, Hugh. *The Life and Letters of Emma Hamilton.* London: Victor Gollancz, Ltd., 1963. (2000.069.00.0001)

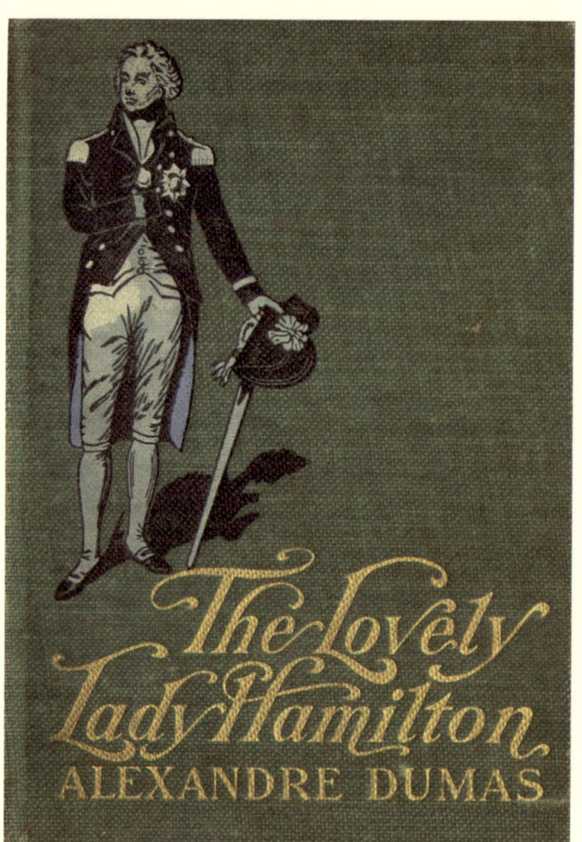

# The Lovely Lady Hamilton

("*EMMA LYONNA*")

OR

## The Beauty and the Glory

AN HISTORICAL ROMANCE OF ROYALTY
AND REVOLUTION

BY

### ALEXANDRE DUMAS

AUTHOR OF
"THE THREE MUSKETEERS," "MONTE CRISTO," "THE REGAL
BOX," "THE KING'S GALLANT," "ALL FOR A CROWN," ETC.

Translated from the French by HENRY L. WILLIAMS

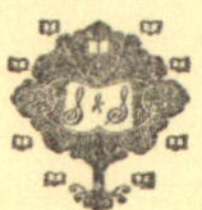

NEW YORK AND LONDON
STREET & SMITH, PUBLISHERS

---

EVENINGS at 8.30
MATINEES: THURSDAYS and SATURDAYS at 2.30

By arrangement with Miss MARY MOORE

BRONSON ALBERY

PRESENTS

## EMMA HAMILTON

A Dramatic Chronicle in Three Acts
by
TEMPLE THURSTON

*Characters in order of their appearance:*

| | |
|---|---|
| Captain Willett Payne, R.N. .. .. .. | D. A. CLARKE-SMITH |
| The Hon. Charles Greville .. .. .. | ION SWINLEY |
| Mrs. Kelly .. .. .. .. .. .. | ELLEN HARE |
| Mrs. Notley .. .. .. .. .. .. | MARY COBB |
| Mr. Notley .. .. .. .. .. | WILFRED BABBAGE |
| Sir Henry Fetherstonhaugh .. .. .. | FREDERICK LLOYD |
| Mrs. Ransome .. .. .. .. | MARY MACDONALD |
| Mr. Ransome .. .. .. .. .. | RICHARD GRAY |
| Emma Hart .. .. .. .. .. .. | MARY NEWCOMB |
| Hilt .. .. .. .. .. .. | TOM REYNOLDS |
| Manservant (to Sir Henry Fetherstonhaugh) .. | BASIL BEALE |
| Mrs. Cadogan (Emma's Mother) .. .. | RENEE DE VAUX |
| Sir William Hamilton .. .. .. .. | NORMAN MacOWAN |
| Captain Trowbridge .. .. .. .. | EUGENE LEAHY |
| Manservant (to Sir William Hamilton) .. | LAWRENCE EDGLEY |
| Nelson .. .. .. .. .. .. | LESLIE BANKS |
| Josiah Nisbet .. .. .. .. .. | JAN BUSSELL |

Guests : LAWRENCE EDGLEY, MARJORIE MacINTYRE, FRANCES RUTTLEDGE

Play Produced by LESLIE BANKS.

---

ACT I.
*Scene I.* Mrs. Kelly's House, Arlington Street, W.
1781

*Scene II.* Captain Willett Payne's Rooms, Piccadilly.
*The same night.*

*Scene III.* Dining Room, Fetherstonhaugh's House in Sussex.
*Some months later.*

ACT II.
*Scene I.* Charles Greville's Rooms at Edgware.
*Two years later.*

*Scene II.* The same.
*Six months later.*

ACT III.
*Scene I.* Room in the British Embassy, Naples.
*June, 1798.*

*Scene II.* The same.
*September, 1798.*

*Scene III.* Bed Room in Lord Nelson's House at Merton.
*September, 1805.*

Preludes and Interludes by NORMAN O'NEILL.

### AUTHOR'S NOTE.

There has been practically no adjustment of historical events in this play. There is no record of Sir Henry Fetherstonhaugh having seen Emma at Mrs. Kelly's. This also applies to Charles Greville. But since every one in the fashionable world visited the Abbess of Arlington Street, it is quite reasonable to suppose these gentlemen both went there.

Here and there a slight transposition of the scenes where events took place has been made. The events themselves are not changed except in the case of Admiral Nelson receiving the Queen of Naples' letter from Lady Hamilton. This letter was actually sent by Captain Bowen, but as no importance attaches to the fact, I have considered this a permissible alteration.

E.T.T.

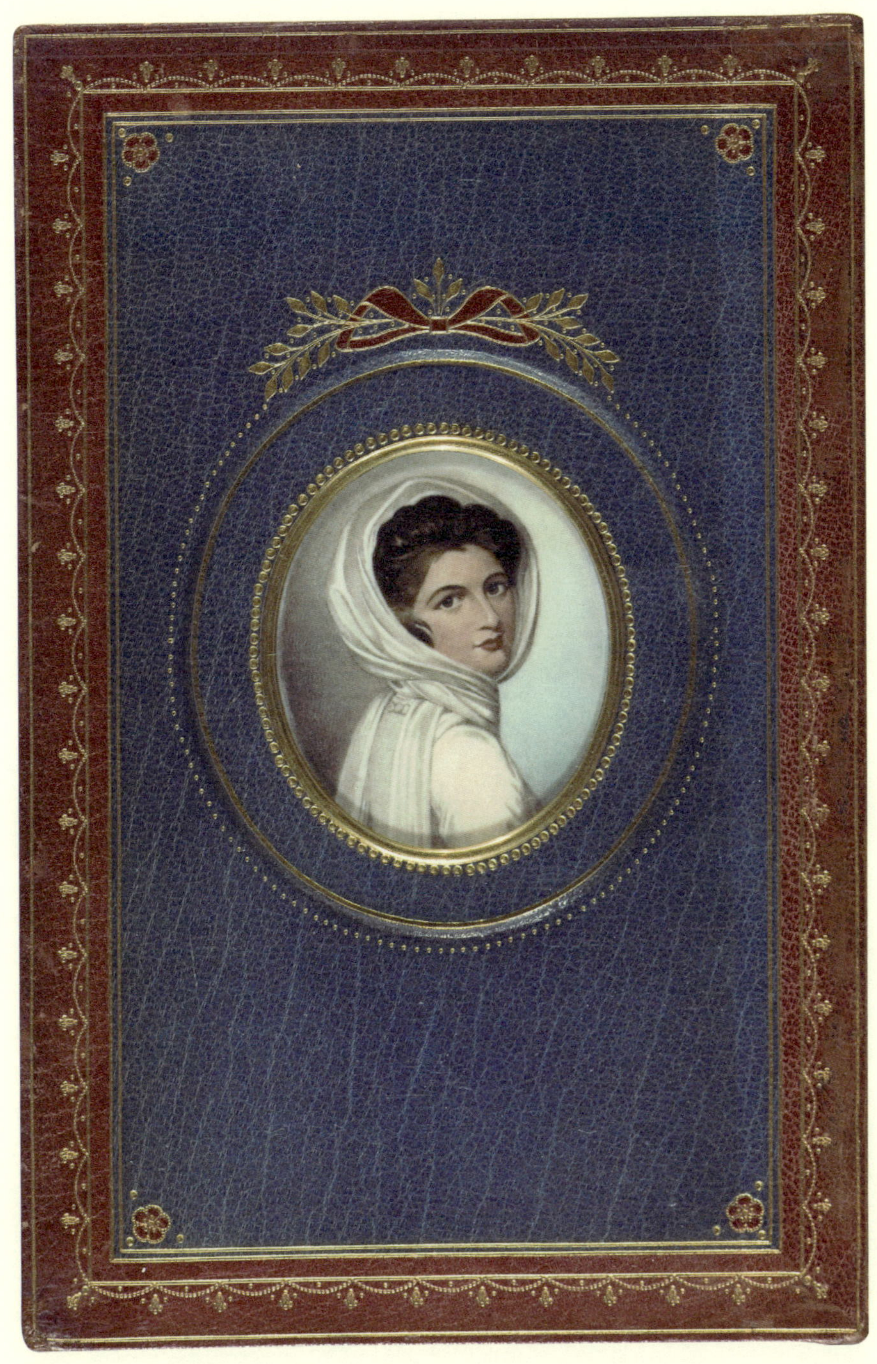

*Opposite, top:* ALEXANDRE DUMAS, *The Lovely Lady Hamilton ("Emma Lyonna"), or The Beauty and the Glory.* New York: Street & Smith, [1903]. (2010.076.00.0001)

*Opposite, bottom:* [THEATRE PROGRAM] TEMPLE THURSTON, *Emma Hamilton: Souvenir Theatre Program Performed at New Theatre, St. Martin's Lane.* London, 1929. (2010.104.00.0001)

*Above:* EMMA AS SPINSTRESS (see page 18), from the binding of Walter Sichel, *Emma Lady Hamilton: From New and Original Sources and Documents.* London: Archibald Constable, 1905. (1992.004.00.0004)

1965 LUTTRELL, Barbara. *The Prim Romantic: A Biography of Ellis Cornelia Knight 1758–1837.* London: Chatto & Windus, 1965. (2000.089.00.0001)

1965 WARNER, Oliver. *Nelson's Battles.* London and New York: B. T. Batsford and The Macmillan Company, 1965. (2000.082.00.0001)

1966 LEGG, Stuart. *Trafalgar: An Eye-Witness Account of a Great Battle.* New York: John Day Company, 1966. (2000.081.00.0001)

1969 FOTHERGILL, Brian. *Sir William Hamilton: Envoy Extraordinary.* London: Faber & Faber, 1969. (2000.090.00.0001)

1969 HARDWICK, Mollie. *Emma Lady Emma Hamilton: A Study.* London: Cassell, [1969]. (1991.356.00.0001)

1969 RUSSELL, Jack. *Nelson and the Hamiltons.* New York: Simon & Schuster, 1969. (2000.060.00.0001)

1970 BRYANT, Arthur. *Nelson.* London: Collins, 1970. (2000.071.00.0001)

1970 GERIN, Winifred. *Horatia Nelson.* London: Oxford University Press, 1970. (2010.030.00.0001)

1971 RATTIGAN, Terence. *A Bequest to the Nation: A Play in Two Acts.* Chicago: The Dramatic Publishing Co., 1971. (2010.019.00.0001)

1972 [EXHIBITION CATALOGUE]. JAFFÉ, Patricia. *Lady Hamilton in Relation to the Art of Her Time.* An Exhibition Organized … at the Iveagh Bequest, Kenwood, 18 July–16 October 1972. London: Arts Council, 1972. (2010.085.00.001)

1972 BENNETT, Geoffrey. *Nelson the Commander.* New York: Scribner, 1972. (2000.072.00.0001)

1972 RATTIGAN, Terence. *A Bequest to the Nation.* Original script of first-draft screenplay, 8 March 1972. (2010.082.00.0001)

1974 HATTERSLEY, Roy. *Nelson.* London: Weidenfeld & Nicolson, 1974. (2000.073.00.0001)

1977 HARDWICK, Mollie. *Beauty's Daughter.* New York: Coward, McCann & Geoghegan, 1977. (2010.090.00.0001)

1978 LOFTS, Norah. *Emma Hamilton.* New York: Coward, McCann & Geoghegan, 1978. (1992.005.00.0002)

1983 SIMPSON, Colin. *Emma: The Life of Lady Hamilton.* London: Bodley Head, 1983. (1992.005.00.0004)

1986 FRASER, Flora. *Beloved Emma: The Life of Emma Lady Hamilton.* London: Weidenfeld and Nicolson, 1986. Inscribed by the author. (2000.096.00.0006)

1986 FRASER, Flora. *Emma, Lady Hamilton.* New York: Knopf, 1987. First U.S. edition. (2010.003.00.0001)

1987 GILL, Edward. *Nelson and the Hamiltons on Tour.* Gloucester and Monmouth: Sutton and Nelson Museum, 1987. (2010.028.00.0001)

1988 HOWARTH, David. *Nelson: The Immortal Memory.* London: J. M. Dent & Sons, 1988. (2000.096.00.0007)

1992    MCKAY, K. D. *A Remarkable Relationship: The Story of Emma Hamilton and Her Impact on the Lives of Charles Francis Greville, Sir William Hamilton, and Horatio Nelson, including details of the Pembrokeshire Connection.* Private publication by the author, 1992. (2010.087.00.0001)

1992    SONTAG, Susan. *The Volcano Lover.* New York: Farrar, Strauss, Giroux, 1992. 1st edition. Autographed by the author. (2000.096.00.0001)

1994    HIBBERT, Christopher. *Nelson: A Personal History.* London: Viking, 1994. (2000.075.00.0001)

1994    HUDSON, Roger. *Nelson and Emma.* London: Folio Society, 1994. (2000.074.00.0001)

1995    CARR, F. Benjamin. *Nelson, Nisbet, and Nevis.* Nevis: The Nevis Historical & Conservation Society, 1995. (2010.031.00.0001)

1995    MCCARTHY, Lily Lambert. *Remembering Nelson: As Told to Lt. Commander John Lea, R.N.* Portsmouth: Royal Naval Museum, 1995. Limited edition of 120 special bound copies/No. 57. (2000.096.00.0008)

1995    WHITE, Colin. *The Nelson Companion.* Portsmouth: Royal Naval Museum, 1995. (2000.096.00.0009)

1996    [EXHIBITION CATALOGUE]. JENKINS, Ian, and Kim SLOAN. *Vases and Volcanoes: Sir William Hamilton and His Collection.* British Museum, London, 13 March – 14 July 1996. London: British Museum Press, 1996. (2010.075.00.0001)

1999    HICKMAN, Kate. *Daughters of Britannia.* London: Harper Collins, 1999. (2010.023.00.0001)

1999    POCOCK, Tom. *Nelson's Women.* London: Andre Deutsch, 1999. (2010.096.00.0001)

1999    UNSWORTH, Barry. *Losing Nelson.* London: Hamish Hamilton, 1999. (2000.092.00.0001)

2000    FENWICK, Kenneth. *Southey's Life of Nelson.* London: The Folio Society, 1956. First edition. (2000.083.00.0001)

2002    [EXHIBITION CATALOGUE]. KIDSON, Alex. *George Romney 1734–1802.* Princeton, N.J.: Princeton University Press, 2002. (2010.039.00.0001)

2003    VINCENT, Edgar. *Nelson: Love and Fame.* New Haven, Conn.: Yale University Press, 2003. (2010.018.00.0001)

2004    DOWNER, Martyn. *Nelson's Purse: The Mystery of Lord Nelson's Lost Treasures.* London: Bantam, 2004. (2010.015.00.0001)

2004    SCHUTZE, Sebastian, and Madelaine GISLER-HUWILER. *The Complete Collection of Antiquities from the Cabinet of Sir William Hamilton.* Cologne: Taschen, 2004. (2010.074.00.0001)

2005    KNIGHT, Roger. *The Pursuit of Victory: The Life and Achievement of Horatio Nelson.* London: Allen Lane, 2005. (2010.017.00.0001)

2006    WILLIAMS, Kate. *England's Mistress: The Infamous Life of Emma Hamilton.* New York: Ballantine Books, 2006. (2010.004.00.0001)

2007    ELYOT, Amanda. *Too Great a Lady: The Notorious, Glorious Life of Emma, Lady Hamilton.* New York: New American Library, 2007. (2010.027.00.0001)

PRINTED BY
FINLAY PRINTING
BLOOMFIELD, CONNECTICUT

BOUND BY
ACME BOOKBINDING, CHARLESTOWN
MASSACHUSETTS

CLOTH AND SLIP-CASE COPIES BOUND BY
THE CAMPBELL-LOGAN BINDERY
MINNEAPOLIS, MINNESOTA

DESIGNED BY
MARK ARGETSINGER
ROCHESTER
NEW YORK

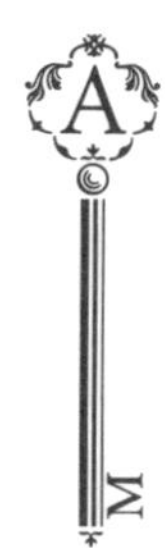

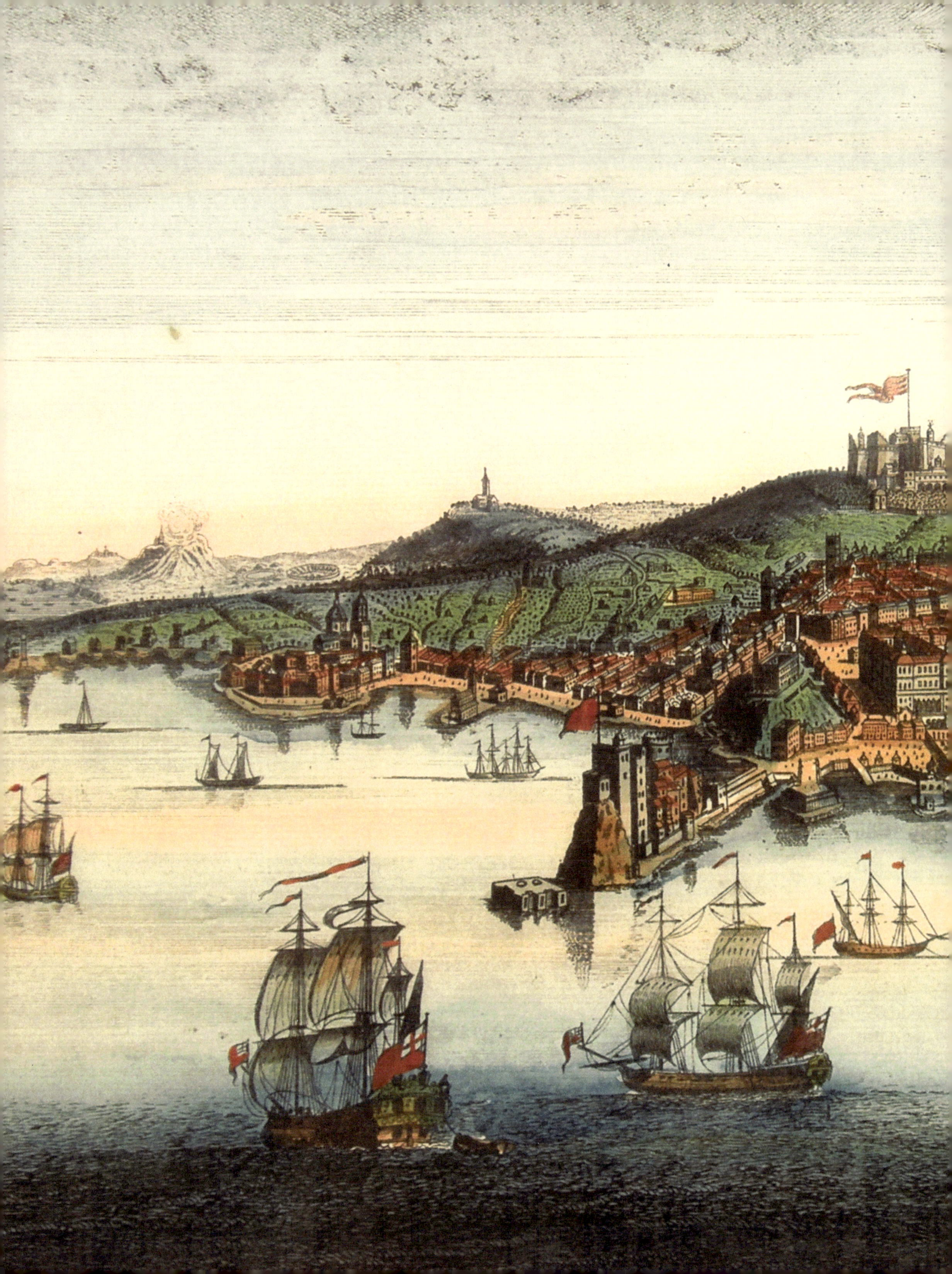